I, THE ABORIGINAL

As told to

DOUGLAS LOCKWOOD

NEW
HOLLAND

Books by Douglas Lockwood

Crocodiles and Other People
Fair Dinkum
Life on the Daly River (*with Nancy Polishuk*)
We, the Aborigines
The Lizard Eaters
The Front Door: Darwin, 1869–1969
The Shady Tree (*with Bill Harney*)
Up the Track
Alice on the Line (*with Doris Blackwell*)
Australia's Pearl Harbour: Darwin 1942
My Old Mates and I

I, THE ABORIGINAL

As told to
DOUGLAS LOCKWOOD

First published in 2004 by
New Holland Publishers
London • Sydney • Auckland
www.newhollandpublishers.com

131-151 Great Titchfield Street London WIW 5BB United Kingdom
1/66 Gibbes Street Chatswood NSW 2067 Australia
5/39 Woodside Ave Northcote Auckland New Zealand

First published by Rigby Limited 1962
Reprinted 1962, 1963, 1964, 1965, 1966, 1968, 1973, 1979, 1984
Reprinted by Seal Books 1971
Reprinted 1972, 1973 (twice), 1975, 1976, 1977, 1978, 1980
Reprinted by Lansdowne Publishing Pty Ltd 1996
Reprinted by New Holland Publishers (Australia) Pty Ltd 2004, 2013, 2018

A CiP record of this title is available from the National Library of Australia.

ISBN 9781742575001

Printed by Toppan Leefung Printing Ltd (China)

*This book is dedicated
with gratitude and affection to*
WAIPULDANYA
*of the Alawa tribe of Australian Aborigines
whose story it is.*

He sat with me during more than one hundred hours of interviews while he patiently told me the details of his life and explained the customs and rituals of his people.

He then listened and criticized through many more long hours as, together, we read and checked the manuscript.

For his sake, therefore, I hope the author has been worthy of his subject.

Waipuldanya began life as a piccaninny on the Roper River in the south-east corner of Arnhem Land.

He was born in the bush on a paperbark couch.

Since then, by his own efforts, he has raised his status until today he is a sophisticated and educated man, but one who has never forsaken the culture of his primitive ancestors.

Recently he was decorated by the Australian government. We gave him the Medal of Freedom—citizenship.

Throughout the Northern Territory he is known as

PHILLIP ROBERTS.

But whether as Waipuldanya or Wadjiri-Wadjiri (another of his tribal names) or as Phillip Roberts, I will always remember him as a great man, a fascinating story-teller and—especially—as a proud aboriginal.

DARWIN, N.T.   *Douglas Lockwood*

List of Illustrations

Chapter One

IT was one walkabout time at Mount Saint Vidgeon in the Never-Never Land south of the Roper River that the Medicine Man, the Doctor Blackfellow, tried to kill me.

I lived to tell the tale. Allabout hear 'im:

My father, Barnabas Gabarla of the Frilled Neck Lizard totem of the Alawa tribe, was away from home on a droving trip with a white man. In his modest, itinerant way he was earning his family's bread, although in those days our staple food was more likely to be wild yam, goanna, snake, kangaroo, or lily roots.

I was living with my mother at Roper River mission station, four hundred miles south-east of Darwin and fifty miles west of Port Roper on the Gulf of Carpentaria, an uninhabited estuary fed by a thousand tidal rivers and creeks . . . uninhabited, that is, except for the sharks, the crocodiles, the mammoth sawfish, the stingrays, the Manta rays, the Portuguese-men-of-war, the stonefish, the giant groper and the octopuses.

The water was poisoned with these monstrous killers, lurking, waiting for young aborigines to swim incautiously past or be cast from their canoes. The land itself was less lethal; harmless and edible kangaroos and goannas were interspersed with a few venomous taipans, hundreds of death adders, and a multitude of pythons which we ate by the yard. When we swam we had to be careful not to be eaten by our natural enemies; but on land we were the enemy, the eaters of all living things, hungry indigoed hunters who ate our food when and where we found it, never conserving, never thinking about tomorrow in a limitless country succouring Stone Age people who knew how to use it.

My greatest delight at the age of seven was to be taken on holiday walkabouts so that I could practise stalking and killing with the toy spears my father made for me. At that age I was as murderous and cruel as most young boys, whether black or white; nothing pleased me more than to be allowed to give the *coup de grâce* to some small reptile or animal which my elders had trapped.

Then one morning in the cold-weather-time my mother said we were going to Mount Saint Vidgeon, twenty-five miles away, to inquire when my father might be back from his travels to the ends of the earth and beyond—even into Queensland.

I was in an agony of impatience at once. The moment she spoke I was ready to go. I had been naked from the day I was born, and I would remain so throughout my childhood. I therefore did not have to concern myself with getting dressed. Not only were there no Sunday-bests or Going-away clothes; I had no clothes at all. Once I had picked up my spears I was ready to move—and waiting.

My elders, fortunately, prepared almost as quickly. My mother, Nora, wore a simple lap-lap. Her breasts were bare, heavily laden with the latent milk which would soon feed an infant brother. Her long black hair blew unconcernedly, untended, in the breeze.

Like all of us, she was barefooted. The soles of her splayed feet were calloused and leathered from a lifetime of intimacy with stones and pebbles and prickles and the rough red-and-black earth.

She had never owned a dress or shoes or stockings, or even a comb; never a bead or bauble, powder or paint. She was a human being, female but unfeminine, unadorned, perhaps unattractive, but the only kind of woman who could share the life of a nomad.

She did not feel the need for the fripperies I have seen aboriginal women wearing today. She was entirely subservient to her husband, my father Barnabas—a chattel, an incubator for his sons, her role ordered for her by the dictatorship of the tribe according to the inflexible sociological pattern.

At puberty she had gone to the man who beckoned her to his campfire, the man who knew by tribal right that a particular woman was his, to keep and to hold, to punish and banish and scold, and to impregnate mysteriously with the seeds of his body, from which children would grow when the Rainbow Serpent, the Giver of Life, had made the Road.

My grandfather, Ned Weari-wyingga, was with us. He was an Elder, a gnarled and pitted old man with a flour-bag of white hair; naked, too, except for his brief narga. He had lived here on the Roper during the First Coming of the White Man when the Overland Telegraph was built. He was here during the First Coming of Christ to the Aborigines with the arrival of the missionaries. But he was also here Be'Fore . . . before the country held humans other than the Alawa, the Anula, the Ngulkpun, the Nungubuyu, the Mara, the Rembarrnga, and the faraway Balamumu and Andilyaugwa tribes at Caledon Bay and Groote Eylandt across the Arnhem Land deeps.

My younger brother Silas Ngulati of the Bungadi skin came along, too.

We walk.

We walk and we walk and we walk and we walk.

At midday we sit down.

All right now, we walk again . . . and we walk and we walk and we walk, hunting on the way, laughing, playing, happy to be alone on our tribal ground, the land which gave us our totem heroes, the land which would for ever belong to the Alawa even after it had been alienated by the white man and his cattle.

And then, in the evening, with the smoke-grey sky flecked with purple light-rays from the Dream-Camp of the Sun below the rim of the earth, we came to Saint Vidgeon.

11

I am not sure how long it was after we camped that I began to feel ill. During the hunt my mother had found some Sugarbag in a tree, and I ate ravenously from this delicious nest of wild honey. That had often happened without interfering with my appetite for the evening meal, but now I was revolted by the burnt-flesh smells of grilling goanna which she was passing end-to-end through the blazing campfire.

Fat dripped from the cooking perentie, its tail alone more than a yard long, paying with its life for the comical mistake it had made earlier that day while we hunted wallabies.

The perentie had seen Silas stalking through the bush and, typically, had raced for the nearest tree, climbing swiftly until it reached the topmost branch only seven feet from the ground. Not until then did it discover that the tree was alive and human.

My grandfather's immobility—he had been standing with an arm upstretched and instinctively froze in that position when wild life moved around him—was transformed into action which was fast indeed for such an old man. He caught the goanna by the tail and killed it with one neck-breaking flick against the ground. Now we were to eat it.

"I'm sick," I said.

My mother had warned me about the penalties of eating too much Sugarbag and was ready to say, "I told you so."

Yet at that moment, child that I was, I knew this to be no ordinary illness. Little explaining of my symptoms was necessary to convince the others.

My skin was hot. My stomach felt as though it would soon come to the boil. My limbs trembled with an ague which might have been caused by malaria. My heart palpitated, my head ached, and I sweated profusely. But none of these tribulations equalled the crazed fear I knew when my grandfather, who was looking down at me, whispered one word:

"Maraworina!"

I was still a piccaninny, but I had listened to enough tales around our campfires on the Roper to know instantly that he believed I had been deliberately poisoned.

Who would want to poison a seven-year-old boy? And why? What possible sins, apart from his natural mischievousness, could have been committed by a so-small aboriginal lad to induce someone to poison him?

The answers to these questions were not difficult for any of us to understand. In the year nineteen hundred and sixty-two the eastern tribes of Northern Territory aborigines still have an abiding, unreasoning fear of the western tribes, not unlike the distrust most white people from what is called the Free World have for their tribesmen from behind the Iron Curtain.

We are afraid of the Malak Malak, the Brinken, the Nangomeri, and the Murinbada because down through the centuries, from that mystical age we call The Dreamtime—prehistoric antiquity—they have been symbolized as poisoners of immense cunning and inventiveness, and experts in the ancient art of removing a man's kidney fat while he is unconscious.

We are careful today how and when we sleep if a Malak Malak or a Brinken is within effective range to practise his black art of witchcraft. Too often we have seen them at night with a piece of human fat or a thighbone from a dead person, dissembling, manoeuvring, and sneaking stealthily until they can approach the windward side of a hut where their victim lives, then to burn the fat or bone in a fire and wait while the smoke is wafted slowly but menacingly to the nose of the person inside.

This is a primitive anaesthetic, an ethereal ether which quickly envelops the victim and plunges him into a deep sleep. Now the poisoners and the surgeons who come for kidney fat can go about their grisly business unhindered.

"Maraworina!"

It meant that they had been at me while I slept, nobbling me with a deadly mixture of putrefaction: red ochre and white clay kneaded with dogs' excrement and perhaps a little powdered glass.

How could I live after a dose of such terrible medicine! It had often been used to poison dingoes, and did so effectively. There seemed little chance that a young picca-ninny might survive, especially as the shock of knowledge was almost equal in severity to the poison itself.

This is not a fable or a mythical aboriginal legend that I am recounting. It happened to me, and I remember it clearly.

Well, of course, I was given the antidote recommended by our own Doctor Blackfellow for maraworina. Any puny protest I might have made would have been useless, and so I remained silent for that reason as well as for the fact that I was too ill to object.

Young boys become young men, virile procreators who ensure survival of the tribe. Without them the tree dies. To lose one, in my grandfather's view, was like lopping off a healthy branch. He did his best, with my mother and Silas helping him, to see that I lived.

I watched, fascinated and fearful, as they quickly scooped a large hole in the sand, filled it with dry wood and leaves, and put a firestick to it. When the furious blaze died away they brushed off the coals and ashes, leaving the sand too hot to touch. Coolamons filled with water were now dashed on the sand, and sizzling clouds of steam were given off. At a moment which my grand-father chose, the sand was judged to be the correct temperature, a blanket was spread over it, and I was laid there to baste . . . to cook until the evil juices trapped inside me began to drip away.

I sweated profusely, the very gravy of me dripping from my skin. The heat was barely tolerable. I wanted to cry out, to jump up, to run away. Yet at no time did my grandfather or brother need to hold me there; I was caught in the massive grip of fear, weighed down by oppression, clinging to my bed of fire so that I might be purged, tem-pered like steel in an open furnace while the dross was burnt out of my system. This was only one of the trials by ordeal I suffered in my youth, but I think it was the severest.

14

Now my mother, my grandfather, and Silas watched for the poison to emerge with the sweat. My black body had been coated lightly with white ochre so that the driblets of moisture could be more easily seen. My mother had the meatless shoulder-blade of a kangaroo. My grandfather had a flat stick. And together, as my skin salivated, they scraped it off, hoping that by doing so the emission of poison would be wiped away.

But all this, I was soon to discover, was nothing more than a clinical test by a primitive pathologist. As it happened I had not been poisoned at all.

Ah, no, incomparably worse!

My grandfather was eventually satisfied, when I showed no improvement, that his early diagnosis of maraworina was wrong. He re-examined the symptoms and pronounced profoundly:

"Waipuldanya, he has been sung!"

If I was frightened at the prospect of dying from maraworina, now I was terrified.

A belief in our own kind of voodooism is strong in the heart of every tribalized aboriginal, and of most who have been detribalized.

I have been living with white men and as a white man for ten years, but I still have not conquered the innate fear and inherent conviction I have of existence of the supernatural powers of certain elder tribesmen.

I have seen the eyes of my tribal friends rolling in terror. I have seen them frothing at the mouth. I have watched them run amok and be struck dumb: all because they believed too readily when confronted with inexplicable phenomena. It is necessary to understand this to appreciate fully the reaction of any aboriginal who suspects that he has been "sung" to death by a man of his own race —the Doctor Blackfellow . . . the Sorcerer.

Being "sung" is known in other tribes as "pointing the bone." I have seen strong men wither and die as imbeciles within a few days of affliction with this terrible mental illness, for that is what it is

15

And now it was happening to me at the age of seven. Why?

The complex course of the aboriginal mind is seldom understood outside the tribes. There comes a time during any white man's analysis of an aboriginal act when logic disappears and he runs into a solid wall of superstitions. The two are irreconcilable.

But to the aboriginal mind there is no such thing as an insoluble problem. When a native exhausts the logical explanations for any set of circumstances, especially if they should be phenomenal, he can always fall back on his strong belief in the supernatural.

"Might-be Something!"

How often I have heard that said! It is, at once, an expression of fear and an admission of belief in black spirits. Let me say that my recently acquired sophistication has not freed me of the conviction that they exist.

But why, and again why, was I being punished? I had done nothing wrong. I did not possess the evil eye. I was not an idiot who had to be killed to prevent him impregnating tribal women with more of his kind.

To this day I do not really know why, although there are several theories. In my family we have always thought that I was "sung" because a mistake was made during the ceremonial decoration of bodies for our ritual corroboree, the Yabudurawa. That is a serious offence.

The Yabudurawa is danced by the Kangaroo, the Goanna, the Wild Plum, the Wild Orange, the Snake, and various other totems of the Roper River tribes. It extends east to the Gulf of Carpentaria; west to Elsey, the Never-Never cattle station; north to the Mainoru border of Arnhem Land; and south to the headwaters of the Hodgson River.

In the Alawa tribe it has no songs and no didgeredoo accompaniment—nothing more than the beating of sticks. It continues spasmodically from January until June, but unlike most other ceremonies, which are danced at night, the Yabudurawa is performed during daylight and must

16

end no later than four o'clock except on the final night, when it goes until dawn. That is the law.

The corroboree is banned to all women. They must remain at least half a mile away. If a woman went close to a Yabudurawa in my grandfather's youth her head would have been chopped off at once. Even today death would be likely.

On the final night the women are allowed within fifty yards, but they must have their heads under blankets so they cannot see the hundred or more painted men performing their last secret rituals.

My male cousins paint my body in accordance with the instructions given them by the Elders. The intricate patterns must be exact. The corroboree could not go on if a mistake were made. The Master of Ceremonies would prevent it, and the celebrants would simply sit down until I was repainted. But if a tribesman was harbouring a grudge against another he might make a deliberate error so small that it would perhaps not be noticed until after the ceremony had begun. Then it would be too late to stop and trouble would develop.

At the age of seven, of course, I was too young to be a participant in the Yabudurawa. How, then, could I be "sung" for having an inexact decoration?

Long before the First Coming of Christ to the Aborigines we were practising many of the laws since given to us in the Bible. One of these was the exhortation of Moses that the iniquities of the fathers would be visited upon the children, even unto the third and fourth generation.

That is an ancient custom among most of the aboriginal tribes. A boy has often been killed for the sins of an old man. In that way the punishment takes greater toll. An Elder may have passed the age at which he can beget children, but a boy has his procreative life before him. By his death many other potential lives are lost, even to the third and fourth generations and beyond. That is especially so in a community with a rigid system of moieties ordering an undeviating marriage pattern such as ours.

And so it was that I became singled out for death by auto-suggestion.

Until the moment when I first felt ill I was happy and carefree. I was as healthy as any aboriginal boy can be. I had no thought of violence or malevolence or death. Yet within a few minutes I was running a high fever and my stomach was boiling.

I have been asked how such an illness can be attributed to auto-suggestion when I had been unaware of symptoms until the very moment I was struck down. I can say only that that is how it happened to me and has happened to others. I believe that a person who has been "sung" knows about it instinctively and begins to react physically long before his conscious mind communicates the reaction to him.

I looked up again and saw my grandfather, Weari-wyingga, watching me gravely. Unless a miracle was performed quickly, what he had pronounced amounted to a sentence of death.

"Waipuldanya, he has been sung," he repeated.

My mother wailed piteously and began to beat her chest. I knew that later, if I died, she would cut her head with stones until rivulets of bloody tears poured down her face. It had ever been thus with deaths in the Alawa tribe.

The curse was upon me, insidiously destroying my mind and body.

I would reject all food and water.

I would defaecate where I lay.

I would groan and grovel, twitching in an agony of muscular contraction until the day, perhaps a week, perhaps two weeks hence, when I would scream at the hideous picture in my mind, ignoring the equal horror of my physical degeneration, and die the most terrible of deaths.

I could be saved only if the curse was removed by another Doctor Blackfellow with powers more potent than those of the evil man who had perhaps danced around a drawing of me on a white-gum tree, had then thrown his curse into the tree, and projected a red-hot star from there into my body.

18

"Gudjiwa!" my mother screamed. "Gudjiwa!"

Gudjiwa was our Medicine-Man, a friend of the family.

"Yes, get him quick-time!" my grandfather ordered. He pointed at my brother Silas. "Run for your life to Saint Vidgeon's station. Find Gudjiwa! Find him! Find him! Bring him here, running! Tell him that Waipuldanya has the curse upon him and will die unless he comes quickly."

Like me, Silas was naked, but the old man's order was electrically urgent. He ran into the bush towards the cattle station five miles from our camp. I was unaware of the passage of time. My body, deprived of a brain, functioned involuntarily. I lay in my filth and waited, unknowingly, for the death which came slowly, for the penalty which was mine because it was through me that my tribal relatives could best be punished by their tribal enemies.

Gudjiwa came. I do not remember his arrival. I do not remember anything of what followed until I was cured. But my grandfather told me:

Gudjiwa made a herbal mixture from wattle bark and yams, mixed it with more of the wild honey I had eaten, and forced it down my throat. My stomach rebelled, but he thrust it upon me until satisfied that I had retained a small quantity.

Meanwhile he danced around me, beating the ground with green bushes, yelling imprecations at the nameless people who sought my destruction, chanting to me, chanting to my ancestors, placating his totems with extravagant promises of tribute, and calling malediction on the sorcerer who had brought me to the verge of the Djarp, the predestined path that leads from life to death.

Gudjiwa carried a piece of tree bark made into a coolamon. Now he put his hand over my heart and began sucking my arm near the shoulder. His cheeks swelled, and in a moment he spat a mouthful of blood into the coolamon. Then he sucked again . . . sucked and spat . . . until the coolamon was dripping with blood.

My eyes regained their focus. The muscle-twitching eased. I stopped my insane noise and had recovered from

19

deep hypnosis to consciousness when Gudjiwa rubbed his bushes over my chest, spat out a final mouthful of blood, and took from his mouth a red, star-shaped shell.

Instantly the great oppression lifted from my mind. My body relaxed. The nausea passed. I spoke coherently.

In a week I was clean and whole.

In the years since then I have managed to escape the evil attentions of other Doctor Blackfellows. In fact, I have been able to win their confidence and use it to help white doctors in their attempts to eradicate tribal diseases and cure the ills which my people have inherited from Europeans.

On one exceptional occasion which I will discuss later I even cured a Doctor Blackfellow, his wife, and his son with conventional medicine. That was a triumph indeed.

I have been asked where Gudjiwa could have obtained the blood he spat into the coolamon while my life was in the balance.

The cynics claim that he killed a kangaroo and had a mouthful when he arrived at my side.

That is unlikely. In the first place, he chanted while he worked on me, opening his mouth wide without disclosing the presence of blood. Secondly, while sucking my arm he emptied his mouth more than once.

My advent into civilization has taught me that certain things are physically impossible. I have had medical training and I understand the basic precepts of anatomy. I know that you can't get blood from a stone. And yet I know that Gudjiwa got it through my skin by sucking. I know that, by doing so, he convinced me the bad blood in my body was being removed.

I was "sung" to death by a primitive Doctor Blackfellow. I was saved by another who was equally primitive.

I do not know how it was done. It may have been a trick. If so, it was an exceptionally clever one. But need it have been an illusion? Couldn't Gudjiwa have performed a miracle? After all, God created Woman by taking a rib from Man. Christ cured the lepers, caused the blind to see, made cripples whole, produced loaves and fishes to feed a multitude, and ascended into heaven.

We have our magicians, too. Is it inconceivable that they should also be able to perform miracles?

The qualifications of a Medicine-Man vary from tribe to tribe. Perhaps the most usual condition among the Roper River people is that the aspirant should have slept in a cemetery. It is from such places that much of their power is derived, although other qualifications are also necessary.

Since my emergence into the Big White World I have learnt that Europeans are just as unhappy at the thought of passing a night in a graveyard as the average aboriginal. They are frightened of apparitions, the ghosts that we call spirits.

A few years ago at Bathurst Island mission station a group of Tiwi tribesmen were asked to lay down a flare-path consisting of tins of kerosene-soaked sand for a Flying Doctor plane which was due at night on a medical emergency. But when the missionary went out to light the tins he found they had been placed at short intervals and extended only half-way along the strip. The far end—the vital landing and take-off area—remained in darkness. The missionary had to put the tins there himself. No aboriginal would go. Beyond the half-way mark the cemetery lay in wait!

Anyone who sleeps in such a place, therefore, is regarded as a superman. He has not only conquered terror but overcome evil spirits. Consequently he can do little wrong in our eyes. He is credited with extraordinary powers. He is a man to be reckoned with, and his wrath studiously avoided.

We have constant proof, even during this period of galloping detribalization, that the influence of the Doctor Blackfellows remains paramount.

An aboriginal woman named Maisie Nambidjimba died near Tennant Creek. Police and qualified white doctors examined her body and found no apparent cause of death, so an exhaustive autopsy was performed. At a subsequent coroner's inquest Dr Beryl Rich said that in spite of the post-mortem examination she was utterly mystified.

But the tribal Elders might have enlightened her. Maisie's death showed that aborigines never forget. All wrongs must be set right by a system known as *Pay-Back*. The Lord God had the same idea when he said to Moses: *"Eye for eye, tooth for tooth, hand for hand, foot for foot. Burning for burning, wound for wound, stripe for stripe."*

Maisie's story began on a fiercely hot day when her husband, Snowy Jambadjimba, took two boys from Warrabri settlement on a hunting trip to Singleton station. The boys perished from lack of water, and Snowy, who survived, was blamed.

I can imagine the diabolical whispering campaign that would have begun immediately among the old men at the settlement. Snowy and Maisie were subjected to an intensive war of nerves which finally caused them to flee in terror.

But that did not save Maisie's life. She died a few days later, showing no symptoms except that she frothed at the mouth. The doctors could find nothing wrong with her.

And yet Snowy Jambadjimba saw no mystery.

"She bin die when spirit stone grab her heart," he said.

Spirit stone? Yes. For one of the Doctor Blackfellows' methods of execution is to administer to his victim a belly-ful of magic stones.

A person who is "sung" and remains within his tribe inevitably dies unless reprieved or treated by another Doctor Blackfellow, as in my case. Several people have been saved in recent years after removal from the tribal environment.

The most notorious of these was a young Gomaid tribesman, Lya Wulumu, who was completely paralysed after being "sung" at Yirrkalla mission in north-eastern Arnhem Land.

Wulumu's mother-in-law had complained to the Doctor Blackfellow about her son-in-law's philandering. His woomera and spear were stolen and placed in a hollow ceremonial log, where he later found them. Simultaneously, Wulumu was shown his nulla-nulla at the top of a tall tree, a positive indication to any initiate of the tribe that he had been "sung" to death.

Within a few hours Wulumu lapsed into unconsciousness. A Flying Doctor aeroplane brought him to Darwin —and not a moment too soon, for his respiratory system collapsed and he had to be put in an iron lung. Each time he was removed his breathing stopped.

I know the details of this case, because at the time I was studying as a medical orderly at Darwin Hospital with Dr Jim Tarleton Rayment, who treated him with a mixture of white-feller medicine and his own brand of incomprehensible hocus-pocus.

Whatever he did, Wulumu must have been convinced of his superior power because he slowly began to reject the poisons of the mind which were killing him. He made a remarkable recovery and returned to his tribal land.

People have asked me if the scientific training I have had as a medical assistant (I am still working in a hospital) hasn't cured me of my own belief in the power of life and death which we attribute to the Doctor Blackfellow.

I can say only that in the civilized hospitals I have seen miraculous cures effected on men and women who were evidently near to death.

I am invariably astonished at the skill of surgeons who open an abdomen, remove what I would have thought was a vital organ or part of it, sew up the incision, and have the patient walking around again within a few days.

I have seen amputations, broken limbs mended, and blood transferred from a bottle to a man who would otherwise have died. More remarkable still, I have known about the complete change of the blood of a baby whose parents' blood was incompatible.

All this has impressed me deeply. I believe in the immense skill of white surgeons.

But how can I not believe in the evil abilities of the Medicine-Men and the sorcerers?

I have the evidence of my own eyes to persuade me.

I have the memory of my own harrowing experience.

I have my tribal traditions.

I am confused, but not disillusioned.

Say, if you like, that I'm just a superstitious aboriginal.

Chapter Two

A MOOK-MOOK owl hooted solemnly from its perch in a paperbark overhanging the Alawa camp where Barnabas Gabarla, my father, dozed fitfully with his dogs.

The first blush of piccaninny daylight tinged the eastern sky. The great Stockyard of Orion's Belt and the Dreamtime Cave in the Milky Way, brilliant in the unpolluted air, paled with the lifting light.

A frilled-neck lizard, inviting death, peered inquisitively from behind a tuft of paragrass at the stirring tribesmen. It was safe from my father because it represented his totem, but it scampered to the safety of a distant tree before other hunters armed themselves with boomerangs and spears.

My father sat up, and as he did so he slapped his right arm, just below the shoulder, where a muscle had twitched involuntarily.

"I have a son," he said, emphatically.

Meanwhile, in the pink sand of a creek called The Women's Place, my mother had been deflated and immensely relieved by the mystery and agony of birth. For several hours she had pressed and groaned on the tribe's ancestral couch of leaves and paperbark. For another day and night she would lie there, attended desultorily by phlegmatic midwives who were more concerned with the traditional presents they could expect than with the urgent duties confronting them.

Drought was heavy on the land. Red dust eddied sluggishly, matching the colour of the water they brought from the billabong. My mother drank, ignoring the grit,

25

watching proudly as the wailing baby before her was rubbed with cold ashes, patted fondly, and wrapped in a primitive shawl of paperbark.

Many months had passed since that night when she lay across my father's thighs, tenderly caressing, mutely obedient, consummating as he wished, as the women had instructed her when she reached puberty.

The Road was Made.

Next day she had gone to the lagoon to swim, there receiving from the Rainbow Serpent, Giver of Life, the spirit to supplement the male-child seed which would quicken with life and emerge when the heart was beating and the milk was ready.

In such lowly fashion was I born, without a crib, without a manger, with a pink-brown skin which blackened as I grew, with two hands, two feet, two eyes, and a heart which would throb for the tribal culture I would one day leave.

But now my life was governed for me in a complex but rigid pattern. My name was the first word my mother spoke when she heard me squalling.

"Wadjiri!" And then, because she repeated it, my personal name became Wadjiri-Wadjiri.

The men, never satisfied with anything done by the women, called me Waipuldanya.

My wife, the promised woman for every man, was known to all my relatives, even though she didn't yet live. When she was born, and when she was grown, she would come to me as my mother had gone to my father, when I beckoned, because she would know it was the Dream-time Way. Actually it didn't happen quite like that . . . she was late in coming and I was impatient. I married another and gave her away.

I already had a mother-in-law.

As my mother lay there on her crude couch, recovering from her contribution to survival of the tribe, she may have wondered what the future held for her full-blood aboriginal boy in a white community where tribal life was disintegrating.

Did she worry about us feeding on the opiates of civilization?

Did she foresee our assimilation?

I doubt it. The cares of a tribal wife and mother are confined by the horizon. She does not see beyond.

I fed at her breast for much longer than the average white child. Aboriginal babies, especially boys, are spoiled in that way. And I did not have only my mother's breasts to suck. Any woman who carried me offered her ripe nipples, and I drank contentedly, perhaps for too long. I was two years old before being properly weaned. I was fat and awkward, and needed more exercise than the women allowed me.

When I cried no attempt was made to stop me. "He likes to cry, so let him cry," the women said.

My earliest recollection of solid foods is of lily roots, a hard, fibrous tuber which the women harvested by diving into the muddy lagoons along the Roper.

Although it was late in my life my mother fed me in the mouth-to-mouth fashion, so common in the tribes, which resembles the feeding of a small bird in a nest. She also taught me to drink mouth-to-mouth because I had difficulty in doing so from the bark vessels which were our only alternative. If that is thought to be unhygienic, the practice of Alawa mothers who sucked out the congested nostrils of piccaninnies suffering from colds was infinitely worse, although nobody regarded it as sufficiently unusual for comment.

For eight years, except for the time when I was "sung," I lived as a child, playing happily along the river bank, swimming in safe waterholes where the crocodiles wouldn't get me, fighting mock wars with toy spears, camping always with nothing more than a blanket to protect me from the rain and the cold, hunting through the bush with my parents in search of the food we must find to live.

We were fortunate to have a river near by in which fish abounded. I often wondered how the desert people west of Alice Springs managed to survive through droughts which sometimes lasted five years.

They had neither river nor fish, and often they didn't have enough water. But they not only survived. They multiplied.

Little did I know, after my eighth birthday passed unnoticed, how close I was to being subjected to a series of indignities as I grew from childhood to youth and must face initiation for the responsibilities of adult life.

My testing came and the realities began one dry-season day soon after the turtle-egg harvest at Port Roper, just before the burnt-grass time.

I think I was nine years old. My brother-in-law, Mardi, approached me stealthily from behind, blindfolded me with his hands, and said:

"Waipuldanya. Your time has come. Barnabas, your father, has told the Elders that his son is ready to be made a man."

I suppose that any nine-year-old white boy would be flattered if told that he was ready for manhood. But for all aboriginal boys who are living by the tribal law it is a time of fear and banishment, of brutality and monkish self-denial—and silence.

In my case it involved circumcision with a razor-blade, without anaesthetics or antiseptics, a ban on speech with specified tribal relatives for two years, a lifetime prohibition on eating certain foods and a temporary taboo on others, and, finally, I was required to sleep with a group of women —my sisters-in-law!—without molesting or even talking to them.

Poor feller me.
Poor feller me.
Poor feller me.

I did not realize then that my circumcision was a relatively painless and particularly hygienic operation if compared with the methods used before the First Coming of the White Man. Among his gifts to us have been sharp implements. But my father was cut with a stone; my grandfather's operation was performed by a surgeon who used his teeth!

28

Today a young initiate is correctly bandaged. But my dressing was a lump of wet clay—margira—which dried and cracked in the sun and had to be replaced daily.

After I had been blindfolded a group of Elders surrounded me, tapping boomerangs and chanting ceremonial songs. While they were singing other brothers-in-law painted me with margira and red ochre—on the forehead, cheeks and body—and then placed around my neck and torso a string of possum hair and feathers.

This indicated that I was Wulugurr: about to be made a man by ritual circumcision.

When that was done they took me to my sisters-in-law. It was with them that I first became conscious of ordeal and indignity.

"You must sleep with one of them, in her blanket, while the others sleep around you," I was told. "They are your protectors. They will feed you and do your bidding. But it is forbidden for you to talk to any of them!"

"Wadjiri-Wadjiri. Do you want water?" they asked.

I nodded my head.

"Do you want food?" I nodded or shook my head as I felt inclined.

"Do you want to go to the toilet?" They asked me that, too. I answered with my head.

"We will sleep now," a sister-in-law said. She indicated my position beside her on the blanket. I must not touch her. She talked interminably with her sisters, often about me, but I must not utter a syllable.

It was written thus, in the tribal law.

I was having my first lessons in self-control. My mind and body were being disciplined so that I would always have both under iron control, unless I was unfortunate enough to be "sung" again by a sorcerer.

Once I had been handed over to these women my father, my mother, my brothers and all my close relatives stayed away from me. I was not taboo for them; this was simply another lesson in self-denial.

And, of course, I didn't like any of it. I hated every moment. Imagine how any nine-year-old white boy would react to an order to sleep with a group of women, every one quite naked. I was shy and I cried miserably, but I avoided speech and I didn't run away.

The ceremonial began with a women's dance called Wunguduwa—the Mermaid. My sisters-in-law took me to the corroboree ground and I stayed there all night while they danced, clapping their legs together, gesturing, quietly miming.

My bed was made for me at the rim of firelight—in the front stalls, so to speak—where I could see easily the only women's dance that would ever be performed exclusively for me.

But the next night when the men danced the Mundiwa, though again for me alone, I was allowed to see nothing.

Throughout that day I stayed with my sisters-in-law while the men painstakingly decorated themselves with intricate patterns in ochre and margira. At mid-afternoon the women re-touched my own adornment and added a white band of rag, surmounted by a single feather, around my head. An hour before sunset my head was covered with blankets.

Thus blindfolded I lay at the edge of the ring and listened. Women were singing to the men that I was in my appointed place.

There was a great tapping of boomerangs.

Children were crying.

Dogs were barking.

And everyone waited expectantly for a signal from the near-by creek where the chief actors in the corroboree were vainly primping their matted hair and examining their elaborate, stylized body designs.

"Hurry, hurry!" I whispered urgently, for I sweated profusely under the heavy blankets.

The tapping and the chanting stopped at last. I felt rather than heard the awaited hush. I couldn't see them, but I now know that the starring players, posing un-ashamedly, were emerging from the dry creek. They were painted to represent turkeys, yams, lily roots, wild oranges, wild plums, kangaroos, snakes, and catfish, according to the Dreaming of each man—the pagan totems which we credit with unlimited influence.

I belong to the Kangaroo totem. I therefore believe that the kangaroo gave me my language, waterholes, food, hills and valleys, and much else. Certain parts of a kangaroo carcass are taboo to me as food, including the forelegs and hindlegs. A tribesman belonging to the Snake totem will not eat any of the reptile because one part of its body looks like any other part, and he might make a mistake.

As the painted men came into view of all but me, one of the singers at the ring called out the "country" of each. We all belong to the Alawa tribe and the Roper River district, but every man among us owns a particular plot of tribal ground which he calls "My Country."

Mine is an area of sixty square miles—nearly forty thousand acres—just south of Roper River mission. I call it Larbaryandji. I know a white man who grazes his cattle there and thinks it is his.

My brother, Jacob Wuyaindjimadjinji, owns country on the Hodgson River inside the boundaries of a cattle station run by Lord Vestey of England, who thinks it is his.

When all the performers were out of the creek the singers began a marching song:

Kunamanda-manda
Kunamanda-manda
Kunamanda-manda
Bira bira
Oi! Oi!

This means simply: "Here we are together, gathered at the corroboree ground, waiting for the ceremony to begin."

From my dark and stifling prison beneath the blankets I heard the approving comments as the snake-like file of painted men moved towards the ring. On arrival there a woman rubbed each man on the legs with a human-hair string, thus releasing them from the proscription under which they had been denied association with their families.

They were also pelted with ashes as a symbol of regeneration.

Two of the men were painted as dogs. One of them would be officiating surgeon tomorrow, and the other a kind of untrained theatre nurse who would hand him his surgical instrument, the razor blade, and the highly septic dressings—muddy swamp water and white clay.

Each man emerged from the creek only when the name of his own dog was called by a chanter. These men walked and listened, walked and listened, quickly, slowly, hearkening, miming with cupped hands behind their ears, the beating sticks changing tempo as they changed pace, the dogs' names constantly called by the singers.

The dogmen wore hair-belts, which they rubbed under their armpits. When they reached me I felt them rubbing the belts on a piece of paperbark laid on top of my blankets, indicating to the women—my sisters-in-law—that their duties were ended. By this single symbolic act they knew it was time for them to leave the arena. Henceforth the ceremony was strictly men's Sunday-business—Yunguwan—in which they could not take part.

My blankets were then removed. For that I was grateful. The men returned to their camps, but I was not allowed to leave the ring. I stayed there with my Uncle Stanley Marbunggu and two boys who had already been circumcised.

The psychological pressure was increasing. Not knowing what was ahead made me anxious. But the two boys whispered reassuringly and, although it was forbidden, told me a little of what I might expect. You know how secrets will leak out.

"Don't be afraid," they said.

"Don't cry out."

"Be strong and brave."

"Make the men believe that pain means nothing to you. Make them proud that you are an Alawa."

"Don't be weak like a woman."

"They will cut off your foreskin. . . . "

" . . . it will hurt. . . . "

" . . . but not enough to make you cry out. . . . "
" . . . it will be over quickly. . . . "
" . . . not like the Gobaboingu. . . . "
" . . . and the Jambaboingo at Yirrkalla. . . . "
" . . . who knock out a front tooth with a hammer. . . ."
" . . . that must hurt badly. . . . "
" . . . so remember. . . . "
" . . . be a Man. . . . "

After dark the singers returned and resumed their chanting. When they heard men whistling at the camp I was put back under the blankets. This was a signal that the painted dancers were ready to return. I was still not allowed to see them.

The two dogmen led the Mundiwa, but at a shouted word they went into hiding behind bushes. I was alone again with the two boys. With the start of another song they pulled the blankets away and a man appeared to blindfold me with his hands.

A dancer approached, put his mouth to one of my ears, and blew. That was symbolic of the fact that I was now permitted to hear things I hadn't heard before. He then rubbed sweat from his armpits on my eyes, symbolizing my right to see the Number One Dancer.

This was repeated—the blindfold, the blowing in the ear, the smearing with sweat—for each dancer separately, so that I might be able to look at them, too.

Then the chanters sang the Munggun, a song about the Road of my Dreaming. Now the dancers came out in groups of two, three, and four, brothers together, with bushes tied to their legs. This was one of the secrets of the ceremony that the initiate must learn to keep.

And immediately they bombarded me with instructions and swore at me in Waliburu—the Alawa language. The verbal assault was led by my Uncle Stanley Marbunggu and my cousins. . . .

"Don't chase after women."
"Don't throw spears at dogs."
"Obey when an Elder instructs you."
"If you're told to run a mile, run a mile."

"Don't argue."

"Don't answer back."

"Don't hit your playmates or your brothers and sisters."

"Avoid your female cousins."

"Don't lose your temper."

While I was being thus harangued the singers and dancers were reminding us about the billabongs and rivers made by the Rainbow Snake.

We regard The Snake as The Boss. His symbol is the rainbow. He is the Roadmaker, bringing young girls to puberty, forming the roads to their wombs so that spirit-children may pass to be born of their flesh. My people do not believe that conception occurs through sexual inter-course. It is achieved immaculately by the spirits, much as happened to the Virgin Mary.

Now the fires glowed.

The women in the camp had their faces hidden.

The children dare not look in my direction.

Like the instinctively understanding dogs, they were all struck dumb.

A tribal Man was being Made.

That was an augury demanding the utmost silent fervour.

It goes on. It goes on. It goes on. On and on, over and over, repetitive, religious, fundamental, according to the Dreamtime Way, until daylight.

My ordeal approached its end as the dark curtains of the night parted so that we could see the early birds, and the surgeon might have enough light upon his operating table.

A paperbark bed was prepared, and my brother-in-law, Mardi Munggunding, lay face-down upon it, acting as a human mattress. I was lifted by my Uncle and laid on Mardi, back-to-back. This was where the anaesthetist should have entered with his antiseptic paint and his welcome injection of pentothal to give me peace.

Alas. Our Medicine-Men practise supernatural killing and healing, but the ceremonial surgeons have never studied anaesthesia.

The Number One Dogman approached softly. I saw him looming above me, grotesquely painted but benevolent.

"Bite hard on this," he said. "It will help you not to cry out."

He handed me a crude dillybag made of grass, reeds and fabric.

"Bite it well," he repeated.

I clenched the bag between my teeth and instantly felt the searing heat of cold steel as I was sanctified. The operation lasted less than a minute. It was painful, but I savaged my biting-bag and did not cry out.

My Uncle Stanley carried me away to a shadehouse and stayed with me there for five days while I recuperated.

If I thought that my testing time was now ended I was soon disillusioned.

Marbunggu, tribally appointed to "grow me up" like a Christian Godfather, laid down the law:

I must not eat fat goanna, fat turtle, fat scrub turkey, or any other fatty food. Whatever meat I ate must be lean.

In no circumstances could I talk to anyone other than my father, my mother, my uncle, my brothers, and a few other close relatives.

I must camp with my male cousins and not approach my sisters.

While healing I was forbidden to swim in any river, billabong or flooded creek, on pain of being swallowed by the mystical Rainbow Snake. I believed that implicitly. In spite of Christian education I have since had, I still believe it.

I could talk to other boys, my male mates of the camp-fire circle, but if a man approached I must be silent. If I was asked a question—and that was often done to establish my faith and alertness—I must answer with a nod or shake of the head.

Above all, I must avoid speech with the dancers who performed at my initiation.

I was to remain under these taboos not for two days or weeks or even two months, but for two long years. The penalty for breaking one was rather more imagined than real, but I was well aware that presents being made for me —toy spears, boomerangs and canoes by the men, feathered bangles by the women—might be given to other boys if I was wayward.

That was unthinkable, so I accepted the discipline, deliberating always whether I was entitled to speak before I did so, ignoring my sisters, sisters-in-law, and aunts, and forsaking the fatty foods I loved to eat.

I waited two years for my humble presents, but I waited well. I am proud that I passed my tests in self-denial and self-control. I believe I am a better man for having done so.

Perhaps this speech-taboo explains much of the reticence of the aborigines. A man who is half-dumb for two years is seldom garrulous thereafter.

I know of other tribes whose people would benefit from similar interdictions.

And they're not all black!

Chapter Three

MY early life was not always grim.
Tribal initiation and the attempt to
"sing" me to death occurred during my most impression-
able years. I am therefore never likely to forget either
episode. It is because they loom so positively in my
memory that I have written about them first.

But the mind of an aboriginal piccaninny is no less
receptive than the mind of a white child, and I have a
clear recollection of other events in my youth.

Today I am supposed to be a civilized man. I think I
am. I can read and write. I speak English as though it
were my mother tongue, even though I learnt it as a
foreign language.

Citizenship has been conferred upon me. I studied the
Christian religion at Roper River mission and was baptized
in the Anglican Church. I have acquired a number of
sophisticated skills: I am an ambulance driver, a motor
mechanic, a medical assistant, a hospital orderly. I sleep
in a bed, eat with a knife and fork, wear clothes, and bathe
regularly.

Yet I have never lost my primitive instincts.

At weekends I take my wife and our six girls on hunting
and fishing walkabouts to Buffalo Creek or Casuarina
Beach or Lee Point or other pleasant places near Darwin.
After working as Europeans do during the week I like to
throw off the silken fetters of civilization on Saturday. I
stride through the bush with spears and boomerangs
poised, my family following behind with camping gear
and water.

If my aim with a spear is not as good as it once was, that is explained by lack of practice. Nevertheless, I still get an occasional wallaby which has been careless with the cardinal rule of the bush: caution. If I spear nothing it doesn't matter. I earn enough money to provide food for my family. These walkabouts are holidays, the equivalent of the white man's shooting and fishing expeditions.

And yet . . . and yet . . . they are much more besides. To me they are also a symbol of times past.

With civilization all around me I am happiest when I walk out as a scantily clad manly hunter, forgetting the present and future and easily projecting myself into the past, using the hereditary gifts of bushcraft and tracking which the modern age has been unable to alienate from our keeping.

And it is during these hunting holidays that I find myself in closest affinity with my ancestors, living by the laws they taught my great-grandparents, alert for the same evils, believing in spirits as they did, still afraid. . . .

Yes, afraid. In the bush within a dozen miles of the city of Darwin I am never less instinctively alert than I was in Arnhem Land when I lived by my skill as a hunter.

Why should I be alert and afraid when the necessity to find food is gone and the city's proximity should have banished the evil spirits?

The fact is that as I walk along I stop constantly and listen intently. I freeze, immobile as a totem pole, at the slightest movement of a tree or bush not apparently caused by the wind.

I look behind me every few steps, believing that I am being followed. If a twig snaps I might stand on the one spot for several minutes before moving on. I will avoid passing close to caves or small clumps of jungle for fear that they hold an ambush.

In all the years I have been hunting I have not yet seen anything to substantiate these fears . . . but I know that something, someone, is there. I must be careful, watching always for—I don't know what.

Who could be there?

Perhaps the pygmies, the little people who live in the mountains north of the Roper. We call them Burgingin. My tribesmen have seen them.

I first learnt about the Burgingin as a gullible white child learns about a bogyman. A boy or girl whose parents have talked seriously about a bogyman in the dark will believe the story throughout childhood and, especially in the girl's case, may retain a fear of darkness throughout her life.

In much the same fashion, I was cautioned about the pygmies by the Elders of the tribe.

"Be very careful," they told me. "Never let one get behind you. They are Little People, three feet tall, but immensely strong. A Burgingin man can crush an Alawa's bones and break him in half. A Burgingin, like an ant with a beetle, can carry a bullock on his shoulders. Be on your guard! Look behind you as you hunt! Beware! Take care!"

In all my life I have not seen one, but I have never failed to look for them when I'm hunting.

The fable of the Burgingin—if it is a fable—extends from the Roper down east through the Anula and Garawa country into Queensland. They believe it at Turn-off Lagoon and Doomadgee Mission, on the Nicholson, as we do on the fringes of Arnhem Land five hundred miles away.

The geographers say that Australia and New Guinea were once connected by a land bridge . . . and there are strong warrior-pygmies in New Guinea today. Why should we not believe that they are still on the mainland in places where few white men have been?

Before my initiation an old tribesman told me this story:

"One day I go on hunting walkabout. I go and I go and I go and I go. And I sit down. Camp.

"Arright. Sun-up I go and I go and I go and I go. And I sit down. Camp.

"Arright. Sun-up I go and I go . . . ah! what's that! Kangaroo! Quietly sneak-up . . . woomera on spear . . . swish! . . . got 'im!

"But that kangaroo not dead first-time. He hop away, blood dripping, crooked track, go here, go there, go everywhere. I run after him.

"I run and I run, chasing blood trail he leaves on the ground. Then that 'roo lie down properly-dead-finish. I run up, I see big pool of blood where he die. I see tracks where he thrash about, and my spear there, too.

"But that 'roo not there. Him gone. Then I look close-to and I see piccaninny track . . . only him not piccaninny track at all . . . him pygmy!

"Burgingin bin carry that kangaroo away and I properly fright. I run and I run and I run no-more-little-bit and I not sit-down till dark. And all-a-time I got plenty pimple-along-skin, all-a-same goose."

I laughed loudly when the old man told me his story. Nevertheless, I remembered it well. I watch for the pygmies today, especially in the rainy season when they might be hiding behind the misty clouds hanging on the hills.

Many of my friends on the Roper told me they had seen Burgingin. I have no reason to doubt their word. Moreover, the Elders would not have warned us to be alert for them while hunting if they didn't exist.

One aspect of the Burgingin fable has puzzled the younger members of the Alawa tribe who are perhaps not so blindly credulous since the dilution of our faith in the weakening waters of civilization: in all the stories we were told about them there was never a reference to a pygmy woman or a pygmy child.

Without women there can be no children. Without children there can be no men. We found this especially hard to explain because our hunting walkabouts are family affairs. Everyone goes along, the hunter leading in his lordly fashion, the women, the piccaninnies and the dogs behind.

Although we were puzzled our faith in the story was not destroyed. I still believe it. It was a law brought down from the Time of Dream by the Succession of Elders. My Uncle gave it to me and I have given it to my nephews.

It will remain part of our culture until assimilation deprives us of it for ever.

Deride us if you will for believing in the existence of such people. But remember that ghosts, gods, devils, dwarfs, giants, wraiths, bogymen, and flying saucers are also supposed to inhabit the earth today.

Another of our parables concerns the Malanugga-nugga, the Stone People who lived near The Ruined City in the Arnhem Land escarpment.

They were flesh-and-blood aborigines who were normal in all respects except for an intense timidity allied, paradoxically, to a murderous blood-lust.

They were true nomads: Stone Age people who lived in the rocky escarpment, but seldom remained long in any one locality. Their descendants have since been absorbed in branches of the Ritarnngu and Rembarrnga tribes who have come south to the Roper River to escape the privations of their tribal land.

The Arnhem Land escarpment is incredibly rugged. It reminds me of pictures I have seen of the Mountains of the Moon. Tortuous granite and sandstone outcroppings of the most devilish intricacy make it almost impassable to humans. To my knowledge, it has been crossed only once by white men, and they followed the river valleys to avoid penetrating much of the Stone-Country itself.

Every five miles or so the range stops abruptly at a precipitous cliff, razor sharp, and extending beyond the horizon. Perhaps half a mile, sometimes a mile away from the first cliff there is another equally steep, identical in its forbidding symmetry, the two forming a majestic Death Valley floor reaching back like a dry river gorge into the neverness.

It is uncanny and repellent country, and within it there lived the Malanugga-nugga. We did not like them; not only because they often raided the Alawa for women, but also because we associated the escarpment with evil and devils.

We had a particular abhorrence of a place we knew as Burruindju—The Ruined City—on the Rose River. This was an immense bluff of white sandstone that strikingly resembled the collinear façade of a European castle. There was not one of these; there were dozens, each a mute attestation of the origins of architecture, each geometrically perfect, eerie, and odious.

When I came to Burruindju one day on a horseback walkabout—even for my calloused feet the country was too rough—I was overcome with revulsion and a foreboding that here, unless I turned about, I would meet evil spirits and their fleshly cousins, the Malanugga-nugga.

I camped with my friends on a ridge about two miles from the city but clearly within view. We were afraid to go near it at night, and after what we heard and saw even our daylight approach was one of fear and trepidation.

I had not long rolled out my swag and was lying on it, idly sipping from a pannikin of tea, when the air was rent by high-pitched demoniacal screaming.

The very skin of me crept and tingled with fear.

"Devils!" I said.

"Yes," my friend Gurugul said. "Black devils! What will we do?"

There was nothing to be done but stay there. The escarpment was barely passable by day. At night it was a maze from which there was no escape.

Scarcely had we recovered from the first fright when the walls of Burruindju, in the places where windows might have been, came alight!

This was a phenomenon, indeed. I had never seen such brilliant lights. They flicked on and off as though electrically controlled: first one window, then another and another, a ceaseless neon in a place where no electrician has yet set foot.

Was the screaming really the mournful wail of a pack of dingoes baying to the moon?

Were the lights turned on and off by giant fireflies, their luminosity magnified in a land where artificial light was unknown?

Was it radioactivity?

All I can say is that I imagined a Black Mass of the most horrifying kind, and demented Malanugga-nuggas running around with huge lanterns.

Nor was my peace of mind helped when I heard a far-off roar, which was inexplicable—until the wind that caused it, racing along the valley floor, climbed the Jump-Up and reached us. I was least of all fortified by the profile of my horse, his neck stretched forlornly, neither sleeping nor alert, neither grazing nor drinking, but standing stupidly still, waiting docilely for the end in this most distasteful of all pastures.

After our terror of the night we were all rather proud of ourselves next day when we mustered the courage to ride down and examine Burruindju.

What we found was that which might have been expected: the sandstone walls, chiselled by the Master Masons of Time, crenellated by darting winds whose flow was broken by the inconsistencies of the geology; immense caves with hungry mouths able to swallow a man and his horse at one bite; a million stylized paintings in ochre and white clay, the work of another generation of Malanugga-nuggas . . . and human bones but no other humans!

Believe me when I say that we did not linger there. We looked and we left, like men with vertigo on a canyon verge. If our horses were rowelled grievously that day it was because we had urgent appointments elsewhere. The "elsewhere" might be north, south, east, or west, just as long as it was at maximum range from Burruindju.

I did not return there. I never will.

My father told me that in his father's time the Mala-nugga-nugga came in from the coast to raid the Alawa, carrying off our women and killing our men. Perhaps that accounts for the fact that today the Alawa is not a numerically strong tribe.

Our women were taken back into the escarpment, perhaps to places like Burruindju where we found the human bones. There they were impregnated and kept alive while they continued to produce children. But barrenness inevitably meant death.

It required extraordinary cunning and stealth for any group of people to make an undetected approach on the Alawa, but the Malanugga-nugga could do it. They moved quickly between waterholes, never showing a smoke, never talking, careful that they did not flush big flights of birds, until the moment when they flung themselves upon my people, slaughtering the men while they slept and making off with the potential mothers of their children.

The raiding parties were known as Gulgar. No more terrifying word existed in the Waliburu language. They descended upon us in hundreds, throwing spears and boomerangs indiscriminately and thrashing about them with nulla-nullas which cracked skulls and limbs. There were times, of course, when the Alawa carried out reprisal raids, but from what I have been able to learn they were not often successful. Our blood is still relatively pure.

There came a time, too, when we switched our attentions from marauding aboriginal tribes to the early European intruders, first because they were unwelcome in our land and then because they had many things we coveted: knives, axes, mirrors, combs, flour, and fresh meat.

The Singing String—the Overland Telegraph Line— was thrown across the country in my grandfather's day. The heavy poles were brought up the Roper for unloading at Roper Bar. We took our share of their goods and our share of their lives, but we paid dearly in the only currency we had: our own blood.

The Alawa once believed themselves destined to rule all the aborigines, a fantasy not unknown in the white world. To achieve this, one of our raiding parties stole a number of rifles from an O.T. Line camp and went looking for the Mara people at Wadanardja below the Roper. They had recently raided us and this was to be their moment of truth. The Malanugga-nugga would be next. But the only people killed that day were hit with spears and boomerangs. My people fired the rifles aimlessly into the air, unaware that the bullet and not the explosion of a cartridge was lethal. Their avaricious dreams of power and influence were dashed. The Mala-nugga-nugga were left in peace.

A similar incomprehension marred our first experience with flour, the basic food of half the human race. Instead of eating it, my people used it as a substitute for white clay to paint their bodies for corroborees. It was much later, long after the raids against the linesmen were forgotten, that an understanding traveller showed us the uses of flour as a food. Thereafter every black raider of a white man's camp had two enemies: the white man himself and the aborigines from other tribes who were trying to beat him to the storeroom.

Perhaps it is poetic justice that the descendants of the Malanugga-nugga, now assimilated in the Ritarrngu and Rembarrnga tribes, have had to leave the Stone Country and come to live along the Roper. Some went the other way, north to Yirrkalla, Elcho Island, and Millingimbi on the north coast of the world's biggest aboriginal reserve. Their own tribal land—thirty thousand square miles of it —is an empty waste.

They could live there still, if they wished, but civilization is heavy upon them. They want education for their children, and that can be had only at the mission stations and government settlements.

So the nomads have disappeared, the raiders have stopped raiding, and the culture and the corroborees are slowly being lost.

Nevertheless, the tribal traditions remain strong in their breasts. Though their blood is diluted, the Ritarrngu and the Rembarrnga still go back to the Stone Country every year on hunting walkabouts, drawn by loyalty to the Malanugga-nugga they assimilated. But I doubt if they go to Burruindju, where I found their languishing but frightening spirits.

Chapter Four

MY contact with the Big White Way began in a limited sense from the very day I appeared in the world as a true bush baby.

Some years earlier the Church Missionary Society had established an evangelical mission twenty miles downstream from Roper Bar, so named because that was the navigable terminus of the river for almost any ship bigger than a dugout canoe.

After resting in the bush for two or three days, my mother carried me proudly to the mission.

My father, Barnabas Gabarla, had found work there as a stockman and saddler, earning with the skills he had learnt from the drovers and surrounding pastoralists enough food to keep his growing family alive.

Our permanent "camp"—and I doubt if it deserved any more pretentious title—was a bark hut, twelve feet square, consisting of but a single room.

When our family was complete I slept there with my mother and father, my sister Mercia, and my brothers Silas and Jacob.

Such togetherness was something of an embarrassment. The building was too small to accommodate six beds, and so we all curled up on the floor with a few blankets the missionaries gave us.

Privacy was impossible. Long before my initiation I was aware that a man and his wife lay down at night not only to sleep; but my education in this respect would have been no less graphic had we lived in one of the many tribal camps on the river flats where the act of physical union, if not quite a public spectacle, was seldom concealed.

Our needs were simple. We were entirely without money. I don't know what we would have done with it if one of us had suddenly found a hundred pounds. There was no shop, and no other way in which we could spend it. I doubt whether I saw a silver coin—and certainly not a banknote—until I went to school. Money was something we couldn't eat or wear; therefore we had no use for it. When this basic aboriginal yardstick was applied it became valueless. Even in the currency of the bush, which was food, our spending power was circumscribed by the tribal laws.

Any substantial food was carefully and strictly divided in accordance with the rules. A kangaroo, for instance, was invariably carved so as to allot the various portions to predetermined owners whose right was inalienable.

The hunter himself was traditionally entitled to the back, the tail, and the head of any animal he speared. The right leg belonged to his maternal uncle. And there were nominated cuts for his parents and other close relatives. As the Lord commanded Moses: *"Thou shalt take of the ram the fat and the rump, and the fat that covereth the inwards, and the caul above the liver, and the two kidneys, and the fat that is upon them, and the right shoulder . . . and thou shalt put all in the hands of Aaron and in the hands of his sons."*

Normally, a relative of mine who killed a kangaroo would send me my portion by a messenger, perhaps an aunt or a cousin. But my entitlement was so well established that I could, without fear of remonstrance, walk into his camp and cut off my share before he had touched it.

That kangaroo had eaten grass which belonged to the tribe as a whole. The tribe had kept it alive. The tribe could therefore claim its communal tribute.

None of us ever disputed the right of another to his fair share, even though it was occasionally thought that some lazy men might have done a little more hunting.

47

I suppose that in this respect the aborigines were among the world's first practising communists. We lived by a form of collective security, giving to each according to his needs, expecting a contribution of every man's hunting ability as the price of his equity in the common ownership. Even so, our deeply religious philosophy—though fundamentally pagan—eliminated us as contemporary recruits to dialectical materialism.

My maternal uncle—the Gardigardi—owed me a living in more ways than the division of food. I could borrow literally anything of his—canoes, spears, boomerangs—without permission. They were his. Therefore they were mine.

The Aranda artist, Albert Namatjira, had the same problem. He found in his lifetime that he was Rich Uncle to more indigent nephews than he had known existed. These nephews were old enough to be uncles themselves, with their own crop of relatives to support. The result was that Namatjira became Aranda Bank Unlimited, a utopian enterprise in which withdrawals were easy and deposits unnecessary. His hangers-on included a horde of claimants whose blood relationship was obscure but who were nevertheless fed and feted.

They began by insisting that Albert should buy a motor truck for communal use. No native had ever owned a truck before, and the mystery of motive power, plus the fact that four wheels made easier work than two legs of the eighty miles between Hermannsburg mission, where they lived, and Alice Springs, where they played, endeared itself to the Aranda heart. It also carried tremendous prestige when they were visited by or, as more often happened, they visited neighbouring tribes.

Namatjira's family tree was explored to its roots by every Aranda who knew that by proving remote relationship he could attend the artist's Court and add himself to the retinue of princes.

In nineteen hundred and fifty Albert was earning one thousand pounds a year. Five years later the figure was three thousand five hundred pounds. By nineteen hundred and fifty-nine he was making a fabulous seven thousand pounds a year from his painting, plus an unknown amount for reproduction rights.

But he died penniless, preyed upon by tribal wolves who stripped him of his last shilling and even caused him to go to gaol by insisting that he also share his liquor with them. As a citizen, Albert was entitled to drink. But his relatives were wards of the State, for whom alcohol was forbidden. The minimum penalty for anyone giving it to them was six months' imprisonment. Albert, inevitably, had to share with his tribesmen. They won and he lost. Such a penalty was imposed upon him in a white man's court.

I have mentioned this only to emphasize the vulnerability of aboriginal uncles. The law was the same for Namatjira as for my Gardigardi. It applied in reverse, of course, to my father. His nephews exploited him unconscionably.

The arbitrary division of our food did not apply to snakes. A hunter who caught one, if it wasn't taboo to him, could eat it all. In practice, however, most of the snakes were given to old men and women who were no longer able to chew the tough kangaroo steak.

Snake was known as "soft tucker." If none was available the old people pounded kangaroo meat on stones until it was soft enough. In isolated cases it was masticated for them by close relatives, so that all they had to do was swallow it! I suppose it was like living on vitamin pills, with all the pleasure taken from eating.

My father was one of about fifty natives employed by the mission and entitled to his family's subsistence. But he never knew how long it might be before we were again required to live by our wits as hunters. We therefore practised our spear-arms whenever possible. Each Saturday we walked out to hunt kangaroos and dig lily roots from the lagoons. It was a rule that we fasted unless we killed game. That did not often happen. Nobody is hungrier than a black hunter. Our trackers' eyes were sharper and our shafts flew straighter with the knowledge that a missed target meant a missed meal.

My naked childhood passed pleasantly, although my own children would complain if they lived as we did. One of our chief amusements was a game called Horses-and-Men in which we play-acted the work of the stock camps. We were familiar with all the stark realities of cattle raising because the mission owned a substantial herd —and wasn't my father the best stockman?

We made toy stockyards of stones, matchsticks, and pieces of string or wire. Boys riding on their friends' backs then mustered other boys, who acted as calves. They were roped and thrown, branded OTC—the mission's registered mark—with spittle and sand, and were even subjected to mock bangtailing and castration while they bleated mournfully.

We fought with toy spears, the ends bound with rag so that anyone who was hit wouldn't be badly hurt. A boy struck by a spear was obliged to fall down. The girls then ran in and wailed over their dead brothers. This was the only part the girls were allowed to play. Young aboriginal boys probably have a greater contempt for girls than white boys. We wouldn't be seen near them. But we didn't mind them crying over fallen relatives. That seemed appropriate to their station in life.

We also fought with boomerangs and nulla nullas. The idea was to hit without hurting—but you know how it is with boys: taps which began as slaps became clouts and wallops as one boy accused another of hitting harder than was allowed by the rules, and he therefore had to retaliate. But if someone was really hurt we adopted the Pay-Back system of the Elders.

The wounded boy was entitled to a Johnny-cake or a plate of rice from the offender at meal time. This meant that one fed too well, and the other remained hungry. If the wound was especially severe and obviously deliberate the culprit could be deprived of something he prized, perhaps a fish spear made for him by his father.

That was considered harsh, indeed, but unless he paid up the plaintiff was entitled to tell his father that Waipuldanya, if it was me, had made him bleed. I would do anything to avoid the inevitable consequences of such a disclosure: a thorough thrashing with a stick which hurt the pride almost as much as the hide.

Small canoes which carried three or four boys were our lasting joy. My father had cut one for me from a paper-bark log, and with my brothers and friends I spent endless hours on the placid Roper River, paddling lazily along the half-mile stretch of water between two points we knew as "camp jetty" and "mission jetty."

Young boys, whether they're black or white, invariably extend the boundaries delineated for them by their guardians, but I can say with absolute truth that we never once went off-limits. We stayed where we were under observation by the Elders for the excellent reason that we were afraid of the crocodiles sharing the river with us.

"The crocodiles will get you if you don't watch out!" was our constant warning. And we had evidence to prove just how true that was.

One evening a sixteen-year-old girl, Girigbal, went with her cousin, Gurtima, to draw water from the river in billy-cans. Normally this was a daylight task performed by bigger groups of women, but the camp was short of water, and the girls were sent to get it.

The bank was steep, matted with grass and reeds, and eerily sinister in the moonlight. Girigbal dipped one billy-can in the stream, leaning well out from the bank while Gurtima, who also held a paperbark firestick aloft, clasped her cousin's wrist so that she didn't overbalance.

As Girigbal's billycan touched the water a crocodile grabbed her wrist with its claws. She dragged it away, screaming with pain, terrified by the suddenness of the attack, blood pouring from wounds which had laid bare the bones on the back of her hand. Of course, if the crocodile had had time or been in position to strike with its fearful jaws Girigbal would not have had a hand; in fact, we would not have had Girigbal.

"Yak-ai! Yak-ai! Yak-ai!"

I remember Gurtima dragged her up the bank while she yelled for the Elders. They came with torches blazing, searching the shallows, probing with spears for the man-eater, which had disappeared.

I never forgot that episode. When canoeing I kept the scene in mind and had no difficulty obeying the injunction not to go beyond the jetties.

I knew that the crocodiles were immensely cunning, lying in wait for hours and often days before being satisfied that danger was eliminated and the time to strike had come.

My father tried to catch one with a poisoned bait he had attached to a line from a Leichhardt pine hanging over the water. He had strychnine the missionaries gave him to kill dingoes. But why poison tough dingoes when you might get a tender crocodile? So my father set his traps.

Days passed without the bait being taken. He replaced it with meat, which he forgot to poison. It was taken the same night.

I remember that this process was repeated several times, deliberately at last because my father was trying to establish whether the crocodile could really distinguish between pure meat and poisoned bait.

He proved it beyond doubt. The fresh meat invariably disappeared. The bait was always left alone. We knew then that we were dealing with a saurian enemy capable of thought.

Nevertheless, its thinking was sometimes faulty. I remember well the day when Alan Gumalamalay, an athletic Ngandi tribesman, trapped a crocodile into attacking him by imitating the yelps of an injured dog.

His distressed canine howling was perfect. It must have been so to fool a crocodile. When it ceased he tapped gently on the water with his woomera, lap-lap-lap-lap-lap, like a dog drinking. The crocodile fell for it, sliding quickly out of the water and around a small point of land which had concealed Gumalamalay and two of his friends.

The crocodile was right out of the river, moving revoltingly towards its victim, when it died. One man's treble-pronged spear caught it under a leg, penetrating to the wicked heart. Startled, mortally hurt, its pride also wounded for having been caught, the crocodile reared and slashed with its gnarled tail, exposing the softer underbelly of hide. And at that moment the second spearman fell upon it, driving for the base of the spine with a shovelnose that inflicted a terrible wound.

The immense carcass, twelve feet long, its tail and snout dangling, its stumpy legs now paddling air, was borne aloft by ten men, five on either side, like a coffin to a grave.

Proudly they passed down an admiring aisle: old men, young men, boys, women, and girls, in that order.

"Fat one," we exclaimed, the ultimate in compliments to a hunter.

"Cheeky one."

"Big one."

"Dead one." Allabout laughed.

We patted it, felt its two canine teeth protruding from the snout like elephantine tusks, and marvelled at the double row of serrated, saw-like spines along the back and tail.

So that was what had cut down the tree!

Yes, the power of a crocodile is little understood. We had seen plenty of them in the distance. We had seen them submerging like sinister U-boats as we approached in our canoes, emptying their tanks of putrid breath.

In later years, as a professional crocodile hunter, I was to have intimate personal battles with man-eaters. But this was the first big one I had seen close-to.

Now I knew what it was that had cut that tree off a foot from the ground, the one near The Place Where the Horses Drink, slicing through a solid six inches of Leichhardt pine as though it was a chain saw. I had seen another tree, a eucalypt, with a hole three inches deep in the bole.

"Crocodile bin knock 'im," my father had said.

Having seen the cutting tool and felt the muscle power behind it, I understood.

I knew at last why our men used the long stringy muscles from crocodile tails to bind metal heads to their spearshafts, preferring them when available to the more conventional kangaroo tail muscles.

"Suppose you put crocodile muscle around spearhead, him never shift," my uncle taught me.

So this, I thought, is what kills horses!

Often during the dry-season months when the river level was receding and the billabongs were drying out, our men found the tracks of horses. The animals had been bogged in the mud while stretching for a drink, stunned by a blow from such a tail as this one, and then dragged into the river.

A crocodile could drag a horse from a bog? Certainly, and bullocks too. It happened every year along the Roper, where life had not changed very much since those days, millenia ago, when the Dravidians crossed from Asia and were trapped in Australia, perhaps by cataclysmic up-heavals which formed new seas where land bridges had once existed.

The horses liked to feed in the lush grass and reeds on the river flats, but this greener grass changed colour when they found themselves helplessly bogged and a crocodile approaching. One blow of the huge tail shattered a skull. The saurian propelled itself backwards on the tail, drag-ging the animal out of the bog and into the river where there were no rules about horse meat being unfit for croco-dile consumption.

But on the Roper there was also no rule about crocodile meat being unfit for human consumption. There was nothing to stop us eating the eater. This one was obviously too big to be cooked whole, so it was skinned and cut up according to the tribal plan.

My father carried his portion to our camp. Anticipating this, my mother had been firing the stones in the ground oven in which we cooked most of our food. They were now thoroughly heated. She had lined the base of the oven with white-gum leaves and tea-tree bushes, in order to minimize grit in the meat and to add that dash of herbs that crocodile à la Gumalamalay really needs if the piquant, distinctive flavour is to be highlighted. The hot stones were then replaced, the meat was committed to their care, the whole delicious entrée was spread with ashes and driblets of water to make it steam, paperbark and sand covered that, and we sat back to hold our patience and our salivary glands.

When is a crocodile cooked? When is a kangaroo cooked? When is a goanna cooked? It depends entirely on the appetite and the will-power of the guests. I have come in from a hunting walkabout and insisted that my kangaroo should be lightly done, say ten minutes on the stones to char the fur. At other times, on a full belly, I don't mind if it cooks for two hours. That also applies to crocodile: it's done when you can't wait any longer.

I soon became an adept hunter myself. Before I was ten I could have subsisted on the food I speared, trapped, found, or hi-jacked—like milk from a nanny-goat's udder.

A favourite game was to go out with the shepherdesses —the old women of the tribe—and drive them to distraction by riding the goats and unsettling the herd. Sometimes we offered to act as shepherds while they went off to find lily roots in the lagoons, but it was only a ruse so that we could have our daily ride.

That kind of exercise made us thirsty. Water was common old stuff we could get at any time, but milk was food as well as drink, and here it was on tap!

One or twice I tried sucking a nanny-goat's teat, but I couldn't get a drop. I was puzzled to know how their kids managed to stay alive. But there were other methods: one of us would hold a teat and squirt a jet of milk into the open mouths of our friends.

And not only into the mouths! It was hilarious fun to deliver a fresh vanilla milkshake into a mate's eye or up his nose. We were soon covered in it. The nanny-goats betrayed us by bleating miserably, and the women would come back to chase us away.

At one time the mission had four hundred goats for us to molest and rob of their nectar, but the numbers rose and fell alarmingly if the shepherdesses allowed them too near the river.

The goats, inquisitive and lacking cunning, were easy marks for the crocodiles—a delicious mouthful of mutton. The women were supposed to keep the goats away from the river, but the animals were recalcitrant; they ran off to the greener pasture over the hill and many did not return.

Of all our diversions, I enjoyed canoeing and fishing most of all. They offered us danger, pleasure, food, and an outlet for our sharpening skill with spears.

The small dugout was nothing more than the name implied: a paperbark or pine log, which had been hollowed out with knives and axes—our ancestors did it with stone! —to form a crude canoe.

It had no keel, and having been made from a round log was alarmingly unstable in the water. Yet with practice we learnt how to balance it even when one of the three or four occupants stood upright to spear a fish.

In reaching perfection, of course, we had many upsets. But the thought of a crocodile tickling our toes while we floundered in the water helped to train us to right the canoe quickly and to scramble aboard.

That was the most difficult trick of all—for three boys, each wanting to pull or shove in a different direction, to co-ordinate their struggles so that the canoe remained upright while they clambered over the gunwale.

The river became our Arcady, a happy valley of tidal water, and no place for tedium; its banks echoing with liquid language as we drifted and shouted along, one boy paddling, one boy bailing, one boy poised with treble-pronged spear cocked and ready.

S-s-s-h! A movement of the mouth rather than a whisper. S-s-s-h! The paddle becomes a rudder, correcting the canoe's course. S-h-h-h! . . . Whish!

"Got 'im! Got 'im! Got 'im! Waipuldanya got 'im! Look-a-look-look. Rifle fish, that one. Rifle fish, yes. The fish that spits at insects and knocks them into the water.

Now Waipuldanya got 'im, look-a-look-look. He got 'im with spear-spit. E-e-e-e-e! A-a-a-h-h-h!"

The goat shepherdesses watching from the bank laughed uproariously.

The silly fish wriggled ineffectually on the three points of my spear. Soon we would bake it in a ground oven we had secreted on a sand-bluff overlooking the river, just far enough away from camp to be seen by the Elders, just far enough away for privacy. We were not bound to divide our fish with the tribe. To encourage boys to hunt with spears they were allowed, as a reward, to keep and eat their own fish. But it always tasted better if the Elders didn't know what we were doing.

How miserable it must have been upon the river in the days before fencing wire and thin steel rods! A Space-Age white child has difficulty in comprehending the horror of a world without radio and motor cars. But the aboriginal world which existed before fish spears is just as incomprehensible to me.

My grandfather, Ned Weari-wyingga, told me about the alternative he used as a boy: a conical basket net made of loya cane. This was placed in billabongs, and the fish were invited to trap themselves. Many did. Their hauls —if my grandfather's fish stories are to be believed—were immense.

"But you missed all the fun, grandfather . . . the fun of throwing a spear at a silver barramundi and watching it wriggle," I said.

"We didn't miss as much fun as you think," he said. "Boys make their own fun. While the traps were catching fish for us we could be hunting kangaroos with our stone-head spears. A trap left in the water overnight would often be full at dawn. No! We had no need of fish-spears. If we wanted diversion we caught them with our bare hands. . . ."

"With your bare hands . . . ?" I said, disbelievingly.

"It was easy," he said. "We held a crayfish in the water, making it flap its broad tail. That is like a dinner gong to a barramundi. Within a few minutes they swam up with their mouths open, straight for the cray, and eased their huge mouths over it as a python swallows a wallaby. Barramundi can hear well, but their sense of smell is poor. They are gluttonous. After swallowing the cray the fish began to swallow the human hand holding it—until it got to the wrist. Then we quickly snapped our fingers through the gills and threw them out of the water.

"If fish could express surprise those barramundi would have been full of exclamation marks. One moment they were gorging on a huge meal of cray and aboriginal arm, working themselves slowly along it. Next moment they were gasping on the bank. And you say we missed our fun! I haven't seen a boy catch a fish as we did since the first coil of wire arrived."

Well . . . maybe that was true. But we did have variations in the use of the three-pronged spear. Sometimes we built bush barricades across a stream, with a single gate through which fish must pass. There we stood, knee deep in water, and picked them off in dozens as they swam through. We stirred up the muddy bottoms of lagoons and billabongs until the dirty water forced the fish to the surface for air. That was like shooting sitting ducks.

We poisoned waterholes with bark from the Murnganawa tree—a fresh-water mangrove which abounded along the Roper. Many times did I help to strip the bark, to place it in an earth oven with layers of red-hot stones, to bind it all with the Bunbungari creeper, and then, when the bark began to exude its sizzling poisonous sap, to throw it all into the water. Next day the billabong was coated with dead fish.

And, of course, we occasionally found the kind of mischief that got us into serious trouble with the missionaries and our Elders.

There was The Case of the Leaking Carbide. . . .

One day tins of carbide used in the mission's lighting system were being unloaded from a boat at the jetty. As usual, the boys sat around on the bank, watching the bags of flour and the tins of jam and the cases of tea coming up in truly enormous quantities from the hold. This day the lid flew off one of the tins of carbide and dropped into the water. It began to sizzle.

"Fog!"

"Cloud!"

"Steam!"

"Smoke!"

Each of us had an explanation for the visible gas, but none expected the miracle that happened when one of the white mission workers threw a lighted match. Our eyes popped as it flashed and flared.

"I'm a magician," the man said. "I can make water burn."

That created a greater impression on my juvenile mind than any other white-feller magic I had seen. I knew that water was used to douse fire, yet here was a fire burning in the river.

"Look a' that!"

"Geez! See that water burn!"

"That must be properly devil-water, might be fresh water from hell, eh?"

We expounded our childish theories, but one of my mates, Jimmy Yudbundji, was strangely silent. Jimmy was the primitive scientist of my gang, a boy who was always inventing an easier method of making a spear or spearing a fish. And that night around the campfire he sat with his chin in his hands and stared endlessly into the coals, watching the changing pattern of colours of disintegrating timbers as they flared and smouldered and died.

At last I asked him, "What's wrong with you? Are you sick?"

"No," he said, "I'm thinking about that carbide."

"Yes, it was funny. But you're not laughing."

"I wasn't thinking about anything funny."

"What were you thinking about? What's wrong with the carbide?"

"Nothing," he said. "Nothing at all. I think we can use it to blow up fish."

59

The inventor, the brains of the gang, had been at work. We were delighted.

"How? How? How now, Jimmy?"

Jimmy produced a long thin tin with a screw top, like the case of a torch. "We will put carbide and water in here and wait for gas pressure to explode it," he said. "If that happens under water it should kill a lot of fish. Maybe there'll be some big barramundi sticky-beaking or trying to swallow it when it blows up."

We were enthralled by the plan, but Jimmy also warned us of the dangers. "We must get the top on and throw it into the water quickly, otherwise we might be blown up instead of the barramundi," he explained.

Finally it was put to the vote, and the Council of Juniors decided that the project should proceed.

The tin was half-filled with carbide we stole from the mission store, a pannikin of water was added, the top replaced, and the device thrown like a hand-grenade into the water. We were overwhelmed with tremulous excitement.

"Big fish for dinner tonight . . . coming up," Jimmy said.

We waited. We waited. We waited endlessly. We had thought that the ground would rumble and the water gush within a few minutes. We were convinced that we had built a fizzer. But then it exploded weakly, blowing the lid off, boiling a few bubbles and a trace of gas to the surface. The only fish we had killed were minnows.

Jimmy was not satisfied. "We can do better than that," he said. "Next Saturday, after school, we'll set off a double-bunger, a gallon tin of the stuff with the lid sealed on."

"You might blow up the mission," I said.

"I might blow myself up, too, but we must find out what happens." Jimmy was a true scientist.

That week was one of whispered secrets, of knowing looks, of sign-talk that only the members of my gang understood. Eventually the sun rose on Saturday, a flaming portent of the man-made fury we were about to release in the depths of the river.

This time we reduced the carbide and water content, leaving ample room for expansion and build-up of the gas. We screwed the lid down tightly and bound it with hemp until we were satisfied that it would not be blown off. We wired rocks to the outside and threw it into the river, more than a little afraid that we had produced a mine as lethal as any sown in the wars of white men.

I had a deep respect for Jimmy Yudbundji as an inventor, but I wasn't sure that he knew how to control his inventions. I therefore took prudent refuge behind a tree during the expectant suspense-laden minutes while the pressure-pot came to the boil. And I must say I was rather surprised that Jimmy also demonstrated his lack of confidence by getting behind another tree.

The wait seemed endless, especially as we dared not leave our hiding places and return to the river. But then it blew like a grampus, spewing mud and debris, water and fish in the maelstrom of bubbles we had created.

We ran down to the river's edge, and there was the unmistakable evidence of our success.

"Looka'look!" Jimmy shouted. "Barramundi . . . fat feller."

"Dhu fish! Properly-number-one!"

"Bream!"

"Trevally! Big one, big two-three."

"Schnapper, looka'look Jimmy!"

Our delight was unbounded. Here was a new way to catch fish, one we might be able to hand down to our tribal heirs just as our ancestors had given us spears and boomerangs.

Unfortunately that is not quite how it worked out.

Jock Buckley, one of the mission workers, had heard the explosion and felt the earthquake—who hadn't?—and came down to investigate. He arrived with almost every aboriginal on the mission as we were taking the dead fish from the water. We were caught gun-running, as obviously guilty of wanton destruction as other more sophisticated armament tycoons.

He took twenty of us before the mission court, which included our tribal Elders.

"Now what have you been up to?" he demanded.

But Jock was a practical man who understood exactly what had happened. We did not have to tell him.

"Who has been breaking into the store to steal carbide? Who was it made the bomb? Who was it killed the poor fish?" He fired questions at us rapidly without waiting for an answer. "How would you like me to fill a four-gallon drum with carbide and let it off in your camp tonight? Now would you like that, you little demons?"

"Yes please no sir, no sir!" We were all agreed on that. We had seen the devastating effect of our bomb, and we did not want them exploding near us.

"Do you want to live?" Jock thundered.

"Yes please—please sir." We agreed on that, too.

"How do you want to live? Like Christian boys or black devils?"

"By eating plenty of fish, please Mister Sir," Freddie said.

"No cheek! Don't be cheeky!" Jock roared. "You're in enough trouble." Then he turned to the Elders. "What'll I do with them?" he asked.

We would have preferred Jock to make that decision himself. We knew from experience that a white man's punishment was often less severe than that of our Elders. They did not hesitate.

"Give them all a whipping!"

"Yes, a belting!"

"A proper-hard belting. They might have blown us all up."

"Get the strap and give it to them all. Legs and backsides. Plenty cuts, properly ones. Kill'm hard-feller!"

And so it was. We lined up disconsolately, and the sentence of corporal punishment was administered at once by Jock. There was no appeal to a higher tribunal.

The first boy through the thrasher whined loudly and came back to me at the rear of the line.

"Boy, that hurt. No-more-little-bit," he said.

"Stinging-one," the next boy said.

"My legs bin burn," another said.

A few moments later I had personal proof of the accuracy of these statements.

"You-SLAP-should - WHAM - be - CRACK - ashamed-WHISH-of-SLASH-yourself-THUD!" Jock and the strap spoke together while I was given six of the best.

That was the end of our carbide bombs. We decided, after all, that fish were tastier if caught on the end of a wire spear. In any case, the mission lighting system was soon converted to kerosene lamps. Lethal material was out of our reach.

If the enchantment of the river began to pall we had only to beach the canoes and walk through the bush to find parrots, peewees, firebirds, galahs, and hawks.

I have speared and eaten all these birds—may I henceforth be preserved from eaglehawk!—but I could never get a crow or a cockatoo. Nor do I know any tribesman who did. The galahs and the others were sleepy ground-feeders, and they paid the price of incaution.

At night the campfires glowed, the didgeredoos droned, the chanters sang to the tapping of sticks. We danced our play-corroborees, the Lunggurr and the Bunggal, distinct in their light-heartedness from the heavy operatic stuff, the symbolic Kunapipi and the sanctifying Yabudurawa in which we sought regeneration.

I suffered derision from my friends and a personal sense of shame because I could never learn to play the didgeredoo. This hollow piece of wood, six feet long and three inches thick, is commonly supposed to be the traditional musical instrument of all Australian aborigines. That is not so. It belongs to the tribes north and west of the Roper. The Alawa, the Mara, the Anula, and the Garawa are singers and stickbeaters. The didgeredoo, to us, is a foreign instrument. Nevertheless, it has been imported and we used it widely in our dances.

Some of my friends, more adaptable anatomically, learnt to play it in fifteen minutes. But I huffed and I puffed, I grunted and groaned, I blew and I wheezed. I managed a discordant noise which sent my friends into maddening paroxysms of mirth, but try as I might I could not get anything either continuous or tuneful from it.

The trick of playing a didgeredoo is in the breathing. Although it is a simple enough matter to produce a noise through pursed lips fitted to the mouthpiece, and to use the tongue as a stopcock to enunciate separate notes, the charm of the didgeredoo is in its organ-like quality of flowing sound. That can be done only by inhaling and exhaling simultaneously.

Try it, but watch you don't choke!

I practised from sun-up till sunset. I went into the bush to try secretly, away from the hauteur and disapprobation of my friends. They tracked me and laughed more than ever.

I had the experts explain it to me carefully. I did exactly as they said. And I very nearly suffocated.

This has been a major cause of mortification all my life: that I never did learn to play the didgeredoo. I cannot play any better now than when I first tried as a child. It is a shameful admission for any tribesman. Nevertheless, it is true.

I was grateful that the didgeredoo did not really belong to the Alawa, for then shame would have become disgrace. There were, moreover, enough distractions to compensate for this disability. I was a champion spearman. I could run like a dingo. I was a skilled horseman. And at an early age I began to acquire white man's skills.

Thus equipped, I was ready to mock the mockers.

Chapter Five

ALAS, even the carefree life of a small nomad is not secure, these days, against the compelling demands of the civilization that is heavy upon us.

One morning not long after my initiation I was confronted with the shocking news that I was about to begin school!

Anyone able to recall the ordeal of their first day at school will appreciate how much more deeply it must have affected an aboriginal boy whose family had no background of academic education, who was embarrassingly shy of all strangers, and who wanted to learn only those basic truths written in tracks in the Book of the Bush.

Most white children, having had some instruction in kindergartens or at their parents' knees, at least know how to spell simple words and to count up to ten before they attend school.

But we were nomads. My father and my grandfather were illiterate, as were my mother and my grandmother. They could not read or write or count, and would certainly be of no help to me when I brought my problem home.

Yet this was only the beginning of my trouble. I was to be taught English, which is easy enough for a white child whose parents speak it, but my mother tongue was Waliburu—the dialect of the Alawa. I would have to learn it as a foreign language while continuing to speak Waliburu in the camp.

Nor was that the only difficulty. Like most aboriginal tongues, Waliburu has no words for figures other than one and two: Wungain and Wuruja. We could count to three and four by saying Wungain-Wuruja and Wuruja-Wuruja. After that we were lost, and indicated higher numbers by using our fingers.

In the broken-English lingua franca known as pidgin which was used inter-tribally and for communication with white people we had such phrases as "little mob," which meant any number up to ten. Between ten and twenty was "little-bit-big-feller-mob," more than twenty was "big mob," and a hundred or so was "properly-big-feller-mob." But thirteen and thirty-three, fifty-five and fifteen just didn't exist.

Our teachers who first attempted to subdivide big-feller and little-feller mobs and to subtract little-bit-big-feller from properly-big-feller were confronted with an exercise unique in elementary mathematics.

We were at a disadvantage, also, because our parents could not help us with the language. They could neither parse nor analyse nor spell, nor could they, in many instances, understand a word of what we were trying to say.

The average white child can tell the time on a clock before he attends school. We had no clocks. To me, the day was divided thus: sunrise, dinnertime, sunset.

The seasons were simply Wet Weather, Cold Weather, and Hot Weather with variations: "The Green Grass Time," "The Long Grass Time," "The Burnt Grass Time," "The Turtle Egg Time," to indicate precise periods. I had never heard of January or June, March or December, but I now know that particular months were marked for us by trees flowering in rotation: the messmates, the nut-woods, the coolibahs, the mountain ash, and one we called Djirilina. We didn't have to be told when Sugarbag would be plentiful in the trees. That was something we knew instinctively. I wonder how many white boys are aware that such a delicacy exists.

It was not long after my initiation that the white missionary, Stanley Port, asked my father to send me to school.

My father replied: "I have nothing to do with it. That is a matter for the gardigardi, Marbunggu, who is growing him up."

Barnabas, of course, was right. My mother's brothers called me Nibarli, meaning son. I called my father's brothers Ngarbinini, which means literally assistant-father. But my guardian was Marbunggu, the maternal uncle, and Stanley Port had to consult him before I could attend school.

Marbunggu ordered me to go. When he spoke I obeyed. I expect that my maternal nephews will also obey me.

Much of my first day in the classroom was passed in sleep. That was my reaction to terror. The mission teacher, Miss Dove, shook me awake several times, but my eyelids were heavy with fear. I yawned once or twice, tried to pay attention, and was sound asleep again within a few moments. Finally she let me hibernate.

Next day, having acquired a little courage, I was alert and attentive. I learnt to spell "cat," and broke through the counting-barrier to five, ten, and eventually twenty. At night around the camp fire I proudly counted to twenty for my mother I might have saved my breath.

"What that talk?" she asked.

"Counting," I said.

"H'm, different one," she said, and thereafter showed little interest in my education. It was incomprehensible to her.

I suppose that our behaviour was average for a class of sixty boys and girls. We were alternately angelic and utterly impish. Perhaps aboriginal boys are more adept than white boys at inventing torments for teachers. Miss Dove often had trouble with her temper—and with fear, too—when she found a young goanna or a pet python approaching her chair. These reptiles were regularly smuggled through the door, past monitors who were watching for them, in lap-laps and nargas.

I never tired of watching the blood drain from Miss Dove's face and the horror in her eyes when she first caught sight of a snake slithering across the floor. To her, all snakes were venomous Taipans. I must say that I didn't blame her, for Taipans, King Browns, and Death Adders were plentiful along the Roper. I should know, because I hunted and ate them.

Miss Dove threatened us with dire punishments when we tormented her, but she never seemed able to resist the well-worn excuse that the snake or goanna had been brought along for Nature Study. After all, hadn't she told us to bring specimens of wild life so that they might be examined and discussed?

Frightening her successor, Miss Cross, was a different matter. She picked up the first python by the tail and threw it out the window.

"I'll kill the next one," she said grimly.

We believed her, and as none of us wanted to lose our pets we gave her peace until the day when a boy named Jorum appeared with a matchbox containing three angry wasps. They partly repaid us for the loss of dignity we had suffered by Miss Cross's contemptuous dismissal of our snakes, but we had to suffer for it.

We had often watched the wasps killing bigger insects with one brief sting from their hypodermic tails. Those of us who had been stung never again turned our back on one. Among the painful hazards of the bush the wasp was known as "Properly-cheeky-feller."

The classroom was fly-wired, so the wasps could not escape. All work stopped while Miss Cross vainly tried to "shoo" them out the door. Finally several boys killed them with bats made of paper. Then the inquest began.

"Who did it?" Miss Cross demanded.

Nobody answered, or even looked up.

"I asked who did it, and I want an answer," she said.

Silence. Jorum wouldn't admit his guilt and, of course, we weren't going to betray him, although loyalty had to be bought dearly a few minutes later.

"All right. Bring Tom to me," she said.

Now Tom wasn't an aboriginal boy whom she suspected of being the culprit. Instead, Tom was a heavy leather strap lying coiled like another snake in a corner of the room.

We all made contact with him that day—on both hands, on both legs, and around bottoms protected only by thin cotton lap-laps. Jorum told us after school how sorry he was to have been the cause of our discomfiture, but that was an hour too late. The searing sting of a hard leather strap can't be cancelled by an apology.

"You can borrow my canoe," Jorum told us. "And my spears. And I've got some Sugarbag you can have."

"Thanks, Jorum," we told him, "but tomorrow you leave the wasps at home. The strap has a far worse sting."

But whether we brought wasps, snakes, goannas, or just ourselves, Tom appeared almost daily while Miss Cross was there. Sometimes we called her Miss Very Cross. She asked for Tom every time I couldn't do a sum and glanced at my neighbour's book for the answer. She said that was cheating, which was difficult for me to understand because in the tribe we shared our knowledge as well as our food.

She hated us to talk, and for aboriginal boys whose playtime chatter seldom stopped that was torture indeed. Anyone caught talking was punished with a paper-clip or a clothes-peg over the tip of his tongue.

"Now talk as much as you like," Miss Cross would say.

Disobedience was another prime sin, but here, at least, our tribal training helped us. Any boy who had been through the purifying fires of initiation, as I had, and the two-year taboo on speech with certain people, had little difficulty obeying simple rules.

Even so, there were times when we rebelled.

One of the delights dearest to our hearts was to be allowed to ride the mission's stock-horses. As the son of a stockman who might follow his father's trade it was fitting that I should be a keen horseman although, as it turned out, my transport has more often had four wheels than four legs.

I couldn't foresee that at the age of ten, and I would fly on to the bare back of an unbridled horse at every opportunity. The horse was naked, and so was I.

I soon learnt how to guide it with my knees, and if I had no curb to make it halt . . . then who cared! I wasn't short of time. The horse could take me where it pleased and stop when it tired. If I was exhausted after a hard gallop I would lie along its back while I floated home.

What greater pleasure could there be for a nomad boy than to have dozens of such horses to ride, to tame, to fly with? Happy Pegasus! The horses knew us and, we thought, seemed to enjoy our fun together better than rounding up cattle.

The stockmen saddled them and concentrated on the prosaic business of mustering, drafting, and branding bullocks, cows, and calves in dusty yards. But we took them into the land of free-flight, into outer space, where the wallabies and kangaroos and emus are; where a horse is unfettered except for a lightweight boy crouched low into the wind, his small spear poised for any wallaby that might slow down to equine speed, or for fat perenties sun-baking on the river flats. If three or four horses raced together, shoulder to shoulder, manes entangled, whipping wind screaming the gait . . . then so much the better.

It happened on a holiday. Stanley Port had given us permission to ride.

"But not beyond the first ridge," he said. "You and those horses . . . !" He shook his perplexed head.

Ridge? Where was ridge? What was ridge? A barrier. A circumscription for a wild horse with a rider it identifies as a playmate! That was unthinkable. And, please Sir, we can't stop the horses because we have no reins. Thank God! The horse will stop when he's tired, Sir, or when we kill a wallaby or a goanna, or if one of us falls off. Not before. The Lord be praised!

We run. We run and we run and we run and we run. Black hair flying, black manes flying, black bodies tingled by the jetstreams of air as heads are lowered, shoulders stretched to go, go ever on, running, come-on-boy, galloping, giddy-ap there, galloping, galloping, don't let that one pass you boy, flying, floating. . . .

The ridge? Oh, yes, Mister Port's ridge. That was it just went by. Hey, you there horse, that was Mister Port's ridge, why don't you stop like he said, you naughty horse you are. And look at those two other horses: they don't see Mister Port's ridge either.

Down to the river flats. Down to the denser timber where we can have fun dodging aound the trees. Down to the greener grass for the horses. Down to Perentie-Land where the big goannas live. Down to the Fat-and-Juicy-Place for reptiles that we would kill and carry home across our horses' manes.

And down on the broad of your back, too, inert and broken, shocked and fearful, especially fearful of the wrath of Stanley Port, who would know that we had disobeyed and gone past the ridge.

Three of us had caught two goannas each, spearing them as we leaned down over the necks of our horses. This was great hunting. We would be feted in the camp tonight. The girls would smile shyly. My father could be proud.

It was then that the wallaby was flushed from its hide. We started after it together, racing still further away from the mission. But pride sits precariously on a bareback horse. Mine turned and crashed into Roger Gunbukbuk's. We all went down in a heap except Roger, who flew into the nearest tree and bounced off it into another. A large bloodwood stopped him.

I had begun to laugh, for I was unhurt. Falls were part of the fun, and we were adept at cushioning our bodies at the moment of contact with the ground. But hitting trees while in horizontal flight was no laughing matter at all. Roger proved that.

"A-a-a-h-h-h! O-o-o-o-h-h-h!" he said.

I crawled over to where he lay. His black face was contorted with pain. His fingers twitched. His surprised eyes looked at me through mists of tears which came involuntarily. A moment earlier he had whistled and laughed.

"I can't move my legs," he said.

"I'll get help. I'll get my father and your father," I said.

"Don't tell Mister Port," he said.

But Stanley Port would know. Stanley Port couldn't help knowing because he had to send the wireless message for the Flying Doctor.

I galloped home and told Barnabas, my father. He frowned. . . . I knew there would be trouble later . . . and began running towards the river. Other men were with him.

He called to them: "Gunbukbuk is hurt. He lies on the river bank near the Fat-and-Juicy-Place. His horse fell. We get him now."

They took the mission dinghy and rowed downstream. I went to show them where Roger lay. They were grim and silent. None of them spoke to me. I might have felt less disquiet if they had upbraided me or joked about it. Later I understood that the possible death of a future tribesman and the discontinuance of his line was no cause for a joke. Rather, it was the most serious calamity that could happen to any tribe.

I found Roger in the long grass where he fell. He had not moved, but was whimpering mournfully, biting his tongue in a vain effort to check his sobs. I knew then, when I heard him cry out in front of the men, that he must have been in agony. Nothing less than that would have allowed him to betray the extent of his travail to the Elders.

"Don't touch me," he moaned, and pressed both hands against his hips.

The men built a bush stretcher of saplings, paperbark, and vines, and moved it slowly but painfully beneath his body. Then they carried him to the boat and rowed back to the camp. None of them, still, had spoken directly to me.

Mister Port was at the mission jetty, outraged righteousness glaring at me from his cold grey eyes.

"Now you know what happens, Phillip, when you are disobedient," he said. "The Lord punishes. The Lord is just."

I wanted to crawl away, but I couldn't leave Roger and stayed with him while he was taken to the mission clinic. A few minutes later I heard the crackle of static as the Traeger transceiver snapped into life in the wireless room. Mister Port spoke at once to the base operator at Cloncurry, seven hundred miles away:

"Cloncurry Base. Cloncurry Base. Cloncurry Base from Roper River Mission. I have an urgent medical for you. An aboriginal boy with suspected fractures of both hips. Can you send the Flying Doctor? Over. . . . Over. . . . "

Roger Gunbukbuk smiled wanly from his bed of pain. Now he would fly in the medical plane and go to a big town. That meant he would be Camp-fire Storyteller-in-chief for weeks after he returned. I was sorry that his pain prevented him from properly enjoying the prospect.

The immediate future seemed equally grim for me. Mister Port was unlikely to forget our disobedience for a long time, and as I was the eldest of the riders I could expect the brunt of his criticism. Eventually it came: a torrent of quiet abuse, which wounded me deeply and depressed me for days. But the wounds inflicted by my family group hurt even more. They were made with a stick.

At sunset I walked alone to the paddock and examined our horses. None seemed to have suffered injury. I caught the gelding I had ridden, and when he began nuzzling me I gratefully wrapped my arms around his neck.

"You naughty horse, you are," I said. "Why don't you look out for Mister Port's ridge? Why do you want to be disobedient like that? All you think of is run, run, run. Too greedy, you are, for gallop. Now Roger must go away in flying machine to get his hips fixed."

Apart from such upsets as that, my school days passed pleasantly enough. I was impatient with the need to remain indoors for long hours, sitting and listening, learning by mere habituation rather than by experience in the wonderful out-of-doors on the other side of the walls.

When the door closed each morning and I was trapped inside with Miss Dove or Miss Cross and the other pupils, I felt as though my ankles were encased in the heavy leg-irons I had seen one day when the policeman came from Roper Bar.

"Two plus five, Phillip?"

"Uh?"

"Three times seven, Phillip?"

"Uh?"

"Phillip, how do you spell sleepy? Phillip, what is the meaning of the word disobedient? Did you wash your hands today, Phillip?"

Should I answer that the barramundi, the Long Toms, the mullet, the trevally, and the schnapper were in shoals near the camp jetty?

Should I say that the goannas were especially delectable this year if you caught them at the Fat-and-Juicy-Place?

Should I say that canoes were for paddling, that horses were for riding, that girls were inferior, that spears were for fishing and hunting, that tracks—not books—were for reading?

For these were the things that filled my mind as the teachers tried to break through my consciousness with sums and words and other white-feller trivia.

Why should it be necessary for an aboriginal boy to say "I believe heavy rain is about to fall, Miss Dove," rather than "Properly big feller rain bin come up, Missus"?

Why should I know how to spell "food" when we always called it "tucker"?

What difference did it make to me if eight and nine equalled seventeen when I didn't have that many fingers?

Why should I say "Good morning, Miss Dove," while cowering beneath the deluge and pyrotechnics of a tropical thunderstorm?

No! I preferred to be an ignoramus if the alternative was to absorb such paradoxical absurdities. And I would probably still be a myall today except for the interest I found soon after the arrival of a coloured girl, Margaret Blittner, as our teacher.

Part of Margaret's blood was aboriginal. She could think like us. Not only was I understood, but I could understand her. My resistance to education was discussed frankly and sympathetically. I have no doubt that Miss Dove and Miss Cross were able teachers. My inability to learn from them and to become interested in learning was entirely my fault.

Nevertheless, with Margaret I was strangely facile within days, and quickly learnt to read and write fluently. In fourth grade I was given a pocket knife for good behaviour and the standard of my work, both of which had previously been unexceptional.

A year later, at the end of fifth grade, my formal education ended. I was cast adrift on the world in my early teens with only the most elementary academic knowledge. Fifth Grade was Top Grade at the mission school.

But my training for the grim battle with life itself had just begun. The day I left the schoolroom my tribal teachers descended upon me. I was soon to learn that the problems in text-books were simple indeed when reckoned against the primary equation on our own blackboards: Survival $=$ Stealth $\times$ Cunning $\times$ Expertise.

My potential as a hunter and a provider—the traditional role of males in our simple lives—was about to be exploited. Miss Dove, Miss Cross, and Margaret Blittner had tested me with books written in a foreign language.

Now I was on trial by the tribe, with the Book of the Bush laid open before me.

It was necessary that I should become its master. For the rest of my days, if I stayed on the Roper, I would have to support myself and my family. As work and money, trade and shops, butchers and bakers were unknown in the Land of the Alawa it meant simply this: henceforth my belly would be full or empty depending solely on how well I adapted myself to secondary education: to the fundamental rules of primordial man.

I was anxious not to fail.

Chapter Six

IN the schoolroom I had been taught by two white women and a half-caste girl. But in the bush my teacher was to be Sam Ulagang, a manly Ngandi tribal hunter ten years my senior. He was my tutor in the tradition of the tribes because his sister, Nora Bindul, had been promised to me in marriage.

If the Alawa and the Ngandi, the Ritarrngu and the Nungubuyu had been Professors of the Art of Living in the· University of the Bush, aboriginal students would always have topped the class. Academic knowledge came to us slowly. The reverse was true in those practical subjects on which our lives depended.

And yet my training as a hunter occupied half my life, and I am still learning.

My earliest recollection is of a day soon after I began to walk when my father first wrote a message for me. Didn't I say he was illiterate? Quite so, but this was a message with a difference.

I sat on a log near the camp-fire while he squatted on the ground with both legs folded in front of him.

"Now I will write for you," he said. "Learn well. Always remember. Always remember that the bush and the ground tell a story—if you can read."

He smoothed a square of sand with the back of his arm. "What is this track?" he asked.

He clenched his fist, and with the thumb uppermost depressed his closed little finger into the sand. Around the apex made by the middle knuckle he touched a finger lightly into the sand four times.

"Dog," I said. I had often seen and identified them near our camp.

He made cat tracks with the tip of a finger, wallaby and kangaroo tracks with the ball of the hand for a pad, and the edge of the hand and little finger for toes. He made the tracks of turtles, goannas, emus, crocodiles, porcupines, birds, cattle, and horses, and told me to copy them. My cattle were calves and my horses foals because my hand was small. But that didn't matter. The exercise impressed upon me for all time the outline of their tracks.

In this way, watching and studying tracks became instinctive with me. Today I read the ground as other people read newspapers and books. The footprints of my wife, my six daughters, my brothers, and other relatives are as familiar to me as their faces. My wife's footprint was the first thing I learnt about her. At the settlement where I now live I know at least fifty people by the track they leave on the ground.

Like most aborigines, I have hypersensitive eyesight and acute hearing. The fact that a wallaby blends well with the colour of dead grass does not conceal it from me. I can see through a camouflage of leaves and point out a bird which has not moved. I can distinguish easily between natural sounds and those made by a moving animal.

It is all much simpler than eight times seven. And there are easy formulae as mathematically precise as the principle of Archimedes to help us solve the most difficult problems.

On hard ground where tracks are invisible it is still possible to follow the movement of an animal by reading the story in trampled grass and disturbed pebbles.

Grass which has been knocked down always points in the direction an animal has taken. A pebble dislodged from its bed in the ground is pushed backwards from the line of flight. The track of a snake might be thought to have no beginning and no end, and yet it is easily followed: at each bend the sand is forced towards its tail.

Possums and squirrels which climb gum trees leave a scratched track in the bark. Getting them down is well worth the effort; the flesh is tender, and aboriginal women prize the fur for belts and other articles of clothing.

During my schooldays I was taught the elementary usage of spears and boomerangs by boys who were several years my senior. I practised with my toy weapons until I could throw them accurately. But when I was big enough for graduation to the traditional killing weapons—the shovelnose spear thrown with a woomera, and the heavy boomerangs—my education was taken over by a professional hunter.

This was Sam Ulagang of the Ngandi. To him I owe my ability to live off the land with weapons I have made. He was a great teacher, a proud tribesman, and the most meticulous tracker I am ever likely to know.

I had thought that after a few days with Sam, or a few weeks at most, I would be bringing home my own kangaroos. I found instead that I must curb my itching impatience for many months before I was so much as allowed to follow Sam while he stalked.

At first I was relegated to the rather unedifying duty of spear-bearing. At first, did I say! Ulagang was my father's friend, the brother of my intended wife, and I expected him to treat me courteously.

"You carry the spears," he said during the first month.

"You carry the spears," he said in the second month.

In the third month he said, "Waipuldanya, you carry the spears."

I was so burdened that when we saw a kangaroo I could do nothing either to help stalk it or kill it. I was a walking arsenal, but otherwise helpless. Now I realized why tribal women, laden with weapons and camping gear, always followed at a distance behind their unfettered husbands.

In the fourth month Ulagang said, "You carry the spears. You wait and watch me closely when I go after a kangaroo."

Ah! So now I could wait and watch! Well, that was an improvement. But what did he think I had been doing all these months?

Ulagang saw a wallaby and indicated with a twist of his mouth that I was to stay behind as usual, to wait and watch every movement he made.

I wanted to learn, so I studied him well. I saw him fight impulsiveness. I saw him curb impetuosity. I saw that he watched the wind carefully, moving quickly when it blew strongly, pausing when it eased, walking always with the freshness of it in his face so that his human smells were not carried down to the animal.

In my mind's eye I mapped out the route I would have taken had I been the hunter, and was chagrined when he selected another. I looked for a reason and saw the tall grass he had deliberately avoided as an unnecessary hazard: other wallabies hiding there might have been put to flight and thus disturbed his quarry. I was beginning to appreciate the reasons for his patience.

"Waipuldanya," I told myself, "you will soon be able to hunt."

I lost sight of him behind dense scrub and trees, but I continued to observe the wallaby for another half-hour. Then it stiffened suddenly, a rigid spear-shaft bisecting it at right angles, its cloven body grotesquely skewered and ready for the grilling spit.

Ulagang walked back slowly and nonchalantly handed me the dead animal to carry, as though killing it had been so boring that he wanted to yawn.

"Next time," he promised, "you can track my tracks."

I was elated at this condescension of the Great Black Hunter. But such patronage! Such insufferable conceit!

So he thought that the son of Barnabas was a fit person to track his tracks! An Alawa, and he a mere Ngandi!

"It is as well," I muttered, "that the Testing Time at the Corroboree Place taught me restraint. Sam would make an excellent base for a right angle."

Had I realized then that my probation was beginning rather than ending, that many weary months of watch-and-wait were still ahead, that Sam was dangling a juicy goanna just out of my reach, I may have been a truant from his school. And yet in my heart I knew that this was the best training I could have. I knew that when he was finished with me there would be little difference between his bushcraft and mine. Whether my spear-arm would be as competent was something which Sam couldn't influence, but that had been schooled since I was a small piccaninny, since the day I was big enough to throw a toy spear.

Next morning Ulagang said to me, "All right. Today we go. Today we go to the Tough and Skinny Place where the grass is rank and the trees are sparse. You can track my tracks."

Thanks, Sam, you pretentious prig. Thanks, Sam, you ostentatious oaf. Thanks, Your Majesty of the Ngandi. So I'm to be allowed to walk behind you! Maybe that's unwise for one so overstuffed with peacock-down. Maybe we'll let a little air in between your shoulder-blades so that humility can enter!

What idle nonsense! Of course it was I who was vain. It was I who needed an injection of meekness. I had speared statued goannas and thought I knew how to hunt. I had speared hypnotized fish and let the entire camp know. But had I stalked and killed an animal bigger than myself, with the odds in its favour, with a millenia of inherent alertness and cunning working for it?

What do you say, Waipuldanya?

No, Sir. Nothing like it, Sir.

All right, then. Fall in behind Sam Ulagang and see if you can learn. Sam is what you might call a demonstration teacher. There are none better, even if he is a Ngandi.

"All right," Ulagang said. "We go now. You carry my spears to the Place Where the Buffalo Wallow. There we will get brown mud to seal the man-smells to our bodies and to make us blend with the dry grass."

"And in the Green-Grass-Time?" I asked.

"You learn well," Sam said. "The Ngandi is pleased. In the Green-Grass-Time you get grey-green mud from the river bank, and moss and leaves."

We smeared ourselves with brown camouflage, oozing and fetid and vile and, it seemed, unnecessary. I remember that Ulagang had not used it when I was simply the spear-bearer.

"Why do we paint ourselves today, Sam?" I asked.

"Because you are tracking me," he said. "You will be unwary. The wallaby will see you unless you are hidden."

The great arrogant oracle again!

"Always, when you are very hungry, you will paint with mud," he said. "It is not good to increase one's hunger with a long stalk and then watch the wallaby jump away when he sees you. The trouble these days is that the Alawa are too well fed. A full belly maketh a careless man. Hunger makes the hunter."

We go . . . and we go . . . and we go . . . and we go . . . and we go. L-o-o-n-g way! Until we are close-to at the Tough and Skinny Place. Come up-wind, climb the hill, and look down.

Ah, there! And there! And there! Three-feller wallaby. Sorry, Miss Dove. I mean three wallabies. Yesterday this would have meant little more to me than that I was to stay there and observe. Today my pulse was beating faster. For now I would track the tracker, stalk the stalker, walk in the Steps of the Master Hunter.

Ulagang ignored me and watched the wallabies. They were grazing into the wind, which meant that their backs were to us. The merest shadow of a smile tripped the corners of his mouth. The wind was good. But three animals together: that was not so good. Three wallabies against one hunter. Or against two hunters? Were the odds three-to-two, or did the fact that I was there make it six-to-one on the wallabies? They had three noses to smell, six eyes to see, six ears to hear. And the speed of light in their feet.

Sam motioned with his mouth and we slipped below the brow of the hill.

"You track my tracks," he whispered. "My right foot, your right foot, same place. My left foot, your left foot, same place. I crawl, you crawl. I sneak along, you sneak along. I stop, you stop. Don't talk. Don't cough. Don't brush grass. Don't brush bush. Stay in shadow, stay in shadow, stay in shadow. The one on the right. It is nearest and we must take it. I will wound it in the leg, then you can track the blood and kill it."

Applause, please. Have a medal, Sam. Boasting again! The unconstrained ego of the man was nauseating.

Although our chance of even getting near three wallabies together seemed slim to me, Sam was so confident of approaching within spear range and then being able to hit one where he liked that he had promised me a blood-trail and a kill.

All right, Sam. Let's go. Let me see how good you are. Let me see The Master Hunter at work.

We sneak up. We sneak . . . and we sneak . . . and we sneak . . . and we sneak. Sam's body formed a right angle at the waist. His legs were vertical, his torso was horizontal to the ground. I watched his feet, only his feet. If I was to do as he said, to step in his steps, to track his tracks, I had no time to look elsewhere.

While the breeze blew freshly, and we were still a hundred yards from the wallabies, he moved quickly, surely, and expertly. But as the range narrowed, his caution increased and speed slackened. I suppose we were still fifty yards away when Sam stopped in mid-stride: so literally with one foot poised that I was reminded of a hunting dog. And with the same foot he pointed . . . at a dry twig he had almost trodden on. His foot was an exclamation mark.

"Beware!" it said.

He avoided the twig and many others like it. I was careful to step exactly in his imprints. Anyone following may have believed that only one man was ahead.

Now we went slowly, knees bent, hugging the shadow, sighting the wallabies rarely. We stopped still, scarcely breathing, when two birds settled in a tree above us. Sam waited until they had flown off naturally before moving again. He didn't want them to give a raucous danger signal.

The next twenty yards across sparsely wooded ground took fifteen minutes. There were times when I thought that Sam would never go on. When he did take a step I noticed the animals had turned their heads away from us.

Sam's objective was a big tree only thirty feet from where they grazed. The last dozen yards to this tree was through tall grass. We inched forward on our bellies, minimizing the movement of the grass tips, dragging the spears horizontally behind us.

Arm forward, knee forward, down, wait.

Arm forward, knee forward, down, wait.

At last Sam was at the base of the tree, its large bole protecting him from discovery. Even so, his motions were still slow and deliberate. He rose to his knees, then on one foot, and finally was standing upright, flat against the tree. He trod on his spear, fitting the shaft between two toes and raising his leg until he could reach it without stooping. He repeated that to retrieve his woomera. Half an hour had passed, perhaps more, since we left the brow of the hill. In that time neither of us had spoken or made a sound. I was proud to have come through behind him without cracking a twig or rustling the grass.

Now Sam fitted the pointed end of his woomera into the base of the ten-foot steel-headed killing spear. With infinite care he edged his eye around the side of the tree, head erect, hair bound, spear-arm poised but not yet cocked. I watched from the ground, where I remained prone, missing no detail of everything this wonderful hunter did—for now I was convinced of his greatness. In my lifetime in the bush I had never been within thirty feet of any wallaby that was unaware of my presence.

Sam's arm came back and clicked. Safety catch off. He had to raise the spear in front of him, a movement the wallaby might have seen. So he did that quickly and threw mightily with the reflex action, almost in the same instant.

The woomera hissed quietly. The spear was gone. Wh-i-i-s-h! And then the dull thud of something hard striking something soft, followed by the frantic flight of two animals and the retarded struggle of another. I knew before I stood up that it was hit.

"Got 'im! Got 'im!" I shouted.

Sam was unimpressed. "You brushed a bush back there," he said severely. "Next time keep away from anything that will make a noise. Otherwise you'll go back to spear-bearing."

I remembered the bush, of course. I hoped that Sam hadn't noticed. But he was the teacher and missed nothing. I had a sense of momentary deflation, of youthful pique, at being thus criticized in the moment of triumph for what I thought was a creditable performance.

Fortunately there was little time for inquests. A wounded wallaby was bounding ahead, a potential feast for the camp, and it had to be caught. Now was the time when I should carry home my first kill, trying vainly not to strut, offering the traditional apportionment to my tribal relatives as it had been offered to me.

"Track it and kill it," Ulagang ordered. "I hit it in the right leg. That will happen to you often when you begin hunting alone unless your aim is true. Remember that every mile you chase a wounded animal is another mile you must walk back with the load, perhaps without water. You are taught this lesson today so that you will always throw to kill. Now go. I will follow."

I began to run, following a heavy blood trail and depressed grass which pointed like a signpost.

"Remember that you are coming back," Ulagang warned. "Conserve your energy. It may be a l-o-o-n-g way."

Nevertheless, I hurried impatiently, my itching trigger-finger pressed on the point of the woomera. As bleeding eased and wild panic ebbed the wallaby recovered some of its natural cunning, climbing from the grass country to the ironstone ridges where tracks and the blood-trail would be fainter.

I go . . . and I go . . . and I go . . . and I go.

Sam was behind me. "Keep going," he said. "This will teach you not to hurry. Perhaps you will knock-up-along-wind and have to rest soon? Perhaps you want rubbing-medicine for your tired legs?"

He was needling me, taunting at the inherent pride of every aboriginal in his physical fitness, in his ability to travel without fatigue.

We followed the trail for an hour, winding for five miles across the red-brown gravel, never once sighting the wounded animal. The day was hot and steamy. We sweated freely and were perishing for water when finally the tracks showed me that the wallaby was crawling and dying. A few minutes later I fired my first shot in anger at the slowly moving target and pierced it through the heart.

"You are about to learn why it is wise to kill close to the camp," Sam said. "You carry it home."

I put the sixty-pound carcass across my shoulders and walked six miles back to camp.

My back ached. I thirsted and hungered. My throat and mouth were dry, but I would not give in. I drank mightily when we reached the river and then walked proudly into the camp. I was now a Hunter Second Class, and anxious for the next lesson.

Ulagang took me with him for another six months, each time wounding a wallaby for me to track and kill.

I was disappointed that after the first two or three such expeditions he did not allow me to lead the stalk and throw the first spear. My sagging patience may have been exhausted except that, invariably, Sam taught me a new trick on every trip.

I remember that on one particularly hot day, with only a light breeze, he began catching and killing the small black flies that settled on his body, and indicated that I should kill those that settled on me.

I had never seen this done nor had I heard of it. I asked Sam why it was necessary.

"Today the wind is variable," he said. "Sometimes it blows from the north, sometimes from the east or the south. If flies smell a kangaroo they will leave a man and go to it. They prefer the kangaroo's smell to ours. But when the flies arrive the kangaroo will catch several in its hands and sniff them for human scent."

And that day, with a change in the breeze, our flies migrated when we were within twenty yards of a kangaroo. As they approached I watched it catch several with electric movements of its hands, smell them, and hop away to safety. The secret was out! A finely tuned sense had warned it that Man, the principal enemy, was within fly-range. That also meant within spear-range.

On the way home, our shoulders naked of game, Sam repeated the lesson. "Be careful of flies on a hot day when the wind is changeable. They can keep you hungry," he said.

Eventually my apprenticeship was ended, but only because I took direct action. I had been with Ulagang for more than a year. I thought I knew all there was to know, yet I was afraid the lessons would go on for months longer unless I was able to prove my ability.

The opportunity came during a holiday walkabout with my parents, uncles, aunts, and friends to the Sandy Place where the Hodgson River flows down into the Roper.

Barnabas Gabarla, my father, called the young men to him. "Allabout go hunting for food," he said. "But be careful you don't bring back a dead Alawa. Remember that a spear which can kill a kangaroo can also kill a man."

Two boys said they would climb trees and find sugar-bag. Others decided on robbing birds' nests. But to me, Hunter Second Class Waipuldanya, that was child's play. I was now Kingsize. Hadn't I killed the wounded walla-bies which Ulagang set up for me? Hadn't I tracked The Master and been his spear-bearer for a year? Didn't I know how to paint my body with mud, and use the shadows, and approach up-wind, and avoid the rustling grass, and not disturb the birds, and catch the flies?

All right. All right then. Let's go. Look out, all you fat and juicy wallabies. Look out, all you kangaroos. The Great Black Hunter is on the march, marching against you, matching his wits with yours because you have eaten and he is hungry. Smell well today's flies. Keep your radar ears revolving and the twitching nostrils open.

Davis Mayuldjumdjumgu, a boy of ten, my cousin, came with me as weapon-carrier. Ah, yes, I now rated my own spear-bearer. I had an apprentice to train, even though I had still not hunted and killed a wallaby alone. Davis hadn't speared anything bigger than a fish.

We covered our bodies with mud and moved out to a ridge where I could watch him, and he could watch me, in case the pygmy Burgingin or the Stone-People, the treacherous Malanugga-nugga, should follow us. Ten-year-old boys are easily frightened in the bush, as I remembered well.

On the brow of the hill I looked down to the valley, and there, one hundred yards away, saw a wallaby grazing.

"Stay here. Stand still!" I told Davis. This was the first order I had ever given, and the authority of my command surprised me.

The air was subdued, but with an unkind variable breeze flicking at the leaves and the tips of the grass. I knew before I began that the stalk ahead of me would have tested Ulagang at his best.

Caution. Caution.

Would I catch him?

Might-be, if the wind doesn't change.

Might-be, if the grass doesn't rustle.

Might-be, if the flies don't migrate.

Well, . . . might-be.

Quietly sneak-up. Quietly sneak-up.

I sneak . . . and I sneak . . . and I sneak. . . .

Ah, the wind changeth!

What was it that Stanley Port had told us in Sunday School about the Lord rebuking the winds? I wished the Lord was here now to govern their constancy.

I approached to within thirty yards, crouching low over rough ground, catching flies, once freezing into an aboriginal arabesque when the wallaby looked up. I stayed there on one foot for several minutes, my right leg extended grotesquely behind me, my arms outflung, motionless while the animal perhaps wondered why it had not noticed the sculptured image before.

It was when I had reduced the range to twenty yards, with only another five to go before the moment of truth, that I saw the whirlwind coiling towards us.

A willy-willy!

Red with dust and dry leaves, convoluting prettily from a pinpoint on earth to dispersion in heaven, but menacing and ugly to the hunter.

How had Ulagang warned me about them? It sounded like one of Miss Dove's theorems: *"A willy-willy sucks the air towards it from all directions, no matter which way the breeze is blowing. If you are close enough to be in that vacuum the animal will smell you."*

In that instant I became Hunter First Class Waipuldanya.

I picked up a small stone and tossed it lightly over the wallaby's head to fall between it and the whirlwind. The unexpected noise of the stone striking the ground startled it. The animal instinctively hopped a few yards away from the sound—towards me!—and there propped and glanced back to investigate, its eyes, its nose, and its ears all diverted from the danger behind its back.

And that was its last free act. I had shipped my woomera and spear while the stone was still in the air, careful that I didn't tap one against the other. I fired at point-blank range and the vicious blade transfixed the body.

"Got 'im! Got 'im!"

For an incredulous moment the wallaby tugged at the shaft with its almost human hands, trying frantically to remove the skewer. Then it fell forward and died.

"Yak-ai! Yak-ai!" Davis shouted from the hilltop.

My spirit exulted. My heart shouted: "You got 'im, you got 'im. And it wasn't easy. That was first-class stalking."

But I remembered Ulagang's nonchalance, his "Oh, it's easy" attitude when he killed, and I repressed the urge to shout back at my young friend. Instead, I took the dead wallaby and dropped it at his feet.

"Carry that to Ulagang. Tell him about the willy-willy," I said.

"Big one," Davis said. "Fat one." There could be no sincerer tribute. He reached down to lift it to his shoulders. "Ah, heavy one," he said, remembering that the camp was two miles away. It was heavy, indeed, so we carried it between us, suspended by its big tail and the tiny hands which this time had failed to catch a fly to warn it that an expert spearman had entered the bush.

My father, my mother, and my Uncle Stanley Marbunggu were proud and surprised.

"We can depend on you now. You are a Hunter First Class," my father said.

"I grew him up," Marbunggu said.

"I grew him along here," my mother said, and patted her belly.

"I trained him," Ulagang said. "Now he is fit to look after a wife and kids. Mayuldjumdjumgu told me about the willy-willy. He told me how you threw the stone and brought the wallaby towards you. I will hunt with you, my friend."

That was the ultimate praise, to tell a younger man that you were prepared to hunt with him. Ulagang seemed proudest of them all. Except me, perhaps, for I was transcended.

Thereafter I hunted and killed regularly. Stalking became instinctive, and I seldom returned to camp without substantial food.

There was one paradoxical occasion when I won the laurel wreath of Master Hunter by hunting and spearing a dingo, the wild dog which is the most timid and cunning animal in the bush, but I had to remain silent about it.

I followed it for a hundred yards to a small creek, crept upon it with infinite care, waited endlessly while it sniffed and listened and, to camouflage the "Whish!" of my woomera and spear, I fired only when the dingo had begun to drink.

Lap-lap-lap-lap-lap. The noise of its drinking prevented it hearing me now, and it died quickly.

Not many of our tribesmen had speared a dingo or even been within range of one. I longed to take it back to camp on the end of my spear and drop it at Ulagang's feet. But the dingo is a Lesser Dreaming of mine, a minor totem.

If it was known that I had killed one I would have had to pay heavy damages to my cousins: my father's sister's children, their stepbrothers and stepsisters. That was the law. If they had demanded everything I owned—my spears, boomerangs, swag, blankets, clothes—in return for my Dreaming, I would have paid without question and been bankrupt.

This system is often used in reverse to get level-feller with a man who has been thoughtless or committed some small indiscretion. Perhaps when I'm hungry-for-smoke a friend may light a cigarette from his own full packet and neglect to offer me one. I can then kill one of his Dreamings—perhaps a goanna, a snake, or a flying fox—and bring it back to the camp.

"The carton of cigarettes," I'll say. "I want them all."

"The ten pounds you won at cards last night."

"Your pocket knife."

"The shirt off your back."

He will pay me anything I demand to retrieve his Dreaming.

And the price of mine is incalculable.

Chapter Seven

DOGS abound in all aboriginal camps. They are friends of ours. Many are half-bred dingoes from camp bitches which have mated with wild dogs. But whatever the purity or the obscurity of their breeding they are useful animals in more ways than the obvious one of helping us find goannas and snakes.

They are, of course, quite good food. Some people apparently believe that eating dog flesh is repugnant. I have never been able to reconcile that view with the willingness of the same people to eat pigs, sheep, and cattle. They are horrified that we eat witchetty grubs and yet they regard snails and frogs as delicacies. Dog flesh is good red meat, neither better nor worse than wallaby. We never eat our pets, although I've no doubt that happens among the Central Australian tribes when prolonged droughts decimate their other natural foods.

We also use dogs as sleeping companions on winter nights. I have slept with as many as six in my blanket and needed the body heat generated by all of them to keep me warm.

"A six-dog night," in the patois of the bush, simply means a very cold night indeed.

For the benefit of those who will exclaim "But what about the fleas!" I must say the belief that dog fleas migrate to humans is mistaken. I've never yet been bitten by a flea from a dog, or found one on my body. They stay with their hosts.

There are several unwritten laws relating to the treatment of our dogs.

One is that we should hide them or send them away on the approach of a policeman or a patrol officer who is armed, not that the warning is really necessary: most dogs know that a rifle means death, and that they will be the target unless they disappear. That is why any dog in an aboriginal camp always appears ready to run.

Another rule is that we must provide meat for a dog that has killed food. I have been puzzled by the strange fact that a dog which kills a goanna, a small wallaby, or any other game will not eat the meat, even though it is cooked and boiled until all traces of its own scent would seem to have been removed. It will only eat meat that has been killed by another dog or by an aboriginal. That, of course, does not apply to dingoes, which kill their own food.

Hawks and crows compete with dingoes for the title of Masters of Cunning. Those which have found their way into our cooking pots have generally been speared through sheer misfortune for them and lucky opportunity for us. Generally, they know when a hunter is in the bush as soon as he enters it, and stay well out of his way.

The kitehawks—we call them firehawks—are inventive hunters. Much of their natural food is caught and eaten on the wing, especially around the perimeters of bushfires where they swoop on fleeing grasshoppers. But they are inclined to regard insects as *hors d'oeuvres*. Both hawks and crows are devotedly carnivorous and do not seem to mind how long the meat has been dead. We think of them as housekeepers, for they keep our camp areas free of rotting flesh.

My eyes are good, but I have often wished they were fitted with telescopes like a firehawk's. It doesn't surprise me that "eyes like a hawk" has become an accepted simile. I have seen them plummet from immense heights on to small mice, rats, lizards, and snakes that would certainly have been invisible to any human eye from such a distance, especially as such things are supposed to be protected by natural camouflage.

Firehawks often confused us in welcoming visitors to our tribal lands by deliberately setting fire to grass and bushland to assist their scavenging. I have seen a hawk pick up a smouldering stick in its claws and drop it in a fresh patch of dry grass half a mile away, then wait with its mates for the mad exodus of scorched and frightened rodents and reptiles. When that area was burnt out the process was repeated elsewhere. We call these fires Jaluran.

How was this confusing to us?

Any native walking through the land of another tribe sends messages ahead to let them know of his approach. This is a survival from the days when tribal land was sacrosanct and any invasion of it was a declaration of war. Even today we are not fond of unauthorized strangers crossing our boundaries. We are still hypersensitive about spies (a fault which the native races do not appear to monopolize), and we intensely dislike interlopers hunting on our territory.

Every tribe had special messengers—diplomats, if you like—who were accredited to its neighbours. If a Yabu-durawa corroboree was to be held at Mainoru, in the land of the Rembarrnga, they would send an emissary to the Alawa with a message stick—the Presidential Note—containing an invitation for us to cross their country.

If I was the emissary, as occasionally happened, I would light a fire every hour to inform the Rembarrnga of my approach. Having seen the smokes drawing nearer from the direction of the Roper they would know that I was on the way and send out an escort to give me safe conduct.

Such fires can be seen up to one hundred miles away on clear days. They mean, invariably, that a traveller is advertising his presence. I have seen comic-books and cartoons which suggest that smoke-signalling is a refined method of communicating messages over long distances. That is nonsense. I have never known a smoke to mean anything other than the publication of a man's whereabouts. And because of this we were sometimes confused by hawks lighting fires in a line approaching our camp.

Like the hawks, we had no matches. All my life until I became a sophisticated citizen I made my fires with Budalarr, a round firestick of soft wood. I never travelled without one.

The Budalarr is held upright between the palms with the lower end pressed firmly against another piece of wood. The hands are moved back and forth quickly so that the Budalarr revolves, creating friction at the point. When it begins to smoke I apply a little wax of goanna fat I carry for the purpose and a dry tinder of grass and leaves. Since my schooldays I have been able to make fire in this way in two minutes.

During the rainy season when dry grass is not readily available I can generally find it by knocking down a termites' nest. White ants use long stalks of grass to strengthen the walls of their huge earthen mounds as builders use steel to reinforce concrete. They also store grass seeds in these larders. A word of warning: it is unwise to attempt my method of making fire unless the hands are calloused and hard. Otherwise blisters may appear before the smoke.

Two men can make fire in less than a minute by rubbing the edge of a woomera across another piece of wood in the fashion of a crosscut saw. And I have also made fire by hitting two pieces of ironstone together until sparks fall on to powdered grass.

But alas! These are the days of safety matches, cigarette lighters, and engine sparkplugs. Aboriginal boys are now growing up without learning to make fire with their hands.

I'm sure there are some who have never seen it or even heard of it being done. And, of course, there are many who do not know how to throw a spear or boomerang, or to track a man or stalk an animal through the bush.

Too many are becoming helpless townies, completely dependent on can-openers for their food, and bottle-openers for their drink. They would starve if forced to hunt. This is one of the tragic effects of our rapidly increasing assimilation into the white community.

Not only the hawks used the ruse of deliberate grass fires as an aid to hunting. We often did so ourselves, especially towards the end of the long dry season when food was scarce and ten-feet tall speargrass, which burnt readily, was a natural haven for game. It is possible that our forefathers learnt this trick from the birds.

The task of setting fire to a semicircle of scrub belonged to the old men who were too feeble to hunt. We, the hunters, concealed ourselves behind trees and bushes down-wind from the fire. When the kangaroos and walla-bies saw the flames and smelt the smoke they ran away from it — towards us. That need not have been too dangerous if they had continued running. A hopping kangaroo is an almost impossible target to hit with a spear. Fortunately for us they generally delayed leaving the fire until blinded with smoke. By the time they reached the line of hunters—and we knew from long experience where to hide—they were forced to stop to wipe away the tears dripping from their smarting eyes and running down their furry faces.

What followed was cold-blooded murder. The kanga-roos had no chance. We thought it a poor day if we didn't kill one each.

It sometimes happened that a kangaroo speared through the top of the back or a fleshy part of the rump hopped away with the spear. Occasionally a mortally wounded animal jumped into the river and drowned or broke the spear while running between two trees. In either case, the weapon was lost.

This was a serious loss to the hunter. My spears were balanced in relation to my height, my weight, and the length of my arm. They were tailor-made to my measure-ments—and I was the tailor. I could not borrow from another hunter without feeling as awkwardly armed as a marksman with a strange rifle.

95

I therefore had to go through the laborious task of making another with inadequate tools. The shovel-nose spear, as its name implies, has a killing-head made of iron. This may be an old horseshoe, a piece of galvanized pipe, or a flat section cut from an abandoned water-tank. In my grandfather's day iron was scarce on the Roper and was highly prized. In his grandfather's day it was unknown. Spears were then made entirely of wood, or with a stone killing-head.

I had two tomahawks. One I used as an iron base, and the other as a hammer. Hammer, hammer, hammer, hammer, hammer. Day and night, night and day, I hammered my precious piece of iron until it was flat, symmetrical, and the correct weight and balance. I pounded around the rough edges and ground it on rocks until it was sharp and straight. All this might have taken me several days or several weeks, depending on the hardness of the iron and the state of my patience.

I then cut a small sapling, one inch thick, a special one called Djindi-Djindi, which was plentiful on the Roper. This was passed end-to-end through a fire until the sap boiled and the wood became pliable enough to straighten easily.

The charred bark was removed and the shaft left in the sun, where it dried straight and hard, tempered in my primitive furnace.

Now came the delicate operation of fitting the killing-head. I made a deep groove in the end of the shaft, fitted the blade, cemented the join with wild bees' wax, and bound it all with natural string made from the bark of a currajong tree. I might bind it all again with stringy tendons taken from the legs of a kangaroo, and apply a last coating of sugarbag wax.

When the manufacture was complete I rubbed the shaft with kangaroo blood and red ochre. Application of the blood was a tribal superstition: we believe that, like a magnet attracting steel, the spear will henceforth be drawn towards kangaroos. I have never known a hunter not to use blood on his spearshaft.

You think that is funny? Perhaps it is. Perhaps it is quite silly. But not more so than the white hunters who kiss bullets before firing them, or the people who spit on a horseshoe and throw it over the left shoulder.

Finally the spear has to be fitted to the woomera and test-thrown, spinning like a rifle bullet as it cleaves the air. If the rear end of the shaft oscillates through too wide an arc it will whistle in flight, advertising its approach to a kangaroo. It must be trimmed and straightened until it is silent and perfect.

The woomera is also made from Djindi-Djindi, with a wooden point bound to the shaft by wax made from the roots of an ironwood tree.

Boomerangs have been identified with the aborigines since the landing of the first white settlers in Australia. My people were then still living in the age of stone and wood. All their food was killed with stone-headed spears and wooden throwing-sticks. But the curved stick—the boomerang—was not a serious weapon in the Alawa tribe. Even today it is of secondary importance.

On hunting walkabouts our chief armaments were spears, which were much more efficient. I carried a boomerang on short walks around the camp area in case I had the opportunity of a quick shot at a running wallaby or a honker-goose in flight. We used them almost exclusively for moving targets, especially against flocks of ducks and geese unwisely migrating over our territory. Dozens of boomerangs were sent up to meet them, and we were unlucky if that night we did not have a change of diet.

Boomerangs came to Arnhem Land in trade and war. At Twin Pinnacles in the country near Roper Bar two bands of warriors, one from the south and the other from the north, clashed fiercely in the Time of Dream. The southerners were armed with boomerangs, and the northerners with spears. They fought a bloody battle, which proved little more than that both weapons were lethal against Man.

Thereafter the Roper was recognized as a boundary line: spears were manufactured north of the Roper, and boomerangs to the south. But because the clash had taken place in the land of the Alawa we could make both. This tradition has survived for centuries. Many of the boomerangs found in Arnhem Land today have been made by tribes hundreds of miles away, and traded north in exchange for red ochre and shovel-spears. Over the years some of these and other trade goods have travelled two thousand miles across the continent. Boomerangs made on the Nullarbor Plain reached the north coast. The spears of Arnhem Land were used on the Nullarbor.

The Djingali, the Waddaman and the Mudbra tribes fought with a fearsome hooked boomerang, the Warradulla, which was as superior to the conventional weapons as the hydrogen bomb is to TNT. A shield, used as a portable tree, and later the nulla-nulla, which was both a weapon of defence and offence, were satisfactory answers to the early boomerangs, but they were useless against the model with a hook on the end. The simple theory of the Warradulla was that the very act of stopping it with a shield or nulla-nulla caused the hooked end to fly off at tremendous speed, decapitating or seriously injuring its victim. Perhaps it was the original secret weapon.

As a Roper River man I made my own boomerangs as well as my spears. I cut lancewood or ironwood into rough shapes with an axe, planed it with glass, and chiselled a grooved decoration we called Minangai with crude implements hammered from pieces of waste iron.

Such ornamentation was not confined to weapons. Our bodies were also grooved and scored with tribal markings on the chest, abdomen and arms. In some tribes these Burrkun marks were part of the initiation ceremony. But in the Alawa they had no significance except to remind one for ever of the torturer who inflicted them. There was no limit to the number of marks a man could have on his body, but fortunately there was no rule that we had to have any at all.

When I was fifteen a distant tribal relative, Lilyarri, told me it was time I was cicatrized. "I want to cut you," he said.

I had known for some time that an approach would eventually be made by a man who wanted me to remember him. I was determined not to submit.

"No," I said bluntly.

"It will make you look good," he said.

"I'm better looking than you are without cuts," I said.

Burrkun was supposed to be attractive to women. "If you don't let me cut you the girls won't look at you," he said.

"Then I'll stay single," I said.

It didn't stop me getting a wife and six children.

I had seen other men recovering from Burrkun cuts, some twelve inches long. The incision is now made with a razor blade, but in the old days it was done with a sharp stick hardened in fire. The open wound is filled with ashes and earth to prevent infection. This also has the effect of causing an elevated scar. I am not sorry that my body is free of such insignia.

Our boomerangs had another principal use: as beating sticks to accompany the Songmen through hundreds and thousands of chants in ceremonial corroborees like Kunapipi.

Thousands? Yes. Perhaps hundreds of thousands, for Kunapipi goes on and on, every night and every day, often until dawn, for six months. During that time the Songmen, to the clack of the boomerang beat, tell their endless, ageless stories in the chants handed down to us orally by the Generations of Men.

Kunapipi is a ritual, a cult which belongs to the Alawa, the Mara, the Mangarai, and other tribes along the Roper. It spreads north to Yirrkalla and Millingimbi on the Arafura Sea, east to Groote Eylandt in the Gulf of Carpentaria, west to the Kimberleys, and south across the desert to the fringes of Warramunga and Wailbri country in north-central Australia. It has penetrated the barriers of language and culture, survived white infiltration, and today is as virile as ever.

Kunapipi is devotedly pagan yet deeply religious, and the bane of all Christian missionaries. They have attempted to eradicate it, with about as much success as the early Romans had against Christianity itself. But the ceremonies thought to be most objectionable have been modified and even submissively abandoned to twentieth-century standards of decency.

Soon after the arrival of the first horrified missionaries the Alawa, for instance, dropped the ceremonial public mating between men and women, which symbolized fecundity and the relationship of intercourse to the reproduction of species.

My father's father and his contemporaries became involved in arguments with Men of God who were affronted by their fervid paganism and appalled by some of its manifestations.

The missionaries tried to banish all corroborees. The Alawa would not hear of it. Kunapipi and Yabudurawa were part of our heritage, and the tribesmen insisted on keeping them.

"It is wrong that men and women should commit adultery," they were told. "This is one of the commandments of God. To do so in public, as part of a ceremony, is scandalous."

These were strong words. What right did white men have to tell us that we should forsake a ritual act which had been practised by the tribes for more than ten thousand years?

What right had they to force upon us a belief in their own God-in-the-Sky, the one who frowned upon us most at the moment of our infinite spiritual consummation?

Nevertheless, they won their point. The mission had become our refuge from cruelty and want, and my people were grateful. When my father was a young man, just through his circumcision, the Elders told the missionaries: "Kunapipi has been purged. Henceforth it will be inoffensive, a censored ritual which will not break your commandments."

I have often wondered if the magnitude of this concession was ever appreciated.

It would be idle for me to attempt a detailed description of what is, perhaps, the most sacred of all aboriginal corroborees. Books have been written about it and I would need a separate one to describe its intricacies, its mysteries, and its magic. It is enough to say that through Kunapipi songs and dancing we honour The Earth Mother—a mother goddess whom we believe was the source of all life, our language, our culture, our food, our laws, our children, our very creation.

It began as a corroboree for tribal women. Subsequently it was recognized by the men as of such profound significance that they not only took it over but banished the women whose invention it was, except when needed to lay down their bodies during the final act of ceremonial intercourse. Wherever it is danced today women are not allowed to take part or even see it.

Instead, they are sent out to collect lily roots, lily seeds, and yams, and from them make dampers, to feed hunters who are preoccupied for months with the solemnity of regenerating ritual.

I am a Kunapipi Headman—a Djungayi—rather than a dancer. Like a square-dance caller, I instructed the others when they were to perform the Catfish dance, the Eagle-hawk dance, the Young Mermaid dance known as Gilyering-gilyeri, and hundreds more. I was their boss. They were my puppets.

"Jaulwoku!" I ordered. "The Owls."

The Songman began his chant about owls and the dancers joined in, weaving, be-patterned bodies glistening in the campfire's light, arms raised in supplication, circling, hissing, beating their calloused feet against the earth in time with the boomerang sticks.

Jaulwoku bandji
Jaulwoku bandji
Mimi bandji
Mimi bandji.

Pugala the Songman gathered the simple story of an owl struck blind by lightning from the pockets of prodigious memory, where he had stored it since the last Kunapipi.

The dancers moved in towards him.

"Eeeee-aaaaaaah!" they shouted.

"Ah-hah! Ah-hah! Ee-ah! Ee-ah! Ho-ho!"

Clouds of dust rose and settled over old Pugala, but he was aware only of the repetitive chant. It folded back to engulf the dancers, but they were oblivious of everything except the voluptuous rhythm, their hearts pulsating with the out-rush of released emotion as the reverberating ground, pounded by tautened legs, called them back to the creative Earth Mother and the Rainbow Serpent, female and male, primeval symbols of fertility and procreation.

Sometimes they danced by day and sang at night. Sometimes the order was reversed. Sometimes it was complementary. Whatever the procedure, I was the stage-manager who manipulated the strings, the curtains, the ancestral lights.

I was also the make-up artist, for it was the Djungayi who ordered the daubing of the dancers' bodies with human blood and white goose feathers.

The blood sometimes came from my own arm, caught in a bottle from a vein I opened with a razor blade. The feathers were plucked from pied geese which the boomerangs of special hunters had found in flight, then reduced to fluff and rubbed in white clay. If the beauty expert's job was thought to be easy it should be known that each dance had its own decoration. Fortunately I had trained assistants.

My position as Djungayi was inherited from my father Barnabas with the approval of the tribe. He is a High Djungayi, a man of stature wherever the Kunapipi is danced—from the north-eastern tip of Arnhem Land through the Never-Never lands to the Roper and south and beyond to the Djingali at Newcastle Waters. Although he is now approaching seventy years of age he still travels around this immense parish of one hundred thousand square miles.

The High Djungayi combines the duties of both Judge and Priest within the ritual, punishing people who offend against its strict laws, admitting new members, and baptizing travellers who pass through our southern districts so they may drink at our sacred waterholes. This is done as a Christian child is baptized by sprinkling a drop of water on the head. And we have been doing it for much longer than the twenty centuries since the birth of Christ.

Some time ago I was told by the Elders that I would succeed my father in this most religious of all tribal jobs, and recently they asked me to assume the office. I was to be the Man of High Degree in a bailiwick extending south from the Roper to Newcastle Waters, and I would have to patrol it, perhaps on foot, every six months.

If there was trouble on the banks of Mahlindji Hole, perhaps because Djingali clans had a difference of opinion on Kunapipi ceremonial, I would be expected to go there at once as arbitrator, walking through for three hundred miles if no other means of transport was available.

Although I belong to the Alawa tribe, the Djingali would abide by my decisions as an Australian Catholic heeds the instructions of an Italian Pope, bound to the ecclesiastic law by his confession of faith.

I would be required to select young initiates as Kunapipi communicants known as Gulawudi after satisfying myself by thorough investigation that each boy was ready: "Is he obedient?" "Does he keep his secrets?" "Does he play-about with girls?"

I must be careful that no loose-tongue who might betray our ritual was admitted. I would accept the recommendation of Elders that a particular boy was responsible and secretive but—and this has often happened—others would be denied until they were eighteen and had learnt to keep the incommutable law of our "Freemasonry."

But my powers as High Djungayi would extend immeasurably beyond the control of initiates and ceremonial customs. I would, in fact, be invested with the right to order the execution of a Kunapipi traitor, or to grant him life on payment of a heavy fine.

The Lower Djungayi, my advisers, might say: "This man has stolen a Kunapipi painting. That man has betrayed a secret to a woman. We want them to die."

I could then give a thumbs-down sign, condemning them to death, or release them with a fine and a bond. In these circumstances the High Djungayi is generally under heavy pressure from the outraged prosecutors for the death penalty. If he refuses too often there may be a move to replace him.

My father, a strict but merciful man, has been through tribal fire from the Lower Djungayi because of his steadfast refusal to order executions. He often told them: "The man will pay a heavy fine only, or you must vote for another High Djungayi." The prestige of Barnabas Gabarla was such that his decisions were accepted or his critics repulsed by the Electorate of Elders.

My father often warned me about this aspect of my duties if I should become a High Djungayi. I attended sacred meetings at which my elevation was discussed. I am under no misapprehension about the difficult decisions I will be called upon to make when I do assume office.

So far I have been prevented from doing so because of my work as a medical assistant with the Northern Territory Department of Health. Whether or not I will eventually return to the Roper to wear my symbolic robes and chain is still in the balance. I am not convinced that I cannot achieve more for my people by helping to minister to their medical needs than by becoming Comptroller of the Ceremonial. We have had a harrowing family experience, which I will discuss later, that makes me favour a continuance of my present work.

Nevertheless, my people already acknowledge me as a High Djungayi although I can practise only casually. My last visit to the Roper with the Flying Doctor coincided with a Kunapipi. The moment I stepped from the aerial —the hair belts, the feathers, the paintings, the body ambulance I was asked to inspect the ceremonial articles decorations—like a General inspecting the equipment and dressing of his troops.

I was satisfied that everything was in order and gave permission for the ritual to proceed. And let me say that while I made my inspection on the corroboree ground the celebrants were as hushed and attentive as the Brigade of Guards at a Trooping the Colour ceremony. We do not recognize Kings or Queens, but the High Djungayi has the equivalent of royal rank. In my own group of the Alawa I am King Pin.

That is something I have had to earn throughout my life. As for all other tribesmen, participation in Kunapipi was not automatic for me until I had passed my novitiate as a Man of Silence and been through the Lorrkun and Yabudurawa corroborees. No man who has not taken part in these may be admitted to Kunapipi.

The Lorrkun is a simple burial ceremony, a funeral service associated with the interment of a dead tribesman's bones in a hollow log and their disposal on a Gulla-gulla tree-platform in his tribal country.

The Yabudurawa, like Kunapipi, is a ritualistic fertility corroboree which goes on for six months. It was necessary for me to have been a celebrant, to have understood its placatory message to the spirits of those animals and birds which were our food, and to the spirits of our ancestors, before I could qualify for the ultimate dignity of a graduate tribesman.

Once that was done I became the White-Haired Boy, favoured by the Elders as a future High Djungayi.

And at that stage, having become a Man, I was ready to be given to Woman.

Chapter Eight

IN the storm-bird time when the mangoes ripen and the flying foxes play, a young Alawa's thoughts may turn to love, or his equivalent of what that means.

All my life I had been aware, of course, that aboriginal girls existed.

Like crocodiles, they were our natural enemies.

From my earliest schooldays and beyond until I became an initiate I thought of them as implacable foes who were to be tormented and vilified on all occasions. If physical torture was possible, so much the better.

I hated them, all of them, with an abiding intensity.

In the segregated community in which I lived the association of boys and girls, fortunately, was difficult. We stayed with the men, they stayed with the women, and we treated each other with the utmost contempt. But at walkabout time when family groups of up to thirty people went into the bush together on hunting holidays, head-on clashes between the juveniles of the sexes were inevitable and premeditated.

I remember that one of our favourite devices was to make toy boomerangs from gumbark and descend on the girls as though they were geese. Feathers were soon ruffled and flying. They retaliated with sharp sticks used for digging yams—and pricking boys. It often happened that a girl who had been hit by a boomerang became so infuriated that she struck out blindly with her yam stick and made a boy bleed.

That meant war.

Aboriginal children like watching fights, whether they are between women or men. In this way they acquire early knowledge of how to parry a spear, a boomerang, or a nulla-nulla. I must admit that the women were better teachers, if only because they fought twice as often.

But being in a fight is better than watching one, and we attacked the girls—and were attacked—on the slightest pretext. Our stick fights were classics in canine ferocity. We rolled around as black balls of naked, howling humanity, and stopped only when threatened by the Elders.

The lurid imprecations which accompanied these fights were learnt mostly from the women.

"Rip that maggot up the guts with a yam stick!"

"Brain that bitch with a boomerang!"

"Break her legs with the nulla-nulla!"

I often wondered what the missionaries thought—and especially their wives—when they saw us go to war, and overheard our battle cries. Perhaps they believed we were playing a game? Perhaps they didn't understand the words? There must have been some such explanation for the fact that they did not interfere.

I understand that white boys and girls overcome mutual enmity in their early teens and then show a disposition to pet and cuddle. There is no cuddling in the Alawa. We would rather fight than flirt. There were no endearments, no fondling, no sly caressing in the dark, and certainly no kissing. Perhaps this explains why I, like many aboriginal men, had no courtship. Perhaps it explains why most aboriginal partners do not kiss even after marriage . . . because residual estrangement has created reticence and destroyed the spontaneity necessary for expressions of tender affection.

Nevertheless, the storm-bird time when the mangoes ripened and the flying foxes played came for me, too.

In the beginning, Nora Bindul became my promised wife. As the eldest daughter of Jupiter of the Balang skin of the Ngandi tribe she belonged to the eldest son of Barnabas Gabarla of the Burlangban skin of the Alawa tribe. That was written. She was the sister of Sam Ulagang. Because he was to be my brother-in-law it was his duty to teach me to hunt.

Soon after she was born, her maternal uncle, Gurukul, said to Jupiter: "Here is the wife of Waipuldanya."

But aboriginal law, inflexible as it is in many respects, is tolerant in others.

When I was twenty years old Nora was still a child, unready for marriage. I would have to wait five years for her, and the tribe, meanwhile, would be wasting the pro-creative power of one of its young men, thus impairing its own chance of survival. In such a situation my Elders were alert for a compromise—and they soon found one.

Her name was Hannah Dulban of the Ngamayang skin of the Wandarang tribe.

It wasn't easy.

Complex tribal interdictions as durable as ecclesiastical law had to be circumvented. Primarily, consent had to be won from my maternal uncle, Stanley Marbunggu, my guardian, the man who called me Nibarli . . . son. Where I was concerned his word was paramount. My father may have preferred me to wait for Nora. He may have been in favour of my marrying Hannah. Whatever he thought was of no consequence: he would simply be expressing a wish. My mother would acknowledge her incompetence to have a view at all by saying: "It is my brother's business."

Similarly, Hannah and I now have six daughters. I have no authority to say who and when they shall marry. That is a matter entirely for Johnny Nanguru, their maternal uncle.

When an aboriginal uncle searches for a wife for his Nibarli he is not concerned with such trivia as her appear-ance, her disposition or her accomplishments. Beauty, fripperies, temper, and culinary art are subordinate to the primary question: Is she Right-Side?

In most tribes there is an arbitrary division of men and women into groups known as "skins" which indicate tribal and inter-tribal relationships. I am of the Bungadi skin although my father is a Burlangban. My six daughters are also Burlangban. The skin of all aboriginal children, both boys and girls, throws back to their paternal grandfather.

It is a grave offence, subject to severe punishment, to marry into any skin-group which is Wrong-Side. I cannot cross the double traffic lines.

The aborigines believe that the marriage of incompatible skins may lead to imbecility, paralysis, and other physical and mental deficiencies. European races have legal and moral prohibitions on the marriage of close relatives. Ours go much further. The skin-group system automatically precludes me from marrying any closer relative than my cousin's daughter's daughter. The ban varies from tribe to tribe, but in the Alawa it is strictly enforced.

I could not marry into the Bulainjan, the Nangari, or the Bilinjan skins. Marbunggu would not waste time looking there. He would know they were across the yellow line. But the Ngamayang skin was Right-Side, and one of its women was Hannah Dulban of the Wandarang tribe. She was single, fifteen years old, and had not been promised to any of a number of men who might have claimed her.

"She will marry Nibarli," Marbunggu said. "I will see her uncle."

Would she, indeed! What would I, Waipuldanya, have to say about that? Would I like her face? Would I like her figure? Had she, perhaps, been an especial enemy in our interminable boy-and-girl brawls?

Such considerations were frivolous. I was not within two hundred miles of the Roper River when my wife was selected for me. When I returned, months later, Marbunggu and my father told me about the meetings which had taken place in my absence.

"I have a wife for you," my uncle said.

"Her name?" I asked.

"Dulban, Ngamayang, Wandarang," he said, giving Hannah's personal name, her skin and her tribe.

Dulban? Dulban? Was she the kid with the cast in one eye? Or was she the one with the club foot? Then I remembered.

"Yes. Hannah Dulban," my uncle said. "What do you say?"

What could I say? The decision had been made for me. Objections would be useless. And, anyway, I did not want to object. I was secretly pleased, for Hannah was attractive by all aboriginal standards: maiden's firm breasts, rounded abdomen, strong thighs, large eyes with long lashes, broad nostrils, full lips, and flashing teeth revealed by a spontaneous smile which broke without cause into melting feminine laughter.

"What does her gardi-gardi say?" I asked.

"He agrees," Marbunggu said.

And I knew that nothing could now stop my immediate marriage, for Hannah had even less right than I to an opinion on whom her partner should be. I knew that whether she liked me or not she would be my wife and bear my children. If she resisted she would be taken on a walkabout holiday by her relatives. Before leaving, her uncle would invite me to a rendezvous in the bush. When I arrived he would point to the girl and say, "Take her away. She is yours." She would then become my wife by force under the Mungu-Mungu law of our ancestors.

Fortunately nothing like that happened. Hannah was apparently satisfied with Waipuldanya of the Bungadi skin of the Alawa tribe.

A few days later her paternal aunts made a camp for me away from my parents: a fire with wood to stoke it, water, food, and a double blanket laid out on the sand.

Then they came to me. "Tonight you will be getting married. That is your camp," they said.

We had no engagement, no kitchen tea, no wedding ring, no bridal gown, no bridesmaids, no groomsman, no banquet, and certainly no champagne.

There was not even a brief courtship or a single word from me to Hannah. In our childhood I had spoken to her as one of a group of infants—as one speaks to babies.

I was five years her senior. If fraternization between the sexes had existed I would have been in another group. In all my life I had not said more than two or three words directly to her, and they were probably rude commands to get out of my way. Now she was to be my wife, to live in my camp until the Lorrkun corroboree for the dead released her from unspoken vows.

As it happened, our wedding ceremony was not quite as simple as it might have been. With five other couples we were married in the mission chapel by the Rev. Norman Woodhart in accordance with the rites of a religion brought to us by white men.

I had attended the mission Sunday School and was baptized in the Christian Church. I have since had trouble reconciling the traditions of my people and our pagan beliefs and practices with the Word of God.

I have been confused. I am still confused. How can I disbelieve what the Elders taught me? How can I reconcile my unimpaired belief in the Earth Mother and the Rainbow Serpent with the Holy Trinity? What must I think when tribesmen who profess a Christian creed on Sunday are fervently chanting paganism on a corroboree ground on Monday?

Are we rice-Christians, affirming a doctrine for its rewards?

If I am asked do I believe in the Earth Mother the answer is emphatically Yes. Am I not a Kunapipi Djungayi?

But when asked if I am a Christian I also answer Yes, though perhaps with less emphasis.

The confusion has left me grasping for the strongest straw, and I sometimes wonder which that is. But I do know that when Kunapipi calls I will be there worshipping the Mother Goddess.

My father appears to suffer from an even greater mental turmoil.

On the day he became a lay preacher in the mission chapel at Roper River and gave an oration about the Tribes of Israel and the twelve stones and the parting of the waters of the Red Sea . . . "a plenty-big water, more-bigger'n this Roper River here . . . " I thought it was time I asked him whether he really believed in God or the Mother Goddess.

"I am now a Christian," he said belligerently. "I believe God made the world, the sea, the animals, our Roper River country, and all our people. I read the Bible. I once believed that my totems, my Dreamings, the Frilled-Neck Lizard and the Jabiru, made the country and the kangaroos and the fish. No-more. No-more. I am a man of God."

"You are a High Djungayi in the Kunapipi," I said "You are a Keeper of the Laws, a Judge and a Priest, an Inspector-General of the Ritual."

"Yes, that too," he said irrationally. "That's different."

Perhaps he wants to be in both worlds, to practise two religions, to have one foot in Heaven and one in the Gulla-Gulla. I wonder has he noticed the quiet smirks of the white men whose belief he professes, the white men who do not themselves, many of them, believe in the white man's God?

To the extent that our marriage was blessed by a priest it was a Christian ceremony, although I have since wondered if the superficial knowledge we have is a sufficient base for professed belief.

In any case, Hannah's aunts did not intend being denied their rights as primitive celebrants. In a tribal marriage it is their duty to deliver a niece to her husband. Having taken Hannah from me at the church door they returned with her when the sun had set.

"This is your woman," they told me. "This is your camp."

"This is your Man," they told Hannah. "Stay with him. Stay with Wadjiri-Wadjiri, your husband."

Aboriginal girls often marry when thirteen or fourteen years old. In such cases the aunts make a camp ten feet from the nuptial blanket to comfort her through consummation. After two or three nights, when she has settled down, the Elders find a pretext to send them with

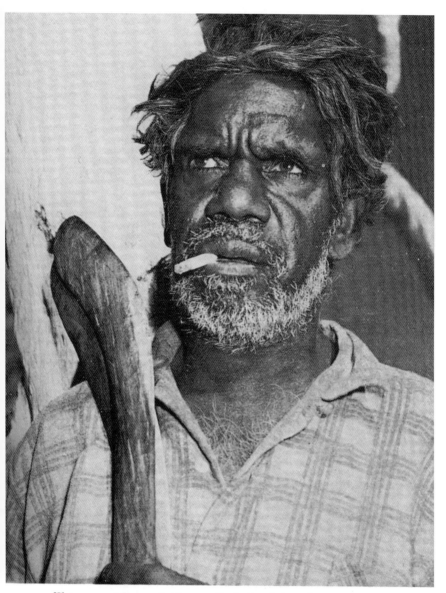

Warramunga tribesman at Tennant Creek, proud descendant of the fierce warriors who first barred John McDouall Stuart's way when he attempted to cross the continent in 1860. There is a monument at Attack Creek to mark the spot of their first clash. But now we live in peace with the white man . . . his cigarettes are good!

"Myself when young did eagerly
frequent . . ."
One of the big fish-and-crocodile
lagoons on the Roper.

And this is what we got for our
troubles . . . delicious king-size
barramundi.

The old T-Model Ford, driven by Les Perriman, in which I learnt to drive. On my first attempt I tried to run it up a tree.

Corroboree. . . . . This was how we implored our pagan gods for favours, and did our best to repel evil spirits, as in this death ritual.

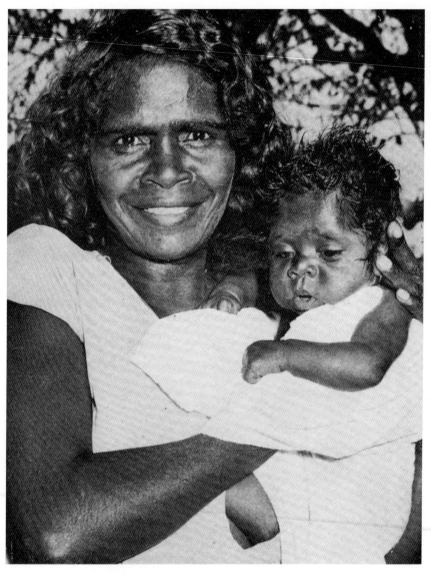

A Malak Malak tribeswoman and baby at Daly River, N.T. I had tribal "relatives" like this wherever I went.

Dr A. H. Humphry.

But for his help I might still have been a primitive tribesman.

Dr A. H. Humphry examines a man for leprosy at Roper River. I did many trips in the Aerial Ambulance shown in the background.

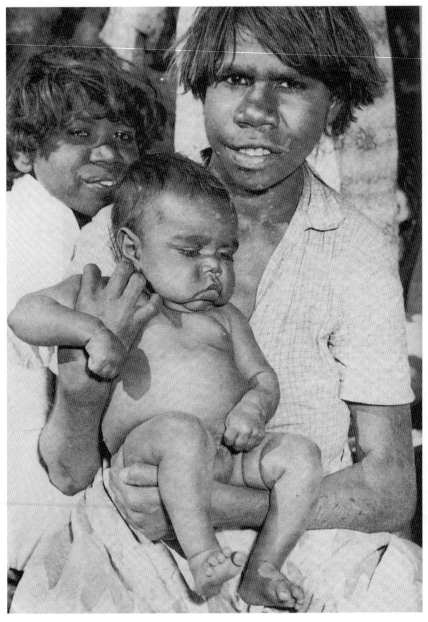

Wailbri women such as these were my relatives, too, although I had never heard of them.

We ate pythons by the yard. But sometimes they tried to eat our dogs. Grilled snake was known as "soft" tucker, and was generally given to the old people.

Two of my uncles! Old primitives of the Pintubi tribe in the desert near the Northern Territory-Western Australia border. The dogs are pure-bred dingoes.

Leprosy patients in Arnhem Land. I walked hundreds of miles searching for them. I regarded leprosy as my Number One enemy . . . it killed my mother.

"Dr" Waipuldanya treating sores on the head of an old man in Arnhem Land. I was often embarrassed by the faith of these people in my medical knowledge.

My uncle, Jambadjimba, of the Wailbri tribe. He is a desert man who has never known what it is to have water to waste.

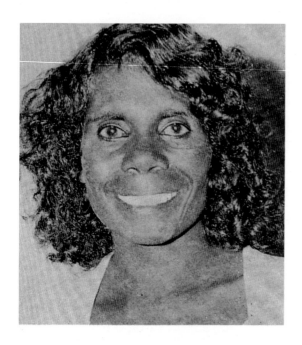

My wife, Hannah, Dulban, was chosen for me by my uncle. I had no say in the matter . . . nor will I be able to choose my daughters' husbands.

This is the white man, Dr "Spike" Langsford, who first encouraged me to leave my country and try my luck in the Big White Way. He is one of my best friends.

A Pintubi man from the desert west of Alice Springs. Only recently some of his tribesmen saw white men for the first time. The Pintubi are the most primitive of Australian aborigines.

My brother Silas and his son, Robert, have always remained on the Roper River. He has shunned civilization; will probably always remain in our tribal country.

My father, Barnabas Gabarla, is a High Djungayi in our ceremonials . . . a very important man. I have been chosen to succeed him. Like me, he has had trouble reconciling our pagan beliefs with Christianity.

Roger Tiwi, of Melville Island, demonstrates a method of fire-making. The vertical stick is rotated by the hands in the hollowed-out part of the horizontal stick. I could make fire in a few minutes by this method.

Be it ever so humble! A hut like this was our house. I lived there with my parents, two brothers, and a sister. Unpretentious . . . but home, nevertheless—and the fire was never out.

Waipuldanya,
Phillip Roberts,
of the Alawa tribe.

Here I am with Douglas Lockwood, the man who wrote this book.
He reckons I'm a first-class ear-basher. I must say he's a good
listener. . . . I talked with him for more than 100 hours, and he
didn't once complain.

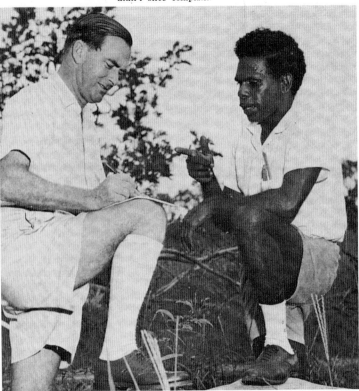

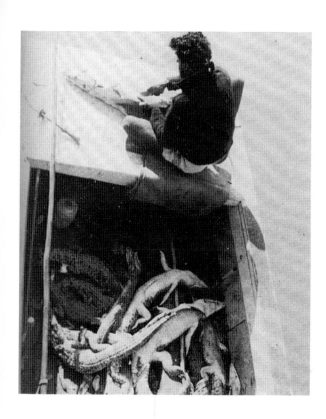

Tucker!
Crocodiles, young
ones, by the boat-
load. They taste
like . . . crocodile.

. . . and more tucker, speared by Tommy Munmulmara (*right*) of the Berara
tribe. What is aboriginal tucker? Meat, fish, and eggs!

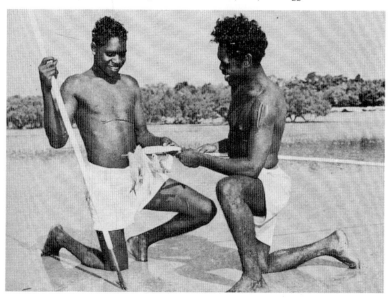

Myself as
ambulance driver
. . . with a young
patient.

Myself (*right*) and brother Jacob, now also a citizen. If you think I'm an
ear-basher you should listen to him. He never stops talking!

a Message-Stick to relatives who may be camping several days' march away. Who blames them for walking slowly, enjoying a primitive honeymoon and their novel status?

My aunts wanted to camp near me, too. I showed them the wide-open spaces. Moreover, the honeymoon I spent with Hannah was one that I chose, walking out to the tribal land south of the Roper which was mine alone, my ancestral country, there to take my virgin woman to me, thighs across thighs, wordlessly but gladly, finding comfort and communion where our spiritual forebears looked down.

I did not then believe, and I'm not sure whether I believe now, that the nuptial couch of bark was the conceptional place of our first child.

I belong to the Kangaroo totem. We all know that the kangaroo made the coolibah tree, called Mutju. We all know that each year the Elders of the Kangaroo clan chew Mutju bark. When it is masticated they spit it out and chant, "The wives of the Kangaroo totem are commanded to have children."

A few months later all the women will be pregnant. Every Alawa believes that his totem impregnates them after the Road has been Made by the Rainbow Serpent.

In recent years I have had medical training and listened carefully to doctors who assured me that conception takes place through fertilization of female ova by male sperm following intercourse. That story would raise a great laugh among the Alawa.

Not all tribal marriages are as easily arranged as mine. We have eternal triangles, too. The system of promissory wives was a major cause of trouble.

I rejected Nora Bindul, or she was traded on my behalf, when I married Hannah. But some of the old men, nearing senility, had more than one wife while young men remained single.

This was a survival from the days when polygamy flourished as it still does in the Andilyaugwa tribe at Groote Eylandt. I know one Andilyaugwan who has six wives, and several who have three or four.

Polygamy among the aborigines is a kind of elementary insurance policy against the discomforts of old age in a tribal community. A man with several wives is sure of messengers to fetch and carry for him. And by selling or hiring his women to the have-nots he has an assured supply of tobacco and food.

Polygamy on the Roper has now been stopped, but even among the Alawa there are still a number of old men with more than one wife. One of these is generally a girl acquired in late life on the promissory system, thus depriving a younger man who may have wanted to marry her.

It also happens that two men from eligible skins want the same unattached woman. Several men were Right Side for Hannah when she was given to me. I was lucky that my inheritance was not disputed. Inevitably, a brutal fight with spears, boomerangs, and nulla-nullas must have followed.

There is just one solution to tribal triangles: the two men go to war until one is either killed or so badly injured that he loses his appetite for women for a long time. I remember one fight in which a man's spine was laid bare by a shovel-spear. And I have seen Wailbri and Pitjant-jarra tribesmen in Central Australia whose bodies were a patchwork of scars from wounds inflicted in woman-trouble fights.

A man may also acquire a wife magically by singing tjarada love songs to her like a primitive Romeo, by dancing before her, by calling her name, and by spitting on a small symbolic bullroarer called Irribinji until she is hypnotized. The result is much the same as a white girl who becomes love-sick and is eventually swept off her feet by a male who showers her with equivalent attentions: flowers, valentines, jewellery, and other white-feller tjarada.

Having laid his bait, the aboriginal Lothario twirls his whining bullroarer on a string until it breaks. That is an omen, like she-loves-me-she-loves-me-not petals, foretelling that the girl will defy her husband and elope with him.

114

Thereafter he wears around his forehead a white band of gumbark. When the girl sees it she drifts into a hypnotic trance, sitting and staring at him, becoming as clay in his hands, subservient.

"Hear this: Tomorrow night when the moon is set you will meet me at the Lily Root Place," he says.

"Tomorrow night . . . ?"

"Yes."

"When the moon is set . . . ?"

"Yes."

"At the Lily Root Place . . . ?"

"At the Lily Root Place."

"Yes. . . ."

The mystic power of the man guides her feet. While her husband sleeps she leaves his fire, as indigent as the day she came, without food, without water, clad in a cotton calico, which is her only garment, which will stay on her body until it falls off. Pervading fear, the terror which would have been with her alone at night in the spirit world of the bush, is gone, suppressed in catalepsy as she floats to her rendezvous. A shadow with human shape moves towards her from the Lily Root Place. Before she is touched, before a word is spoken, she falls on the couch of paperbark, impatient for a lover who is not yet her husband.

The threat of tribal retribution rises with the sun, glowering and passionate and outraged. They know the law of Mungu-Mungu: he who steals another man's wife shall return with her before the next sunset to face the tribe. That is written.

And may the Mother Goddess have mercy upon them.

He walks ahead towards the camp, asserting the dominance he proved in the night, she following in The Docile Path that belongs to woman. They emerge from the paperbarks, culpable but not cast down, defiant but diffident, ready for the barrage of inescapable profanity. And for the spears, the boomerangs, the nulla-nullas and the stones thrown to break their bodies.

Men attack the man, women pummel the woman. Spears are hurled to kill, sticks to maim, and the man had better remember his parrying lessons. The woman is prodded with sharp yam sticks, struck with nulla-nullas, and dragged by the hair. But like all aboriginal women she has been taught to defend herself and she fights back ferociously, screaming dementedly at the shrieks of abuse assailing her.

When the arsenals and the combatants are exhausted the fights stop. The girl, bleeding, spattered and torn, is returned to her husband to absorb his personal wrath. The man is told, "Go! Roll your swag and go!"

Whether he accepts this instruction depends entirely on his heart and his body. A cowed man will leave at once to escape further punishment. But a fighter will stay on the perimeter of the camp, carefully shifting his position at night to avoid encirclement, waiting only until his woman sees him there and acknowledges the sign-talk message: "Tonight! At the Big Yam Place." Her almost imperceptible nod is all that he needs.

And that night, at the Big Yam Place, they wait for the moon.

"Now we go," he says, when it rises. "We go along 'Nother Place, away from tribal land. We no-more come back."

Her heart is his, but it belongs here.

His heart is hers, but it belongs here.

Their totems are here on the ancestral ground.

Her mother is here.

His uncle is here.

Their lives are here, indissolubly bound in tortuous sociological patterns.

'Nother Place is where the dead men are, the living dead who are exiles from their tribal country.

Poor feller my country.

Poor feller my country.

Poor feller me.

Poor feller me.

Gibb'it me 'bacca, gibb'it me tea.

He mutters the Lament of The Detribalized, the Dirge of Miserable Men.

"I'm ready now," she says. "I follow."

They go . . . and they go . . . and they sit down. They go . . . and they go . . . and they sit down. They go . . . and they go . . . and they sit down.

Tired-feller.

Weary-feller.

Sorry-feller.

Properly-sorry-feller longa my country, my poor-feller country, but comforting each other: *"For thou art with me; thy rod and thy staff they comfort me."*

In their hearts there is the eternal hope that beyond the still waters, beyond the green pastures, when they have crossed the valley, their shades will one day be restored to the Roper River from which their bodies are banished for ever.

They go and they go, and they never come back. The law said they must return on the first day of their first elopement. They did that. The law had nothing to say about a second attempt. There was now no threat of tribal pursuit and murder. By-'n-by they would come to a cattle station or a mining camp where food and tobacco and fire-water were to be had for a price . . . for the price of utter degradation, for the price of detribalization, for the price of a woman's body and a man's soul.

Our marriage rules are governed by moieties through patrilineal descent. Compliance with them is mandatory. But there are compensations.

In all the Roper River tribes a man may not look at or speak to his mother-in-law either before or after marriage! As every man has a mother-in-law almost from the time he is born, this saves endless speech.

The ancient tribal legislators may have written this law after a particularly virulent period of what is popularly known as mother-in-law trouble. They insisted that the ban should remain with a man throughout his life. It is still scrupulously observed today.

But like many other laws it has a loophole: a mother-in-law can speak to her son-in-law, although he must keep his face averted and answer her only by nodding or shaking his head.

During his daily life an Alawa tribesman takes meticulous care never to meet his mother-in-law face to face. I am one of very few who have been given a dispensation, and that was done only after the opposition of the women had collapsed under pressure from the men.

It came about in this way. For several years I have been a medical assistant with the Northern Territory Department of Health, accompanying white doctors to remote missions and settlements to help in the monumental task of beating tuberculosis, leprosy, hookworm, and all the other diseases to which my people are heir.

When I began this work it became obvious that I would be at a disadvantage on my home ground at Roper River. The ban would prevent me from taking sputum slides from any of the women in my mother-in-law's group—her sisters were also in purdah to me—or from learning their medical history.

I sent word of this difficulty to the Elders, who discussed it with the women and persuaded them to lift the taboo while I performed my official duties.

When I arrived they approached me in a group. As always, I averted my eyes by turning my back. Then one woman blindfolded me with her hands and symbolically removed them.

"Because of your medical work you are now free to talk to us and look at us," she said.

I opened my eyes and saw my mother-in-law and her relatives. Their faces were unfamiliar even though I had lived in a camp with them for most of my life. I looked at them diffidently at first because the old law weighed heavily upon me. I was painfully shy, unwillingly meeting their eyes when asking a direct question, conscious always of the unspoken thought: "We should not be face-to-face."

But there we were, smiling at last, breaking down another old tradition through a concession by the women, destroying a rule that perhaps pre-dated the commandment the Lord gave to Samuel: *"Look not upon his countenance."*

Another compensation of tribal marriage is that a man can divorce his wife with even greater ease than the Moslem who says, "I divorce thee, I divorce thee, I divorce thee." Any tribesman may obtain instant freedom by saying just one word to his wife: "Go!" Women do not have the same right to divorce their husbands, except perhaps in rare cases when the man is an incurable adulterer.

Adultery, in fact, is the prime cause of all divorces. I have never known a man to leave his wife because she was ugly, barren, ill-tempered, unclean, a poor cook or, in the Hollywood phrase, because of mental or even physical cruelty.

Permanent separation is almost impossible if a couple have children. I have known women to return with a new man to live with her cast-off husband because she could not leave her children. I have also known children to accept such a man as their father, but these cases are rare. A cuckolded husband is redressed by his sons and nephews. Twenty years ago they would have murdered both the woman and her lover. Today, having experienced the application of white-feller law to blackfeller crimes, they are content after the thorough beating with sticks.

But I'm not sure that murder wasn't kinder. Stick-thrashings have often resulted in men never being men again. I have seen them dead in all respects except that their hearts had not stopped beating.

Chapter Nine

I AM taboo not only to my Roper River mother-in-law but also to my mothers-in-law in most other tribes in Australia, from the Andilyaugwa at Groote Eylandt to the Malak Malak at Daly River, the Warramunga at Tennant Creek, the Wailbri and Pintubi in the Great Western Desert, and the Aranda, Pitjantjarra, and Loritja around Alice Springs. I may not, except during medical work, look at or speak to them nor to any of their sisters.

How can a man have more than one mother-in-law?

Simply by being a tribal aboriginal.

I also have a multiplicity of fathers and mothers and more uncles and aunts, brothers and sisters than an oil-rich Arabian sheik.

This happens because of the skin-groups into which all tribes are divided. Wherever I travel I have relatives even though I am a stranger in that country.

If I go to Daly River a Malak Malak man may ask me, "What is your skin?"

"Bungadi."

"Ah," he may say, "you are my uncle."

He will point out my father and mother and other relatives who will care for me during my stay in the district.

During a visit to Central Australia a man asked me my skin. When I told him he said, "There is your family group," pointing to people I had never seen.

I approached them, introduced myself as "Jagamara," the locality-word of Bungadi, and was at once invited to join the camp-fire circle.

I was made welcome, warned of the taboos, told which women were Right-Side for marriage, and which I must avoid because they belonged to the mother-in-law clan. Although I was in a foreign land I was absorbed into the family entity—and yet I could not speak their language. We conversed in broken English and the expressive finger-talk which is common to all tribes.

I can ask a question: Who is it? What is it? Where is it? What is going on? by raising my thumb and index finger and revolving my wrist through a semicircle. That is understood as an interrogative by all aboriginal tribes. I can ask for food by touching my mouth, and for water by bulging one cheek. I can describe most animals and birds with my hands and arms.

A hospitable man may tell one from another tribe to borrow one of his wives without opening his mouth, simply by clenching his fist at the breast and tapping his belly and thigh.

Finger-talk is also constant among men who speak the same tongue. It not only saves unnecessary speech but has the added advantage that evil spirits cannot hear it.

Aborigines also believe in communication through mental telepathy and physical convulsion of the body, the commonest form of which is involuntary muscle-twitching.

If my right shoulder twitches I know that my father has thought of me. If the convulsion persists I think that he may be ill.

My left shoulder represents my Uncle Stanley Marbunggu, because that is where he carried me during the early years of guardianship.

My mother is in my right breast, my thighs belong to my wife, my calves to my brothers and sisters, my right eyelid to brothers-in-law and the left eyelid to my cousins.

When a muscle twitches I throw out my flexed arm violently to straighten it. If the elbow cracks I know that I will soon see or receive news of the person represented by the muscle which has twitched. This has happened to me too often to be coincidental. We do not use such English phrases as "How strange, I was just thinking about you!" and "Talk of the devil and here he is!" We say, instead, "You were expected."

When I visit a strange tribe the Elders will ask me if I have been through the initiation corroborees. If so, they confide their laws and ceremonies to me, explaining taboos, delineating the prohibited hunting areas, trees, and billabongs as a white hunter might be warned about wild-life sanctuaries.

Everywhere I go, in the lands of any tribe and especially of my own along the Roper, there are sacred trees. I cannot throw my boomerang at birds resting in their branches. I cannot eat the Sugarbag hidden in the hollows. I cannot use the bark or the wood or the sap of one of these trees without breaking a taboo, which may darken my Shade and lead to my murder.

I have mentioned this belief to a number of white people, including missionaries. Invariably they have ridiculed our stupid superstitions. But now, having learnt some Christian parables, I refer the sceptics to the Lord God when he spoke to Adam: *"Hast thou eaten of the tree whereof I commanded thee that thou shouldst not eat? And the man said, The woman whom thou gavest to be with me, she gave me of the tree and I did eat. And the Lord God said unto the woman, What is this that thou hast done? And the woman said, The serpent beguiled me and I did eat. Unto the woman the Lord God said, I will greatly multiply thy sorrow and thy conception; in sorrow thou shalt bring forth children; and thy desire shall be to thy husband and he shall rule over thee. And unto Adam he said, Because thou hast eaten of the tree, cursed is the ground for thy sake; in sorrow shalt thou eat of it all the days of thy life."*

Are we so gullible, therefore, when we implicitly preserve the sanctity of our trees? Is it folly that we do not infringe the commandments given to us?

The Lord God spoke to Adam about five thousand years ago. But the aborigines had forbidden trees more than ten thousand years before Christ!

There are other taboos. When my wife is pregnant, as when I was circumcised, I cannot eat fat goanna, fat turtle, fat turkey, fat emu, or fat snake.

When I catch a goanna I search around its ribs with my fingers for a globule of fat. If none is present I may eat it. But if the fat is there I give the goanna to a friend who is not under the Buka taboo.

While I am Buka I cannot crack the leg bones of kangaroos and suck out the sweet marrow, as is customary. I believe that to do so would cause the child to be born with crooked legs, soft bones, and perhaps other deformities.

My wife's pregnancies, even though we have six children, have never been discussed between us. That is strictly Women's Business. I found out she was pregnant on each occasion when it became physically obvious. The fact that she was going to have a child had nothing to do with me, but was a matter for the tribal women only.

It is usual for the father to take the umbilical cord from his child, to paint it with red ochre, and send it to distant relatives as irrefutable evidence of birth.

I did this when my first daughter, Phyllis Mutukutpina, was born. My uncle sent it to family relatives at Newcastle Waters, three hundred miles away. Weeks later the presents arrived: hair belts, bangles made from possum fur, and feathered headbands, both for mother and daughter. But civilization has caught up with that practice. My five youngest—Rhoda Bulilka, Connie Ngamirimba, Mavis Wanjimari, Margaret Gabadabadana, and Miriam Jardagara—were all born in hospitals, delivered by doctors or trained nurses who removed the cord before I could get it.

In addition to particular trees, a number of localities where our totem heroes passed in the Dreamtime are also sacred ground and therefore taboo to hunters.

These are generally small hills which can be easily identified or, more accurately, never mistaken. Profanation of any such area, whether deliberate or accidental, is worse than sacrilege among Christians. It is one of the few offences punished by the tribal executioner—the Mulunguwa who is the Alawa answer to the terrifying Kadaitja Man of the Pitjantjarra.

An Alawa who desecrates hallowed ground knows that someone must die at the hand of the Mulunguwa, whether now or generations later. The offender himself will probably escape, and the punishment be visited upon his children, his children's children, or other relatives.

In this way, for the remainder of his life, he suffers the dolour of not knowing when and where the executioner will strike. The grudge may be harboured through his lifetime and beyond before the Mulunguwa kills a relative who was not alive when the transgression occurred. The Lord God had the same idea when he warned Moses that the iniquities of the fathers would be visited upon the children, and upon the children's children, even unto the fourth generation.

When a tribal killing is contemplated the aggrieved clan approaches the Mulunguwa and recites a typical complaint: "The Gamarang man in our father's day cut a tree on Walinji, the sacred hill, and took Sugarbag. The time for punishment has come."

The Mulunguwa is given a sacred Gulinga stick and hair belt signifying that he is sworn into the act of killing, like a hangman's warrant. He cannot resist. To do so would mean his own death.

I remember one occasion after particularly blatant sacrilege when it was decided that two of the offender's relatives must die. One of the victims was a woman. The Mulunguwa dived into a billabong where she was digging lily roots, dragged her down, and broke her neck under water. Then a brother was slowly sung to death.

For two years I watched that man become an imbecile, his face contorted with fear, frothing at the mouth, muttering unintelligibly, a moron as I had once been, until the morning he screamed and died piteously, thus atoning for a crime that neither he nor the woman had committed.

Legal killers in the white world—the hangman who adjusts a noose and springs a trapdoor, the man who pushes an electric switch, or drops a cyanide pellet or a guillotine —are paid by the government of their country. The Mulunguwa is compensated by the clan whose totem hero was reviled after he has returned the Gulinga and shown that his mission has been accomplished.

Then begins the interminable process known as Pay-Back, or do-unto-others-what-they-do-to-you.

The dead man's relatives issue dire threats. "There'll be more deaths when we find out who killed our brother and sister." Thereafter, and until all grievances are made level-feller in a Kunapipi, a Yabudurawa, or a Banburr corroboree, they will strive to discover the identity of the Mulunguwa and the murdering clan who forced his hand.

That is not easy. Nobody in the tribe except the instructing Elders know who the Mulunguwa is, and there is no possibility that they will betray him. But the aboriginal mind is devious and inventive. Even while the condemned man deteriorates from derangement to insanity he is questioned ceaselessly for a clue to the name of his tormentor, a task that is complicated by his terror of the very name itself and his consequent refusal to utter it.

Nevertheless, a relative stays with him day and night, listening intently to every syllable, assuring him of the needlessness of his fear, and questioning interminably.

"Why do you want to die?"

"Who wants you to die?"

Mental degeneration is rapid, although the man may live for months. It is important, therefore, that the answers should be obtained as soon as possible after the evil spell has been cast.

Direct questions having failed, oblique ones are tried.

"Which country do you like?"

"What is the totem of the man who sang you?"

"From which billabong do you want your water?"

It may be that a question about water will give them the clue they seek if the victim is still able to pronounce comprehensible words.

"Yawurwada!"

Ah! He wants water from Yawurwada. That is on Walinji country and Walinji belongs to . . . Ah! but we must be sure.

His relative says, "Yawurwada is too far, old man. To get your water from there I would knock-up-along-wind."

"Yawurwada! Yawurwada!" Having once said it, the victim is adamant.

"No! Here is water from Mission Hole."

"Yawurwada! Yawurwada!"

All right. The relative, dissembling, walks away and returns with water from Mission Hole.

"This is water from Yawurwada," he says. "Drink it."

The doomed man drinks greedily, and by doing so points the finger directly at the sub-section of people who own the Yawurwada country. The relatives are satisfied that they have tracked the guilty clan through the mental convolutions of their victim, who has gone to them for water. Now he can die in peace. They know which group is due for a retaliatory spear. But there is still a vital unanswered question: who is the Mulunguwa?

May his ghost be transfixed by spears and the wounds cause mortal sores on his flesh!

And, indeed, that is what happens.

I have known it to happen.

While the dead man is being prepared for burial one of the chief mourners, an uncle or a grandson or a close friend, blows a mouthful of smoke into his nostrils and eyes, and paperbark plugs are placed in both ears.

Smoke in the eyes will cause tears and prevent his spirit spying on relatives. Smoke in the nostrils will destroy his sense of smell and prevent the spirit scenting them. The paperbark plugs will stop the spirit hearing their conversation.

All aborigines have a dread that the shades of dead men may return to persecute them. They issue fervent dissuasive commands to a corpse:

"Well, goodbye now, old man. Don't come back."

"You're leaving us now, old man. Don't come back."

"We'll be along later, old man. Don't come back."

"Don't be impatient for us. That 'Nother Place is a good camp, old man. So don't come back. Whatever you do, don't come back."

His hair is cut and preserved. Later it will be used to help track the Mulunguwa. The body is wrapped in paperbark and stringybark so that carrion crows and hawks will not defile it while resting in the Gulla-Gulla. There it will remain for two years until decomposition erodes the flesh and only the whitened bones remain.

They are then collected, painted with red ochre, placed in a hollow log and carried back to a cave or the bank of a billabong in the deceased's own country.

The relative who carries the bones again invokes his Shade:

"Now here you are, in a pleasant glade, with the paperbarks around. I carried you l-o-o-n-g way back to your country, so I want you to do something for me. Fill the billabong with lilies, bring the Sugarbag closer to the camp, fatten the wallabies, tame the kangaroos, make the water clear so we can see the barramundi. A bumper harvest, please, old man."

Transference of the bones and the accompanying corroboree are known as Lorrkun. And it is the signal for what is perhaps the most funereal delirium known to man: incessant hysterical wailing by the women of the deceased's family group.

Although he died two years earlier they now cut their bodies with stones and knives and scarify their flesh with pointed wire.

These sorry-cuts are intended to make the women really feel like wailing, and I must say they succeed. Any woman not sufficiently in travail increases her sorrow by smashing a boomerang on her head. Others use the sharp edge of a tomahawk or knock their skulls against the ground.

The caterwauling is demoniacal in its intensity.

"W-a-a-a-a-a-h! W-a-a-a-a-h! E-e-e-e-e-h! He was my brother! A-a-a-a-a-h!"

"O-o-o-o-a-a-a-h! Why didn't they kill someone else? He was my brother, a-a-a-a-a-a-e-e-h!"

But they can turn it on and off like a tap. Once a woman stopped a piercing scream in mid-note to ask me for a cigarette. "E-e-e-e-you-give-me-cigarette." I lit one for her and after a few puffs she rewarded me: "E-e-e-e-h! Thanks. A-a-a-a-h! W-a-a-a-e-e-e-h!"

The Gulla-Gulla holding the body is studiously avoided by all tribesmen, who fear a dead man's Shade—and that means everyone. Our ghosts, called Djumdjum, are just as active as any likely to be found at a European séance.

But after a man has been executed by a Mulunguwa his uncles and cousins must suppress their natural terror for a few hours to establish the killer's name.

On the day after his death they paint their bodies with white and yellow clay and tie green bushes to their feet, legs and trunk, extending beyond their heads, in a camouflage so complete that they look like moving trees.

At sunset . . . at the very instant of sunset . . . they sneak up to the Gulla-Gulla, quiet-feller, careful-one, inching the trees forward.

"Watchout along that Shade!" they whisper. "Lookout along that Mulunguwa. Quiet-feller, you there boy! Sneak-up properly-way, properly-way. Hey, you there boy, swat that fly, swat that fly . . . you want that Shade to smell your sweat, eh? Allabout lookabout for fly that might carry scent."

No more valorous deed exists in the tribal life than that a man conquers fear and goes with his fellows to the Gulla-Gulla. These men are terrified of spirits and yet they have come deliberately to find one.

And the spirit they seek is not that of their dead relative, although they may be about, but of the murdering Mulunguwa, whose Shade has been taken into the Gulla-Gulla by the man he has murdered. This does nothing to lessen their dread.

As they approach the burial platform there is no creak of unoiled hinges, no wind in the pines, no windows slamming shut, no doors being opened by an unseen hand—

but these clichés of the cinema in natural form must be faced.

Ghosts and spirits are abroad!

"Ah, what's that?" a man whispers.

"A spirit!"

The impulse to flee is overwhelming. Every man wants to run, but none has the courage to start, knowing that the forerunner will be an object of tribal derision thereafter. A tree on the walkabout routes will be given his name, a tree whose very locality will ring with ridicule. So they stand fast.

The wraith they have seen appears again, weightless in space, its smoky outline homing on the Gulla-Gulla.

"The Mulunguwa! It's the Mulunguwa!"

The whispered shout alerts a spearman, the male point of his woomera snug in the shaft of Djindi-Djindi, his trigger-arm cocked for that moment of incaution when the spirit will turn away.

"Now . . . now . . . quick-feller now!"

Whissshh!

The woomera comes forward, exerting its extended purchase on the tip of the shaft, propelling the spear at a speed faster than a spirit can vanish.

The splash of ghostly flesh, the crunch of bone, and the moan of surprise and anger as the shovel-head pierces invisible bloodless matter . . . for there is no doubt in our minds that a disembodied spirit is vulnerable to a spear and can be destroyed.

"Got 'im! Got 'im! We got the Mulunguwa! We got the executioner, the man who sang our tribesman to death and broke the neck of our woman! Where did that spear hit?"

"Below the right breast," the spearman says.

"Where did it come out?"

"At the left kidney."

"Then we shall see . . . then we shall see . . . the man who breaks out in sores below the right breast and near the left kidney is the Mulunguwa. His spirit is wounded and he must surely die."

129

That night the dead man's hair is commanded and sung: "We speared the Mulunguwa's spirit. Now, as his Djumdjum, you make that man have sores. We get level-feller before the Lorrkun."

The Mulunguwa's limping Shade drifts into a siege-camp. The dead man's uncles and cousins emerge from hiding and throw a barrage of spears. Again there is the thuddering smash of steel in flesh and the grind as it scrapes through bone. Again they hear the moan of a wraith before it fades from view. The preserved hair has done its job by enticing the Mulunguwa's spirit to search for it. Now the relatives watch the torsos of opposing clansmen who share the campsite, alert for the appearance of sores on a man's breast and near his kidneys. They know that Pay-Back will not long be delayed.

Two days later, at the Place Where the Stick-Insects Are, an Alawa tribesman is sharpening a horseshoe he has found in the yard where colts are being broken. He leans over his work, hammering the piece of iron between two tomahawks, his glistening body perfect in its male muscularity . . . except, perhaps, for the pinpoint scar near the left kidney.

"How did you get the sore?" he is asked.

"I scratched it on the wire of the stockyard fence."

At that moment he raises his tomahawk and hammers the horseshoe, but the blow is astray and the iron flies up to hit him below the right breast. He sees that it has broken the skin and bleeds slowly. Scarcely interested, he goes on with his work.

But in three weeks he is dead.

I heard the mission sister talking by pedal radio to the Flying Doctor at Cloncurry.

"I have a patient with tetanus," she said. "There is muscular convulsion, a locked jaw, severe pain. One of his wounds was caused by a piece of rusty iron which had been lying in horse manure."

That Mulunguwa died in agony before the mercy plane could reach him, his body racked by fearful contractions, his face contorted, his eyes crazed with unspeakable terror.

I have since had medical training which confirms that the sister's diagnosis fitted the case history. I am not surprised that she suspected tetanus caused the death of a man who was wounded by a piece of contaminated iron. For how could a white woman be expected to know that he was a Mulunguwa whose spirit had been speared by tribal heroes?

How could she know that the precise area of his two festering sores had been nominated by the Gamarang clan he had wronged . . . before they appeared! And, if she had been told, wouldn't she have dismissed it all as pagan superstition?

Sometimes it happens that aggrieved relatives cannot find the Mulunguwa's spirit.

The tribal detectives are then called in to look for signs, rather than a Shade, which will betray him.

If a murdered man has been buried in the ground instead of the more usual Gulla-Gulla they approach the grave carefully, after the piccaninny daylight, carrying small bushes to simulate the elaborate camouflage of the men who speared the spirit. And there they examine the area meticulously, reading the signs, sifting the information until they are satisfied of the Mulunguwa's Dreaming —his totem—and his name.

The Alawa believe that on the grave of every murdered man some sign will point directly to the murderer or his Dreaming.

If I had been the Mulunguwa—and praise the Mother Goddess that I've never been chosen!—the detectives would find a sign indicating the Kangaroo totem. It might be the track of a kangaroo or a fine shred of kangaroo fur. Because there are many Alawas with Kangaroo Dreamings a further sign would be needed to link me directly with the crime. It may be that the track on top of the mound points to my tribal country like a fingerpost. It may be that one of my Lesser Dreamings is also indicated—perhaps the facsimile of a zigzag of lightning. Men trained in the science of deduction now have little difficulty in reaching their conclusions. They have their counterparts for fingerprints and human hairs and bloodstains and microscopes.

The verdict is given: "The Kangaroo and Lightning totems. The Larbaryandji country. The Mulunguwa's name is Waipuldanya."

The signs are rubbed out, symbolic of what is to happen to me. The decision, once made, is never altered. And it is never altered because it is never wrong.

How do the signs appear? How is it possible for our detectives to point out the right man every time?

The answer is simple. During the night the dead man's spirit emerges from the grave and puts the signs there for the detectives to find. He knew the killer and he wants his relatives to know.

Is it so strange that we should follow such signs as these? Were not the Wise Men of the East led by the sign of a star to a lowly stable in Bethlehem nearly two thousand years ago?

Is it so strange that we should be guided by a mark representing lightning, when Christ himself told his disciples to watch for a sign of lightning coming from the east and shining even unto the west, a sign that would foretell His second coming?

We also, we who have faith in the Mother Goddess, believe the portents handed down to us.

Say that we are pagans.

Say that we are unenlightened.

But say, also, that we believe in the Word which has never been written, the Word which has been transmitted from the Time of Dream, centuries before Christ, without stylus, without ink, without papyrus, the Word which has been passed from mouth to mouth by the Generations of Men in hundreds of thousands of ceremonial songs, in the parables of pagandom, the Word which leads our judges to the Herods in our midst.

Chapter Ten

THE Mulunguwa leaves his tribe the moment he is sworn in and becomes a voluntary outcast.

He has no contact with his own people. The very name is an execration, seldom mentioned except by the Elders.

He lives as a hangman must live, secretly, withdrawn, his dirty trade hidden in anonymity, his very body cloaked in the vastness of bush until he kills and is then released from his vows.

How is it possible for a man to conceal himself entirely in a community where every other person, man, woman, and child, is a professional tracker?

That is not so difficult as it may seem.

The Mulunguwa is aided by the existence of sacred messengers known as Gagawar, who are often absent for weeks or months on the official business of the tribe.

Once he is nominated as a Gagawar a man can disappear from his family group without exciting comment. It is a permanent leave-pass and a passport to obscurity, the perfect cloak for someone whom the Elders have appointed as executioner.

Tommy Wururuma, a half-blind, toothless Rembarrnga of High Degree, won recognition as a kind of Secretary-General of the United Nations of Aboriginal Tribes while performing his duties as a Gagawar. He was sent out by the Roper River people, including the Alawa, on a delicate diplomatic mission to foreign lands which kept him away from his own country for a year.

His task was to investigate how ceremonial hair belts and feathers used in the sacred Kunapipi and Yabudurawa had come into the possession of Gunwinggu, Maung, and Iwaija tribesmen in western Arnhem Land who had no right to them.

Tommy was chosen because he is a skilled multi-dialect linguist and an eminent man. He travelled a thousand miles in twelve months, most of it on foot, hunting his own food as he walked, naked except for a narga, without briefcase, without bowler hat, without shirt, without shoes.

Ceremonial articles are beyond price. No amount yet minted, printed, or mined could buy them. Somehow, perhaps through souvenir hunting, they had been acquired by tribes who did not subscribe to the Kunapipi or Yabudurawa rituals—as though the Mace from the House of Commons had been found in the Palace of the Soviets. It was necessary to have a skilled diplomat to recover them.

This, and others like it, are typical of the cover-jobs a Mulunguwa may be given.

He tells his family simply, "I am a Gagawar." Next morning he rolls his swag, making ostentatious preparations for a long walk as a sacred messenger, and disappears.

The Mulunguwa then hides in the bush, living alone, infinitely careful to avoid observation, erasing his tracks, his swag hidden in a cave so that he has nothing to hinder instant flight or assist his betrayal.

He carries only a spear, and a bamboo pipe through which he can drink from billabongs without lowering his head and thereby restricting his view of other Mulunguwas who may be searching for him.

He falls into a trance, aware only of the need for extreme caution and the instruction given him by the Elders: to kill when time will have diverted suspicion from him.

His food is eaten half raw because he will not betray his position with a fire big enough to cook it properly. He uses wood that flares and dies, barely singeing the flesh, and wipes away his tracks with a green bush before leaving

... backwards. No housewife proud of her polished floors was ever more conscious of footprints than a Mulunguwa.

He lives like an animal, going into water at dusk and dawn, freezing to every sound, covering his trail, observing his rear, never sleeping where he eats or drinks, with no blanket to protect him from winter cold, with no thought in his mind except the insistent urge to plan an execution, to decoy an individual into a place where he may kill without danger of discovery.

He becomes a man whom the word Mulunguwa describes exactly: The One Alone.

As a hunter, I have spent a great part of my life alone in the bush. I understand solitude, which is not loneliness. But I have never understood the solitary confinement in an unwalled cell, which is the inevitable lot of every Mulunguwa. If I were asked what I regarded as the biggest single blessing of my years as a tribesman, I would say unhesitatingly: the fact that I was never named by the Elders as a Lord High Executioner.

It could still happen, although my exile in Darwin and my rank as a Djungayi makes the possibility remote. Nevertheless, I must live with the thought that one day the task may be mine. And I try not to dwell on the chance that some of my best friends might already have served a tour of duty.

My father was once nominated as a Mulunguwa and given a jar of poison to kill a tribal relative. Whether it was his position as a High Djungayi or his bravery that saved him, I do not know. But he refused the appointment and is still alive.

He called the Elders together and sat with Old Tommy, the man he had been told to poison.

"Old Tommy," he said, "I brought you here for a reason. It is to tell you that someone has a grudge against you and they want me to kill you. Here is the poison. . . . I put it here . . . in the centre of the ring . . . for all to see. I want to say that in my opinion Old Tommy has done no wrong. I don't know why some people want him to die. Do you?"

If they did, none of the Elders admitted it.

"We are one nation," my father said. "I will not kill this man. If my life is wanted it is here now. Would one of you like to pass me the poison so that everybody will know who killed me?"

Nobody moved. Finally an Elder said: "It is good. You have spoken well. Empty the poison!"

Old Tommy lived for many more years, and died a natural death. My father lives still. But if he had not faced the Elders defiantly, before witnesses, he would surely have died. His courageous outspokenness saved him.

Today I am an Australian citizen, freed from all restrictive laws. I am entitled to vote in Federal elections. I am my own boss. My movements are my own business. Whether I am inside the city limits after dark or have a quiet drink in an hotel is no concern of any policeman, as it once was.

But am I, like my father, free of the tribal laws? Does Australian citizenship mean that the Elders are deprived of the right to dictate to me? If they beckoned now, would I go? If they said, "You are a Mulunguwa; it is your duty to kill our enemy," would I cast off the silken symbols of civilization, the façade of sophisticated conformity, and commit a treacherous murder at their bidding?

Am I not a Djungayi in the Kunapipi?

Am I not an initiate of the Alawa?

Was I not a tribesman before a citizen, a pagan before a Christian?

Am I not bound, therefore, to answer any summons I may be given?

This is one of the unresolved questions that trouble my mind: the division of my ancient and my modern loyalties.

Fortunately it is hypothetical. While I am living four hundred miles from the Roper River and working as a medical assistant it is unlikely that I will be called upon. But if I returned to my tribal country I would certainly be vulnerable and have to decide quickly, if sworn in, whether I intended to invite my own execution or become

136

an executioner. Would I forsake the laws of my tribe for laws which are alien?

I do not know.

But I am grateful to have been spared the task so far.

I will be even more indebted to my Kangaroo Dreaming if he can arrange for me to be overlooked when future appointees are being sought in the Alawa clan to which I belong.

The Mulunguwa who kills outright cannot return at once to the tribe. To reappear too soon after a man's death would invite suspicion. So he delays for further weeks or months, continuing to live alone, until he is convinced that no finger will be pointed at him. Then, after hiding his spears and recovering his swag, he rejoins his family as though nothing has happened, as Albert Pierrepoint, the English hangman, rejoined the customers in his pub after officiating on the gallows.

The man's family are desperately inquisitive about his long absence, but dare not ask questions because of the secret nature of his presumed job as a Gagawar.

But not all Mulunguwas kill outright. On the contrary, most of them prefer to have an intermediary murder the victim in broad daylight, before the eyes of the entire tribe, while he himself is also present and must therefore be blameless. It is because they are so immensely clever at hiding their identities that my people, for centuries, have not been able to uncloak them except through betrayal by their spirits and by magic signs.

What preposterous nonsense!

And yet it happens.

A Mulunguwa who kills through a third person entices his victim into the bush, renders him unconscious with a blow on the back of the neck, hypnotizes him as he recovers, and removes his kidney fat with a knife.

The wound is stitched with string and wiped over with a wax which makes it invisible. While the doomed man is under hypnosis the Mulunguwa implants a message in his subconscious mind: *"Your enemy is Budjirindja. Even*

*his dogs are against you. Next time one barks at you, kill
it at once. Otherwise you will not know peace."*

Back at the camp a few days later one of Budjirindja's
dogs barks loudly.

"Why don't you stop your dogs barking?" the hypnotic
demands angrily.

"Because they like to bark."

"Well, stop them!"

"I won't."

"Then I will." A spear is thrown. A transfixed dog
yelps in pain and fright, biting savagely at the shaft protruding from its body.

It is an unpardonable offence deliberately to kill another
man's dog. Hasn't it helped him on the scent trails of
kangaroos? Hasn't it kept him warm with its body heat
on cold winter nights? Hasn't it become his shadow?

Budjirindja's white-hot rage is unquenchable. He
spears the Mulunguwa's victim at point-blank range while
the Mulunguwa, sitting in his camp, placidly observes a
killing he has arranged but not executed. With his kidney
fat already removed this man would have died anyway,
but who can doubt the evidence of his eyes that Budjirindja
killed him? His blood-stained spear is Exhibit A.

To further divert suspicion from himself the Mulunguwa now takes a leading part in the Lirrgi, our death
corroboree. He wails mournfully and accuses Budjirindja.

The Lirrgi is another corroboree in which a dead man's
Shade is laid. We rub our bodies with smouldering bushes
to establish a smoke screen behind which we are safe from
his spirit.

The wife goes into hiding so that it might not follow
her. She stays away from the camp for at least two weeks.
When we think it is safe for her to be recalled she and
her sisters enter a hole which has been dug in the camp
area. There she is washed by other women and painted
with red ochre. The woman is then free of her husband's
Shade and resumes life in the tribe with a string around
her neck to indicate that she is a widow. Her sisters are

also classed as widows, even though they are married to other men.

A year later we have a further corroboree to "break-the-strings," symbolic of her emergence from widowhood and freedom to remarry.

Meanwhile the missionaries have heard about the murder. Presently the air comes alive with static as the pedal radio crackles with the news.

It is then that Gunanda—The Salt—arrives. He is a white policeman, come to prosecute the European law in a tribal killing, to arraign one of us before the Big-Feller-Boss-Judge. He is told that the victim died in an argument over women. That is traditional because white men readily understand it, whereas they would not understand that a dog was responsible. Budjirindja is arrested and taken to Darwin to face the Court. His evidence will be given like this:

"Your name Budjirindja, eh?"

"You-ai."

"You bin savvy that time big-feller trouble bin come-up alonga that dead-feller longa Roper River?"

"You-ai."

"Arright, now, you tell this Big-Feller-Boss-Judge all you know about that trouble, eh?"

"You-ai."

"No-more what some other feller bin talk-talk. No-more what some lubra bin yabber-yabber alonga you. Just what you do, what you see longa your own eye, what you hear longa your own ear. You savvy, now?"

"You-ai."

"Arright, then. Talk true-feller. Talk loud-feller."

"You-ai."

"Budjirindja, you remember that dead-feller, eh?"

"You-ai."

"You bin kill 'im, ain't it?"

"You-ai."

"You bin kill'm properly-dead-finish?"

"You-ai."

"How you bin kill 'im?"

139

"Longa shovel-spear."

"This one-feller, is this the shovel-spear?"

"You-ai."

"You bin make 'im yourself?"

"You-ai."

"You bin throw that spear at that dead-feller?"

"You-ai."

"And shovel-spear bin hit him in chest, ain't it?"

"You-ai."

"And 'im fall down properly-dead-finish?"

"You-ai."

"What-for you bin kill that dead-feller?"

"Dunno."

"But you must know why you bin kill 'im?"

"Dunno. Might-be woman trouble, I think."

Budjirindja, aware of the futility of denial, admits the offence. The Gunanda, The Salt, The Handcuffs Man, has had his moment of triumph. The white man's law has been assuaged. A tribesman has been sent to gaol for daring to violate a law he does not understand. There he will remain in a steaming cell, a ringbolt in the wall to remind him of harsher treatment given to his ancestors.

He is incarcerated and segregated with a dozen other black men from foreign lands. They probably do not speak his language. He does not speak theirs. The Big-Feller-Boss-Judge, palliating a conscience made uneasy by the conflict in cultures, has as usual handed down a minimum sentence. Even so, in these circumstances, two years is a long time.

Budjirindja's case seemed straightforward: a body pierced by a spear, and eye-witnesses to the throwing excluded complications other than the delusion that woman-trouble and not a dead dog had caused the murder.

Nevertheless, the wrong man went to gaol.

In aboriginal murders, especially those involving Mulunguwas and Kadaitja Men, the wrong man *invariably* goes to gaol.

Oh, yes, it might be the man who threw the spear.

Oh, yes, it might be the man who broke a neck.

Oh, yes, it might be that the murderer was seen to kill, as in Budjirindja's case.

But Budjirindja was simply a Hangman's Hangman, a man goaded by one who had been entranced by the Mulunguwa—and he had been sworn to kill by his Elders! Budjirindja was thus thrice-removed from the legal requirement of British courts that murder can be proved only if there is "malice aforethought."

Budjirindja had no malice.

His victim had no malice.

The Mulunguwa had no malice.

The Elders were without malice, too. They were nothing more than Defenders of the Faith, Keepers of the Dreamings, Custodians of the Culture which insisted that our totems should not be desecrated.

Who, then, has the debt to pay? Does a white hangman incur a debt to his society by doing his duty?

We have never been able to convince The Salts or the Big-Feller-Boss-Judges that the wrong men have been going to gaol. It is many years since we gave up trying.

A Salt will always believe us when we say that a murder has been committed because of woman-trouble.

But we know that neither The Salts nor the Judges would understand Pay-Back: that a young man was murdered by a pledged Mulunguwa because his grandfather had speared a bird which rested in a sacred tree.

On the few occasions when the Alawa did attempt to explain this it was dismissed contemptuously by The Salts as "Blackfeller Business."

Unfortunately for us, the alien laws of England, written centuries after our own, do not list interference with a sacred tree as a punishable offence, although heavy penalties are provided for sacrilege committed elsewhere—whether in a Christian Church, a Moslem Temple, or a Chinese Joss-House.

Is it surprising, therefore, that we resent compliance with supreme laws compulsorily applied to our lives without consultation? We were never asked whether we wished to accept English laws. We were told bluntly that we had no choice. We have always felt competent to deal with our own transgressors. We did so for ten thousand years when Australia was ours, alone. But now we have been denied that right. This is a major cause of indignation among my people, for the laws of the tribes and the laws of England are often incompatible.

The Budjirindja case was simple, but what happens when a Mulunguwa kills in the bush and there is no apparent murderer?

In such cases a Djungayi of the Kunapipi—and I am one—is delegated to fabricate a fable for The Salt.

Unlucky tribesmen have been deliberately sent off to gaol by their fellows on trumped-up stories of woman-trouble, complete with witnesses.

It was their tribal duty to suffer imprisonment in silence, and not to laugh at the solemn fairy tales the jury and the judge were told.

When he returns to the tribe after serving his sentence the scapegoat demands retribution against the Mulunguwa, if he has been revealed and still lives.

Perhaps he is told: "We found a sign of the Kangaroo Dreaming on the dead-feller's grave. It pointed to the Walindji country. His name is Yalga. We waited until you returned before deciding what to do with him. What do you say?"

He remembers the two long years in gaol, and is afraid he may be sent back there if another man is killed.

"That gaol is a No-Good Place," he says. "All-the-time I think about my poor-feller-country. All-the-time I think about my poor-feller-wife and my piccaninnies. I don't want to go back. I would like to fight with this man. I will challenge him to a duel at the Banburr ground."

Yalga is confronted and assumes an indignant "Who, me?" pose. He protests: "I was a Gagawar taking a secret message for the tribe when the man was killed. It couldn't be me!"

"Nevertheless, we will meet at the Banburr."

And so it is arranged by The Elders.

Banburr is a ceremonial corroboree at which grudges are settled in free-for-all fights of extreme violence. The combatants use spears, nulla-nullas and boomerangs, belabouring each other unmercifully until blood runs in rivulets, bones are broken and heads are cracked. But they dare not kill, although I must say they have often come close to doing so.

Banburr is peace-through-war, a ferocious letting-off of bad blood which has reached boiling point. It continues for three days, crowded by men and women who have come from afar to watch and to participate as they might have done at a Roman Tournament.

The arena is first taken by the Mulunguwa and his accuser, who fight until both are utterly exhausted. Then others remember grudges which have not been settled. Within a few minutes the Banburr ground is a bedlam of hysterical noise: the screams of pain, the clash of steel, the dull thud of nulla-nullas, the fearful crack of bones being broken, and the wails of women being cut with yam sticks and tomahawks for the alleged pilfering of husbands and other indiscretions. They are worse than the men, fighting with intense malice, yelling imprecations, and simmering long after the men have quietened down.

But quieten they must, for Banburr is the Peace Table, the battleground where staggering warriors later sign an armistice in our equivalent of legal documents: the exchange of presents. And the most extravagant present of all is likely to be given by the Mulunguwa to the scapegoat he fought. His body may be battered, but his present expresses the relief he feels for having been released from a lifetime of fear. He has paid his debt to tribal society by taking public punishment. He need have no further worry that betrayal by totemic signs or spirits will cause him, one day, to be enticed into the bush by another Mulunguwa appointed to be his executioner. He knows that a spear thrown at his Shade can no longer cause him to break out in sores from which he will die in agony. His heavy chain of office is lifted from him, his hands are cleansed, his mind is free.

Alawa tribesmen fear the malignant Mulunguwa.

The Mulunguwa fears the Alawa tribesmen, believing that eventually he may stand revealed.

But the one who pays in the fires of Banburr earns a tribal pardon.

The price is high: shattered limbs, perhaps a broken nose, perhaps an eye knocked out or hands crushed by hammer-blows from ironwood sticks.

Yet no Alawa Mulunguwa has ever thought these injuries too dear, for they buy life itself.

Chapter Eleven

ALL aborigines smile and laugh easily. We are a naturally happy people. Ripples of mirth are constantly rolling from our camps. A dog chasing its tail, a piccaninny awkwardly learning to walk, a man drinking milk from a goat's teat, a woman suckling two babies at once: such simple matters are likely to cause convulsions.

While I lived in the camps this seemed natural, but lately I have realized that it is probably a cloak of bravado for the many fears that every aboriginal lives with throughout his life.

From my earliest youth I have been afraid of the Doctor Blackfellows, the Medicine Men who sing their victims by using hyperphysical powers.

During hunting walkabouts I was afraid of the Burgingin, the immensely strong pygmy people who can crush a man's bones in a bear-hug. They were our bogymen. Their haunting memory has stayed with me always.

I have never lost my inherent fear of the spirits of the Malanugga-nugga, the Stone People who lived near the Ruined City in the Arnhem Land escarpment. Even though they are gone, no Alawa tribesman will gladly visit their country today.

I am frightened of the Shades of dead men, and of the Mulunguwa executioner.

I would commit any sin or pay any price not to incur the wrath of my Kangaroo Dreaming.

But there is another fear, common to all my tribesmen, a dire physical threat by one man to another or by woman to woman: *I'll have your kidney fat.*

This is not an idle curse but a menacing promise to do exactly as he says: to remove the fat around a man's kidneys. And each of us knows that the other has been instructed how to do it.

At my initiation I was taught by the Elders: "If it is necessary to kill a man, take his kidney fat as the Mulunguwa does. Anaesthetize him with a nulla-nulla. A well-placed blow on the back of the neck will keep him unconscious during the operation."

I was told in detail how it should be performed: "Make a small incision with a knife or a razor blade just at The Kidney Place. It should not be longer than an inch so that after you rub it with wax it won't be visible. . . . "

. . . and how I should suture the wound:

"Be careful with the stitching. Make string from the peeled fibre of currajong bark. Thread it through holes in the flesh that you will make with a sharp fish-bone. You must do this quickly, before he has time to revive and see you at work. . . . "

. . . and the oath I should take while operating:

"The man will bleed. Catch some of his blood in a coolamon, rub it on his tongue and say: 'By the Devil's Spirits, you are a dead man, and you won't tell anybody who killed you.' Rub some of the blood on his ears and eyelids so that he will neither see nor hear anything suspicious about you. . . . "

. . . and the instructions I should give my victim:

"You are a spirit now. You can't talk to humans any more. You will go back to the camp and forget that this has happened. You will not remember this place or how you came here or anything you saw."

And so it happens. In three or four days he is dead, unable to name his tormentor, not knowing that a leaf or a stick or a piece of dirty rag was placed inside his body when the incision was made and has caused internal infection.

But why take a man's kidney fat? Why not break his neck or pierce his heart? Why not hold him under water?

Kidney fat is a talisman. It brings us luck, like wishing-wells and horse-shoes, black cats and Chinese, wishbones and mascots.

We rub it on spears and boomerangs to bring us luck in the hunt.

It is carried in a dillybag around the neck, like a golden cross, to repel evil spirits.

We believe that a kidney-fat amulet will bring us continuing good fortune, will fill our food bags, and dissuade our enemies from attacking us.

I have one other major fear: that I may one day be killed by a malicious woman through a process known as Wilgin. For the fury of an aboriginal woman who is scorned assuredly leads to a private hell for the person she blames.

She cuts a small square from a shirt or dress belonging to her victim, preferably from around an armhole where it will be coated with sweat.

She takes it into the bush, perhaps two or three miles from the camp, and with her tomahawk cuts a hole in an ironwood tree. There she places the piece of cloth.

Next she lights a fire and on it heats a number of small pebbles until they are red hot. While doing so she talks directly to her foe:

> "Beguna neya yardi
> Gu maringu minayi!
> I hate you.
> But now you will die.
> I will be free of you."

With her left hand she picks up some of the red-hot pebbles on a paperbark tray, and with an improvised tool rams them into the hole in the tree where she has placed the cloth.

The smouldering sweat contained in the cloth causes her enemy's spirit to wail:

> "Gungu nimanji?
> Ninanimbi yur!
> Why must you do this to me?
> I have never hated you!"

147

The woman realizes that she is playing with fire and takes extreme care not to inhale the smoke or let it touch her body. If that happens the Wilgin woman herself, having breathed her victim's spirit, will weaken and die. I have known women to put themselves to sleep in this way with their own pernicious chloroform.

She gives the cloth another covering of hot pebbles, plugs the hole with a piece of wood so that the spirit cannot escape, and rubs dirt on the scar she has made on the bark to avoid detection.

Finally she throws a curse: *"You will lose weight. In the hot weather you will be weak and listless. You will soon not be able to care for yourself. You will get thinner, and in the cold weather, without fat to keep you warm, you will die."*

Within a few days her victim feels unwell. She will lose weight as predicted and die slowly, perhaps taking a year to do so. But the process will be hastened if she finds a missing square in one of her dresses, for then she worries herself to death in the knowledge that Wilgin is at work.

"Beware of the Wilgin Woman!" my uncle warned me at my initiation. "She is the cleverest murderer of all. She is never discovered because the spirit which may have betrayed her has been destroyed by fire."

I have never forgotten the warning.

Aboriginal women have their own corroborees from which men are banned. The most important of these among the Alawa is the Digga, their equivalent of the men's tjarada: a Love Song and Dance.

I am not supposed to know much about the Digga. It is strictly Women's Business. But women, whether they are black or white, seem unable to keep secrets as well as men. The result is that we know more about their corroborees than they do about ours.

The corroboree is held about a mile from the camp, but they do not attempt effective concealment. Peeping Toms have been known to spy upon them. Uninitiated boys are taken along, and they are notorious gossips, often acquiring more knowledge than the women suspect. Moreover, they have to borrow ceremonial articles from the men, and we know their uses.

In spite of that, Digga retains a veil of secrecy. The corroboree continues for a month. In that time the women chant thousands of songs. But I do not know one secret verse, nor am I aware of any other man who has learnt one.

We believe they are simple love songs, which each woman directs personally towards her husband or lover in the hope that her attraction for him will be increased. The singing is accompanied by the tapping of sticks and the clapping of hands.

I have often been tempted to crawl up to a women's corroboree and learn the secrets which have intrigued us for centuries. But I am afraid. I know that instantly I came within sight of the painted women I would faint and be placed in the undignified position of having to be "sung" back to consciousness by one of their Djungayi.

All aboriginal men except a few who are immune to sanctity would also faint from shock if they approached. We take care, therefore, to avoid their corroboree ground.

Digga women adorn their bodies with red ochre and a mixture of fat and ashes. They wear a Muddamudda—a pubic tassel made from possum fur or, if the local Christian Dior has been active, from a discarded flour bag. Some wear a Garadada breastplate of fur or plaited currajong bark. Others have a Marabibi laurel of painted strings around the head. They carry ceremonial articles and dance with a looped string held tautly between the thumbs.

Unlike aboriginal men who are lords in the camp, married women must obtain their husbands' permission to attend a Digga. Few women would dare leave home without it. Apart from the obvious reason of bowing to the master, they seek his approval because they also want to borrow his boomerangs and his beating sticks.

This sometimes leads to the kind of complaint one might hear from a white husband whose wife has borrowed his golf clubs and returned them broken and dirty. The boomerangs, invariably, are left with a coat of Digga symbols which have not been erased. They must then be kept away from single men to prevent them inducing marriage with a Wrong-Side girl.

A female Djungayi has one advantage over me: she is able to decorate her hair and carry articles on her head. But the head of a male Djungayi must remain unadorned, because it is sacred. Mine belongs to my Bunga, my father's sister's children. If I placed a ten-pound note on my head, or a cigarette behind my ear I would forfeit it to them, for they have charge of my head and my blood. When I need a haircut a Bunga cousin must do it or give permission to someone else. If I visit a city barber I am liable to any fine that they demand.

If I cut myself and my shirt is stained I lose the shirt at once, or they might take the pocket-knife with which the wound was inflicted. In recent years I have lost dozens of shirts and knives in this way. My blood is sacred. In the Kunapipi it is used as an adhesive in sticking feathers to the bodies of my tribesmen. Each ceremony requires at least a jam-tinful. Sometimes it has to be watered to make enough. Women also use men's blood when decorating for Digga. I am then approached by my female cousins.

The backs of my arms, therefore, are scarred with cuts made by pieces of sharp glass where I opened veins for my relatives. I am the professional blood donor in our clan.

Isolated women have personal autonomy and never take orders from a man. A few—though very few—achieve the distinction of talking to men as equals. And I have known one or two aged women who were entitled to offer recommendations to the law-making Council of Elders. That was achievement indeed.

The status of one woman was unequalled. She was a tribal heroine who was once accorded exalted rank by being allowed to discuss Kunapipi procedure with the High Djungayi. The Kunapipi is banned to women, and she could not see it; nevertheless she was able to talk over some of the finer points with the men. This happened in the days when the sacred ritual concluded with cere-

150

monial intercourse. Women's interests were therefore involved, although that had not previously influenced the men. It is perhaps difficult for anyone who is not an aboriginal and living in a community where patriarchal dominance is absolute to understand the degree of such a condescension.

The authority of a woman in the day-to-day tribal life is confined to the control of her children—but even there it is subservient to the wishes of her brother, the children's uncle.

Hannah cannot tell me when dinner will be ready. I tell her when I want it.

She does not tell me when to get out of bed, that I need a shave, or that I should change my shirt. I will do these things when I feel like it.

Hannah is free to say, "I would like to go to the cinema tonight," but she then accepts my decision without question. If I say "No," there is no argument.

The originator of the phrase, "Never underestimate the power of a woman," was thinking of people other than the aborigines, perhaps the matriarchal Polynesians who crawled before important women on their hands and knees.

I believe that when I die my spirit Shade will go back towards the sunset whence it came.

All our totems have moved across Australia from west to east. We believe that, like them, we came from The Sunset Country. The Happy Hunting Ground is out there still, full of brimming billabongs, a huge Fat and Juicy Place where the kangaroos have lost their sense of smell and the Mulunguwas are benevolent.

Many aborigines believe in reincarnation. The Gobaboingu on the Arnhem Land coast insist that their Shade goes to Burolgu—The Waiting Place. But the Alawa do not believe that a dead tribesman returns to earth in another form. We are fundamental pagans even by aboriginal standards.

Our religious beliefs are as diverse as the sects of Christianity, but in one respect they are uniform: none of us calls upon the name of a dead person from the day he dies until at least ten years later. In some tribes it is never used again.

A decade will pass after the death of my father before the name Barnabas Gabarla is mentioned by a member of his family or any other tribesman.

When it is necessary to refer to him I will call him The Dead Feller and identify him from other dead men by using the name of his tribal country. We are exceedingly careful about this. I have never known an Alawa to name a man or woman who has been dead less than ten years. They are all just as concerned as I am that the spirit of a deceased should not be attracted by the sound of his name.

I am now cleared to name my step-grandfather Jalburgulgul, who died a long time ago. Because he was of the same skin group I can even make jokes about him. But my paternal grandfather is still The Dead Feller of the Duwaumandji country.

There is even an aversion to using the proper names of people who are still alive, and a taboo on naming immediate female relatives.

My sister, my stepmother, and my female cousins thereby suffer considerable abuse. If I want to attract the attention of my sister, Mercia, I say, "Garawu," which means Rubbish. Or I may say "Budarindja," which means Devil, or simply "Garai"—You!

Women return the insult by referring to me through the names of my children. I have often been addressed as Connie and Phyllis.

Among the men there is also a reticence about using personal names. If a man has cut his hand with a tomahawk I will call him Muritji Gulgul—literally Hand Tomahawk. I address a paralysed man as Budjurbudjur and one crippled by a fall from a horse as Lamlam, both of which refer to their afflictions. I am often called Larbaryandji, the name of my tribal country.

And I must say that although I have had ten years in what the white man calls civilization I am still super-stitious about the use of my personal name. I prefer that people call me Larbaryandji or Phillip Roberts—my English name—rather than Waipuldanya or Wadjiri-Wadjiri. One never knows when spirits may be listening! As they are aboriginal spirits they would not recognize me as Phillip Roberts, nor would they know the name of my country.

To be on the safe side I have other names which are used when there is any chance that spirits are around. One of these is a secret name known only by me and my close male relatives. It is seldom spoken, and then only when I am performing my sacred duties as a Djungayi in the Kunapipi.

I was a young man of twenty-one when my mother died. I had lived with her in my father's camp all my life. But I never did hear her tribal name, nor do I know it now. In my presence she was called Nora. That is what I have called her in this book. Even if I did know her aboriginal name I could not mention it here.

Her spirit might be attracted and come back to investigate!

Chapter Twelve

M Y mother died in a lazaret, confined like a convict on a barren Alcatraz in Darwin Harbour, abjectly miserable with a motley of other social outcasts, white, yellow, brown, and black, who had committed the unpardonable offence of being infected with an alien disease. Leprosy!

" . . . and the Lord spake unto Moses and Aaron, saying: The Priest shall look upon him and if he is a leprous man shall pronounce him utterly unclean. And the leper's clothes shall be rent, and his head bare, and he shall put a covering upon his upper lip, and shall cry: Unclean, unclean. All the days wherein the plague shall be within him he shall be defiled; he is unclean: he shall dwell alone. Without the camp shall his habitation be. . . . "

Six thousand years after the Lord God put this curse upon the Israelites a Christian missionary looked at my mother and said: "Nora, you are Unclean."

Straightaway then she was cast out of the camp, to dwell alone all the rest of her days in a foreign land, her body stretched on the rack of physical torment and decay, incarcerated in a rocky waterless prison, studded with stunted trees which offered no shade protection from the merciless tropic sun.

They called it Channel Island. There my mother spent her last years, perhaps reflecting on the ironic fate of a pagan woman banished by a Christian society because she incubated a disease of the civilization which she now saw for the first time. Her cell overlooked the city of Darwin,

which she could see but never visit until she was cured—
and that day did not come.

Her crumpled bones lie there now, just above the
mangrove swamps and the tidal strait with its threat of
crocodiles guarding the sacred mainland a mile away, a
land where survival of an evil superstition was matched
by censure of the superstitious.

My mother was taken away to The Waiting Place for
Death. We knew, as we saw her go, that she would never
return. Few of them ever did in those days before modern
sulphone drugs were available. There she was kept in a
stifling iron hut, a stranger among strangers who had just
one thing in common: their limbs were shrinking and
falling off.

A big factor in the successful treatment of leprosy is an
environment calculated to produce reasonable contentment
and a desire in the patient to be cured. Channel Island
had the opposite effect: the Unclean who were sent there
hoped only that they would die quickly. Many were
denied even that consolation, and lived out their useless,
despairing lives.

My mother was there on that hot summer day in nineteen hundred and forty-two when Japanese bombers
appeared from behind cumulo-nimbus clouds and attacked
Darwin. She had a grandstand view of the devastation
being wrought on the community which had banished
her.

A few days later when invasion appeared imminent
she was one of seventy lepers herded by a half-caste gang-
boss, Gregory Howard, a leper himself, to a remote spot
on the mainland thirty miles from Darwin where they
might be safe until the danger had passed.

Howard ferried them across the narrow strait in a
launch, and on the fringes of the mangrove swamps built
bush shelters with assistants who had only one hand or
one leg or one eye.

The halt aided the halt, the blind led the blind; limping
men and women who supported themselves with sticks,
some with only one foot, some with hands so withered

that they had to be spoon-fed. There were times, as they struggled through the mangrove-slime, when they had to crawl.

At night they fell down exhausted and slept where they lay, huddling around camp-fires with which they attempted to dispel the myriads of sandflies and mosquitoes adding intolerably even to the burden of lepers whose sense of feeling was deadened by the attrition of nerves.

My mother was one of these hapless people, lost in a land where most of them were tasting freedom for the first time in many years.

They carried food. Those who were able hunted for goannas, lizards, snakes, crabs, and grubs. When they could no longer support themselves Gregory Howard went back alone to their forsaken island to replenish stocks from the reserve they had left there.

Patrol-Officers Gordon Sweeney and Bill Harney, of the Native Affairs Branch, with an aboriginal named Crab Billy, searched for them endlessly, but the mangrove swamps and the forests of woolly-butts, stringybarks and pandanus, and the ten-foot tall speargrass, kept their secret deeply hidden.

Howard was physically able to escape and might have done so. He might have abandoned the others, telling those who could still walk to return to their tribal countries. Instead, realizing that his charges needed help, he sent one of the outcasts as a courier into the civilization from which all of them had been concealed. He carried a letter written by a leprous hand with a stub of pencil on a scrap of newspaper:

"Dear Mr. Sweeney.—All the lepers are here, except three who have died. Billy will show you where to find us. We need medicine and food."

Sweeney found them in the bush, and with Howard's help took them back to their charnel-house on Channel Island, where they remained until the war ended. When that day came my mother was dead.

. . . . .

Ah, yes, we were tragically susceptible to this and the other communicable diseases of civilized mankind. Never having had leprosy, or tuberculosis, or syphilis, or such comparatively mild ailments as measles, we had no immunity from them when visitors began to arrive from The Brown World and The White World and The Yellow World.

Thirty tribesmen died in an outbreak of measles at Groote Eylandt. More than two hundred perished in another epidemic in Central Australia. When it broke out at Maningrida on the Liverpool River in north-central Arnhem Land the aerial medical service flew forty-three sorties in forty days in a desperate attempt to minimize its spread.

Multiply this by all the tribes in Australia, add the cruelties and the lead-poisoning, and the punitive expeditions against my people who killed cattle or drank Squatters' Water, holier than Holy Water, and it is possible to understand why the aboriginal population of more than three hundred thousand at the First Coming of the White Man is now less than fifty thousand.

My father was a small boy when the first squatters came into the country along the Roper and the Hodgson and the Limmen, long before the missions and the police brought law and order to the land. I will always remember this story he told me about his youth:

"Bad times. Bad times, arright. We bin live like wallabies, frightened-one, allabout all-a-time walkabout, nomore sit-down one place and be happy, all-a-time we go, we go, run away from white man and his bullet. Naked we go, got nothing blanket, nothing food only what we hunt, nothing water only what we steal from white-feller man.

"Ah-h, bin properly bad times, arright. White man bin say him Boss along all that land, all that water. He send us into hills with rifle bullet chasing us proper-fast-feller, can't see 'im. We frightened to make fire 'cos might-be white-feller see smoke and find us, so we eat meat raw. We bin watch from hill country and we see them tracking us like we kangaroo. On horses they are, with rifles ready, playing Hunt the Nigger, Get Three Before Breakfast.

"Arright. One day they bin sneak up on us footwalk, quiet-feller, got nothing horse. E-e-e-e-h! E-e-e-e-h! Women scream. My mother run, run, run. She catch me in her arms and fly into bush, run, run, run, watching Be'hind, frightened along that bullet from white-feller-man-with-the-hot-feller-face.

"Arright. We bin get away. But my father, that Dead Feller now, he take his mob along hill 'Nother Way to bring squatter after him, away from we. He bin see that squatter got Queensland blackfeller with him but he no-more bin see that blackfeller lift rifle. Bang! My poor father, that Dead Feller, he got hit along shoulder. Bullet bin go in front-side, come out back-side. He bin fall-down, but quick-time he jump up and run, he run, he run and he run.

"Arright. We bin get away. Queensland blackfeller and squatter track blood-belong-him like I track wounded wallaby, but they no-more catch my father. That night we find 'im alonga bush. He no-more cry out, no-more talk-talk, but properly-fright allabout.

"Arright. No medical plane. No mission. No truck. Just nutting, only bush and wild blackfeller and white-feller-man with rifle. My mother and 'nother countryman bin treat my father with sap from tea-tree and put red ochre over hole till 'em mend. But my father, that Dead Feller now, he got crippled arm always, not-much-good hunter, but him live an 'im die when ole-man.

"Arright. We bin properly watch-out now. No-matter, more people bin shot, women bin shot. We bin hear white-man shout, Shoot 'em Nigger Women 'cos 'em Breeders! 'Nother time we bin hear white-man shout: Gett 'im lasso longa that young gin, make 'im good stud, get 'im har'cars piccaninny for stockman. They shoot at us for game, laugh loud-feller when we run or when man get hit.

"Arright. All-a-time we frightened longa rifle. All-a-time we stay walkabout, away from that Holy Water, hunting kangaroo, emu, lizard, eat 'im raw-feller. We bin

158

stay l-o-o-n-g time at Langaban Hill close-up Tanumbirini. We got nothing swag, nothing blanket, nothing tomahawk, nothing billycan, nothing flour, nothing tea, nothing sugar. Got nothing only spear and wallaby meat, sometimes crocodile meat, sometimes Sugarbag. Water we bin get in bark coolamon. Fine-weather time we bin camp on ground, man naked, woman naked, nothing blanket. Cold-weather time, wet-weather time we got windbreak, we got paperbark for blanket. But only sleep half-way 'cos might-be anytime white-feller come and must run.

"Arright. Many years we bin live like animal. We bin cover our tracks, walk along grass, walk along hill-country. Can't have corroboree, can't have Kunapipi, can't have Yabudurawa, Earth Mother must wait. Can't have Lorrkun 'cos when blackfeller dead-finish white-feller burn his body.

"Arright. When I boy I got proper fear all-a-time. Nothing happy, just worry-worry, fright-fright, run-run, hide-hide, but not cry-cry 'cos my Mumma she growl, she say White-Feller-Man hear 'im and come.

"Arright now, arright. The policeman bin come. The missionaries bin come and they talk-talk to we: Allabout bin come live along mission. They talk: We friend belong you, we God-man, we school-teacher. They talk: We come to teach about God-in-Sky, we come to teach about write and read, no-more fight, no-more kill. They bin talk: We got no rifle. White-feller missionary is Mister Joynt, is Mister Sharp, is Mister Huthnance. They got tents, like big calico, and they live there. We got fish, we got wallaby. We giv 'im fish, we give 'im wallaby. They talk: Thank you. Big-feller thank you. We got friend now, squatters no-more bin come, we safe here, and we stay and we stay . . . and now we talk Christian way about God-in-Sky."

Not all the dead men were black.

We took our reprisals when the opportunities occurred. My tribesmen raided white men's camps at night and killed them while they slept, spearing them through the heart, battering their heads with nulla-nullas. Sometimes murders were committed because of ignorance of the white man's way and his worldly goods. I remember my grandfather, the Dead Feller with the Crippled Arm, telling me about a man who was speared because he lit a cigarette and blew smoke through his nose. This was the first time my people had seen that done.

"He's got a fire inside his belly!" they shouted.

"Only spirits have smoke inside. He must be a spirit!"

So they killed him at once. Another man was speared when he took a watch from his pocket, opened it, and looked at the sun.

"He's got Gunaru—that Sun—in his pocket!"

"Yeah! He must be a spirit. He's got sun in his pocket!"

"The Gunaru Man. Kill 'im! Kill 'im!"

Even today my people refer to a watch as Gunaru because, like the Sun, it tells us the time.

There were wars and many killings because of women.

After the first violent conflicts the Alawa began to realize that the white man had goods we coveted, especially tobacco. We traded our women freely in return for it, but war broke out when we weren't paid or our women were taken by force.

We had no moral objection to the use of our women by the white men. When the murders stopped we placed them in the category of visiting High Djungayi, men of superior social standing who had to be given hospitality. It wasn't many years, of course, before the women were going to the white men surreptitiously or defying their husbands to do so. The attitude of a tribesman who was thus deserted by his wife was generally: "If she leaves me she must be rubbish, so let her go."

Punitive expeditions could be guaranteed to follow the murder of any white man . . . and the Mother Goddess protect an aboriginal who got in the way of one of them!

Recently I read an account of one such expedition early this century given by a white man named George Conway:

"At Bauhinia we were constantly under attack by wild natives," he wrote. Bauhinia was near Langaban Hill and

Tanumbirini where my grandfather was shot. His story went on: "I always carried a gun to protect myself and my horses. Once I was sworn in as a special constable to join a government punitive expedition against natives who had murdered five white prospectors and eaten their horses. There were two policemen, two other white men, thirteen natives, and myself.

"We were armed with rifles and revolvers. The blacks attacked us every night. We had to shoot hundreds of them—hundreds, I tell you. Some of their camps contained two or three thousand people. We didn't shoot for the love of it, but because we had to kill or be killed. One of our natives, Milky, ran away. We found him later with his head cut off and his penis in his mouth. They were terrible times . . . terrible . . . but the natives were wild people who had to be subdued."

From such as these am I descended.

And then there was Mounted-Trooper George Montague, of the Northern Territory Police, who concluded with this happy inference a report to his Inspector in Darwin about a punitive expedition he led against the Woolwonga natives: "I feel I cannot let this opportunity pass without paying a special tribute to the Martini-Henri rifle, both as to its accuracy of aim and quickness of action."

The bodies lying on the littered fields were predominantly naked and black. They proved beyond doubt that a rifle bullet travels faster than a spear.

These were the crosses upon which we were crucified. But civilized man's most malignant pestilence came to us stealthily with the arrival of the trading prahus from Macassar, long before the first white settlement, the first white rifle, and the first pool of Holy Water.

These great watermen came from fetid villages which had suppurated for centuries in the ordure of Asia.

They crossed the Timor Sea to the north coast of Arnhem Land, trading rattan and knives and axes for pearl-shell and bêche-de-mer. They sailed into the Gulf of Carpentaria, tacking into the south-east trade winds to the mouth of the Rose River where they found our neighbours, the Nungubuyu.

They had many baubles the tribesmen coveted. We had women the seafarers wanted.

Trade was undoubtedly done.

Much later, in the nineteenth century, Chinese labourers were indentured to work on the Northern Territory's first railway from Darwin to Pine Creek. Their half-caste descendants are here today with Chinese names fitting poorly in jet-black faces.

They found the Roper.

They found us soon after we had our first contact with the prospectors come looking for gold, with the cattlemen overlanding their mobs of breeders along the coast "roads" to their visions splendid in the Kimberleys and beyond, and with the linesmen erecting the Singing Strings from Darwin to Adelaide to complete the London-Sydney cable link.

These men brought gifts and bought our women and brought disease. Especially did they bring leprosy, the morbid malady of the Israelites in the time of Moses, spreading its insidious rottenness among my people until their limbs were deformed, their fingers and toes dropped off, their very appearances changed.

In our primitive state we did not understand even elementary hygiene—we had never found any need for it. We slept together in family groups, shared our pipes, drank from the same vessel as a dozen others. Several musicians played one didgeredoo. The dark corners of our camps harboured lice and other vermin. Our dogs were bed-warmers. Public expectoration was commonplace.

None of this mattered in those happy times when we lived remote from the septic world and its tainted flesh. Our bodies were conditioned to resist the diseases our ancestors brought with them from the Land of Dream, although we had inherited more than our fair share of chronic framboesia, the erupting yaws of the coloured races. But our disregard of the basic precepts of hygiene as we now understand it, our very ignorance of it, was to matter awfully when the brown blood and the yellow blood and the white blood came to be mixed with the black. Germ warfare took terrible toll. Microbes incubated unchecked in the environment they relished, and transmission and re-transmission were inevitable in our communal camps.

Nobody knows how many people from the Roper River alone died of leprosy. Today there are two hundred patients at the leprosarium near Darwin, and one-sixth of them are from my part of the country.

One day soon after the end of the war my Aunt Agnes Nganirimba looked at my younger brother Jacob Wuyaindjimadjindji and said, "He has leprosy." Next time the medical plane visited Roper River a doctor examined Jacob and confirmed the diagnosis.

Jacob went to Channel Island, where our mother had died. When that horror was abandoned he was transferred to East Arm, a modern leprosarium near Darwin. He was separated from his family for twelve years, but was cured by sulphone drugs and has since been discharged. Now, like me, he is a citizen, freed of restraints under the white man's law. We were the first two members of one aboriginal family to be acknowledged in this way. We also had the dubious distinction of having two leprosy victims in the family and several others among close relatives.

Like tribal Pay-Back, leprosy struck in unexpected places. My stepmother, my mother, my youngest brother, and a cousin who was his best friend were stricken. My father, my brother Silas, my sister Mercia, and I escaped, even though Mercia lived on Channel Island for several years with my mother. I have had several tests, all of them negative.

It is not so long ago that leprosy patients fled into the bush and stayed there when the medical plane visited the Roper. They knew from experience that most of the people who went to Channel Island were never seen again.

Even with sulphone drugs that are used today the cure is still slow. A man who has the disease in his system knows that he will not get better overnight. He must leave the tribe for a long time. Because of this many aboriginal people are unwilling to be quarantined. I believe that there are now more leprosy sufferers in the bush than in East Arm lazaret. It is said not to be highly contagious; that there must be long and intimate contact for infection to occur. But when I think of all the infected tribesmen along the Roper I wonder if that is true.

Influences other than the desire of a patient are at work in deciding whether or not an aboriginal leper should seek treatment, especially when a woman is involved. A woman does not make decisions affecting her own movement from the camp-fire circle. Her husband, alone, arbitrates on such matters. He suspects, often correctly, that he will not get her back. He has no proof of the doctor's ability to cure leprosy. If he is an old man he will offer strong resistance: he is not only being deprived of a wife, but also of the insurance policy he has against his years of decrepitude, the woman who by fair means or foul will provide him with tobacco. Her departure for quarantine means that he will be without comfort.

In some aboriginal tribes that can be a harsh fate, and I am not surprised that slow death and the risk of further infection are often preferred.

The Medicine Men of the tribe were helpless against the ravages of leprosy. They did not attempt to cure it, apparently realizing that it was deep-seated and beyond them. Nevertheless, we had reputed cures for other ills. Yaws was treated with a poultice of wet earth or red ochre which, if it did nothing else, at least minimized the damage done by flies.

Common colds were treated with a herbal mixture of boiled tea-tree leaves. We had no bottles in which to store tincture of eucalyptus, so the sap was sucked directly from a gumleaf or the leaf itself inserted in the nose.

A glutinous substance we boiled from the Guyia plant was used effectively in treating dysentery. My countrymen use Guyia today if stricken while on walkabout.

We had another herb, a tribal cure-all, which we believed was efficacious in everything from fractured bones to venereal disease. This was Budiga, another concoction of boiled leaves. It would not mend a broken leg, of course, but a patient who drank it lapsed into unconsciousness—which didn't surprise me—and could have his leg bound with paperbark and currajong string without pain. It was our primitive pentothal.

Having since had some medical training I am grateful that I escaped serious injury or illness and did not have to suffer the tribal cures, some of which must have been worse than the disease.

While at school I helped the mission Sister, generally the superintendent's wife, in the dispensary. I had to bathe and dress wounds and sores and supervise the after-care of patients in our solarium of natural sunlight. In this way I acquired an interest in medicine which I have retained to this day.

But it was to be a long time before I could devote my life to its outer fringes as an ambulance driver and personal assistant to white doctors.

That day did come, but first I had to face the realities of life as a stockman, a horseman, a colt-breaker, and a bulldogger.

The fact that during this period I did not once require the services of the tribal bonesmith to patch shattered limbs is proof that my Dreamings were protecting me.

For, ahead, there lay a period of excitement and danger.

Chapter Thirteen

MY father, Barnabas Gabarla, a High Djungayi and a Head Stockman, has a foot crippled by a horse, a rogue colt named Scotland, which bucked so furiously while he was taming it that he had to be helped from the saddle after riding it to a standstill. His foot was paralysed by the jarring impact on his spine as the wild beast leapt and crashed. It has never recovered.

I remembered the episode vividly one day shortly after I left school when Stanley Port said, "Phillip, I think you should be a stockman."

I knew exactly what that meant.

I had seen the bucking broncos in the breaking yard, their angry nostrils dilating and snorting, their eyes mad with terror, their feet flailing wildly in desperate attempts to maim their tormentors.

I had seen men thrown heavily against the wooden panels of the yard. I had seen them trampled and watched their broken bodies being carried away.

I remembered the times the medical aeroplane came to evacuate men to hospital: men with shattered limbs, men who had been skewered by sharp branches in the tea-tree and lancewood scrub, men gored while learning to throw bullocks.

I knew that this was dangerous work, that it was almost inevitable that I should suffer injuries, and certain that I would be bucked-off and jolted until my spine threatened to snap.

Yet I did not hesitate.

I had been riding mission horses since I was old enough to sit on their backs. I had ridden them bareback, naked rider and naked horse galloping along the river flats, black manes and black bodies mingling as on that wondrous day of free-flight when we flew past the ridges and Roger Gunbukbuk broke his hips. If it was necessary for me to work I wanted to work with the horses.

"I would like that," I said.

"Good," he said. "I will get Sam Ulagang to teach you."

Sam! Sam Ulagang! Ah, so I was to suffer Sam's disdain again, the man who had made me his spear carrier for months, the man who had upbraided me if I put a foot out of place when we stalked game, the cavalier fellow whose contempt had once driven me to the edge of despair. So now I was to have more of his sneers, and to be forced to curb my impetuous wish to run-him-through with a shovel-spear each time I caught his derisive smirk as I picked myself up from the dust of the breaking yard.

"Sam, you had better watch your tongue," I muttered.

And when he began needling me at once: "Boy, have you ever ridden a horse?" . . . "Boy, do you know which side to mount?" I believed that Sam and I must one day meet in the peace-through-war Banburr ceremony.

But as the days passed I came to recognize Sam for what he was—not only the best hunter and tracker, but also the best horseman and the best teacher anywhere on the Roper. I settled down to learn from him zealously, and to become, at least, the second best horseman in sight.

Sam was merciless, shaming me with ridicule on the slightest pretext but constantly sharpening my wits so that I might know how to out-manoeuvre fractious colts which wanted nothing better than the opportunity to murder me with their hooves. He was unsympathetic when, as happened regularly, I was thrown like a sack of potatoes.

"Get up!" he would shout. "Get back on! And this time stay there! What do you think this is—a slippery slide?"

And when I did ride my first colt to a standstill—ah, what a day of triumph!—Sam was less than magnanimous. He had been shouting at me for hours: "All right, yard that colt! All right, get the lasso on 'im! All right, pull it up now until he chokes and falls down! All right, slacken off! Now when he gets up start again. All right, get that collar rope on 'im! Now get that other rope around the fetlock! Patient-one. Careful-one. All right, now pull that one foot off the ground. Ah, got 'im. . . . Hey! Never do that again! Never show fear of a horse! You're the Boss! Remember it yourself and don't let the horse forget it, otherwise you're beaten before you start. All right, now handle him. Talk to him. Throw bags over him. Run your hands along his back. See how he flinches at the touch? Keep doing that. Fondle him. Fondle him well until he stops shuddering. All right now, get that saddle on 'im! Gentle-one. Slow-one. Patient now, ah patient now. . . . Get that girth tight! Tight, tighter now! You're going to need it properly-tight in a minute. Now the crupper under his tail. Get the legrope off, quickfeller-way. All right now, stand back! Watch the flying feet! Buck, you beauty, buck! Up you go! D-o-w-n, d-o-w-n. You can't get that saddle off, eh? No, that's because Waipuldanya made it tight. You don't like it, eh? You'll get used to it, feller. You'll get used to a whip, too, and spurs, and galloping after cattle, and eating out of Waipuldanya's hand if he's not too frightened to put it near your muzzle. Eh, Waipuldanya, how do you like stockwork, eh?"

He scoffed at me thus while the maddened colt threw itself around the yard, plunging and rearing in a frantic attempt to dislodge the saddle. Once it rolled on to its back, grunted sickeningly in animal terror, and struggled to its feet again.

"How you like to ride that one now, eh?" Sam sneered. "You got pimple along skin, eh, all-a-same goose? All right now, get that saddle off. Lift his front leg. Grab the hairs on the fetlock and make him hold up. All right now, do that with the other leg. Fondle him, fondle him, always fondle. Make him lead now. Get that long rein on. Drive him and guide him until he knows how to move, until he knows how to answer to his mouth. You ready now?"

"What for?"

"To ride him, of course."

I had no choice. I was in the ring with five hundred pounds of threshing horseflesh, and I could not leave until I had ridden him, until I had tamed him or been tamed.

"Right!" I said.

"All right," Sam said, and now he became even more intensely efficient, all his faculties concentrated on helping me. The sarcasm stopped as abruptly as it began and he encouraged me quietly.

"Easy one this. Can't buck nothing much. You ride 'im like rocking horse, see, smoke cigarette, eh, read a book, eh? All right now, get that leg-rope on again. Lift that leg now so he no-more buck. Ah, good. Now get the saddle on again, gentle-one, easy-one. Tighten girth. Tighten girth. All right now, reins short in left hand, twitch on that ear with the same hand. Ease your weight into the stirrup iron. Now off. Now on again. Now off. All right now, relax! Weight on again and this time into saddle. Sneak-up! Slide-across! Weight down gently. You all right, Waipuldanya?"

"Okay!"

This was the moment of truth.

"Let go!" Sam ordered another stockman. "Let go that fetlock rope! Open the gate! Hang on! Ride 'im, cowboy!"

There was I in the saddle of an untamed horse with the gate of the small yard opening into the larger one beyond where the horse would be able to move and buck with greater freedom. Now the leg came down as the fetlock rope was cast off.

Whether I liked it or not, it was inevitable that I should experience the roughest ride of my young life on a highly temperamental colt determined to repay the insults and indignities of the past few hours.

169

No rocking-horse this. He snorts, rears forward, rears backward, goes straight up, comes straight down, propping with a spine-tingling crash. He has his head down between his legs, heels flying, dust swirling, Ulagang yelling.

"Ride 'im Waipuldanya. You got 'im, you got 'im."

Yes, I got 'im all right. I knew that after the first few seconds. It would take more than the inexpert bucking of this colt to dislodge a man who has reins and a deep stockman's saddle with knee-pads to support him, a man who has been brought up to bareback galloping, clinging with naked legs to horses that took him to the ridges and beyond.

When the colt began to tire I gave him a little of his own treatment with a slap of the reins: "Come on, horse, what are you stopping for? I like this bucking. That's why I'm here. Get on with it!"

He tried again half-heartedly, desperately tired from the maximum exertion of throwing his entire bulk off the ground.

Foam-flecked and frightened, then, he stood quietly. I patted him gently, spoke to him soothingly, the treatment he could expect henceforth when he behaved.

And in a few days, with Sam Ulagang watching, he ate from my hand.

Sam gave me the faint-praise that was the only compliment he knew.

"All right," he said.

Not all the colts were as easy to tame as the first. Sam had the pleasure of seeing me thrown frequently, and invariably greeted me with heavy sarcasm.

"Maybe you think it's a good day for flying?"

"Maybe you think that horse is an aeroplane, eh?"

"Maybe you got bindy-eye or thistle on that saddle, prick your backside, eh?"

But when danger threatened Sam didn't hesitate to run under the feet of a rearing animal to pull me away. Only once did it happen that he reached me after I had been kicked. A demon-colt, a turbulent Pegasus that bounced me out of the saddle like a rubber ball and scarified my back with its forefeet as Sam rushed in.

I was winded and would have stayed there, perhaps to be trampled to death, if Sam had not fought it off and dragged me out of the yard.

After a few such episodes I forgot his sneers.

We never did get to the Banburr ground.

The herd of several thousand cattle grazed on the mission lease of one hundred and fifty thousand acres and, if they wished, in the unbounded, unfenced south-east corner of Arnhem Land to Limmen Bight and north to the Phelp and Rose Rivers. This was our hunting ground—perhaps ten million acres of it.

To the extent that they roamed in this almost limitless land they were wild bush cattle. But their freedom and contented rumination was bedevilled at least once a year by an intrusion of mounted aboriginal stockmen, yelling demons come to inflict upon them the indignities of animal husbandry, the searing scourges of branding and castration.

I was one of these satyrs, a black human form with equine ears and tail, adhesively astride a horse that galloped from the shadows of dawn and used the moon as a Very light, falling upon them from my saddle as they fled in panic, twisting their tails until they overbalanced and crashed.

This was a dangerous trick of the trade which I had to get right the first time I tried it: to abandon the saddle as horse and bull galloped shoulder to shoulder, to grab and twist its tail so that it would not slip from my hand, to run out to the bull's side where it could see me . . . and attempt to turn . . . and go down in a heap.

Then quickly to leg-rope it with its own tail and hold it there until the man arrived with the branding iron and the emasculator.

Arise, Sir Eunuch! Your name is OTC, written indelibly in your hide with a burn which blisters and rises, identical with an inscription in the Register of Brands in a Darwin office so that all who see, especially any duffers riding our boundaries, will know that you belong to the Church Missionary Society at Roper River.

The first beast I thus bulldogged was a yearling heifer, one that Sam Ulagang cut from the mob and told me to throw.

"Nice easy-one," Sam said. "But don't miss, or we might have to carry you home."

It was a grim moment, but I did not miss. In the years which followed I threw hundreds of cattle in this way.

The annual muster was The Hard Work Time, the time of sweaty fatigue for horses and men, while we chased the herd through the virgin scrub, culling and bang-tailing around the quiet waterholes in the Never-Never Land.

For a young aboriginal who owned nothing but his spears and his tribal country—and the squatters had claimed that—the Month of Muster was the moment of enchantment.

I had a horse and a saddle and bridle and a quart-pot and a blanket in a swag and food in packsaddles and a change of clothes and tobacco and danger and a sense of power over animals.

We mustered the open country around the billabongs on the river flats. On clear nights we drove quiet decoy cattle we called "coaches" on to the plains to attract others. This was Moonlighting, the salt of mustering, spine-tingling in the spirit-laden air, goose-pimpling in the eerie shadows where Shades might dwell, sculptured in our saddles through timeless midnights to the edge of the world and beyond.

There were hours of mortal danger for man and beast when our runners tracked cattle to their daylight havens in the lancewood and tea-tree scrub, where they hoped that none would follow.

But that was folly: we tightened our surcingles and thrashed into the jungle of stakes and skewers, guiding our horses as never before, abrased on the branches, which threatened like rapiers to run-us-through.

I often wondered what benevolent spirit protected me from these jagged limbs at helter-skelter-canter. My Kangaroo Dreamings must have been on duty in this Forest of the Deadly Blades, for I was not hurt. But other men were, and horses were killed frequently.

Perhaps they broke a leg in the fork of a fallen branch. Perhaps a courageous barrel was impaled. In either case the animal was shot to relieve its dying agony. I saw my countrymen prostrate with grief, crying bitterly over dead horses with which they had become identified, horses which had answered their whistle, had responded to the pressure of a knee or the gentle touch of a rein. I have seen men cut themselves with sticks and knives and go wailing into the bush when the head stockman came up with a rifle.

"Properly-sorry-feller along my number one horse! A-h-h-h-h! A-a-a-e-e-e!"

But I also saw horses cruelly rowelled by men who lacked feeling, the Master Men of the aboriginal tribes who were demonstrating that the Black Race was superior to the Brown Horse.

We camped beside our saddles and packs, using them as pillows and windbreaks, coddled by these white-feller comforts in a land where, like Jacob the Israelite's, our pillows were normally pillars of stone.

We had rations of flour, tea, and sugar, and we could kill a bullock for meat when necessary. It seldom was. We took with us an aboriginal cook who was also a professional hunter, a man who hunted kangaroos and fish and turtles and searched for lily roots, yams and Sugarbag while we chased cattle. In those days I preferred to eat our natural food, and today, after long periods of sophisticated stews, I hunger for it still.

I worked as a stockman for several years, risking my limbs and my life in the crazy gallops through the witchwood, but I was never once paid a penny in wages.

That is not said critically. I am not alleging parsimony by the mission. I am simply stating a fact: I was First Class Unpaid Stockman Waipuldanya. Nor were any of my friends paid. Never having heard of a fair wage for

173

a fair day's work, we did not expect it. We worked gladly for nothing.

In those days I had seen money only rarely when visitors came to the mission. Until I was an adult I had never handled a silver coin, nor would I have known what to do with it if one had been given to me. I learnt that money could not be eaten, and thereafter lost interest in it until the war came and I was enlisted in the army as a tracker with the North Australia Observer Unit. The army insisted upon paying me seventy shillings a fortnight—a huge sum, a princely sum, and a useless sum to a man ignorant of its value and already kept in food and clothing.

The fact remains that for long periods of exhausting work I was paid nothing. The wage for a day's hard riding, often from dawn until midnight when we were Moonlighting, was food and tobacco. The missionaries had a book which we were told represented our Bank. The names of all the stockmen were in that book, and each had a figure beside it. We could get a pair of trousers from the mission store against our credit, but I never knew how much credit I had or the price of any article of clothing. Until the day I left the mission nobody ever said to me, "Here are your wages," or "You have earned ten pounds." And when I left I went with nothing.

The tobacco was nikki-nikki, black sticks of a powerful narcotic, which we wrapped in newspaper or smoked in a long Larawa pipe. We had no cigarette papers, and on a mission station four hundred miles from Darwin newspapers were rare. A printed page was therefore worth more to us than an entire newspaper to a city reader. The *Encyclopaedia Britannica* would have been a priceless treasure for reasons other than its storehouse of knowledge, especially as it is printed on fine paper. Each volume would soon have been reduced to its two hard covers.

During newspaper famines we rolled our tobacco in paperbark. Sometimes I tapped a piece of green stick until its sheath of bark was loosened and came off as a tube. I filled this with tobacco and smoked what we called Tailor-Mades.

If nicotine is thought to be a poor substitute for regular wages it should be remembered that in the Northern Territory there were missionaries who refused to issue tobacco because they said it was sinful. They firmly believed it to be an evil which had to be stamped out as ruthlessly as ceremonial mating and infanticide, and a few other sins in the eyes of God.

I am sure these views were sincerely held, just as the Roper River missionaries were sincere in segregating aboriginal boys and girls in dormitories, which were locked each night against the eventuality that bush children who had played nakedly around the camp-fires together might corrupt one another.

I was a Dormitory Boy, separated from my parents and my family fire during my early youth to prevent me molesting girls who were also behind lock and key.

Looking back on this act of prudery I can only conclude that the missionaries had no conception of the strict tribal barriers segregating the sexes and minimizing venery. In any case, it had the opposite effect of creating the temptation of forbidden fruit which did not otherwise exist.

But the denial of tobacco on other missions had much more serious consequences. The missionaries must have been well aware that aborigines who had once acquired a taste for it would do anything to satisfy their craving.

They looked around for a fresh source of supply and found it among lonely crocodile shooters, buffalo shooters, half-caste stockmen and native labourers employed in the shooting camps, who did not have women, but had plenty of tobacco and were anxious to exchange one for the other. And so trade was done.

This caused such an outcry that the circumstances were investigated by the government. One mission was told that unless the tobacco ration was restored it would lose its lease of land.

The restoration was possible only after the missionaries responsible for the original decree had been replaced by men whose approach to the Word of God was a little less Calvinistic.

As long ago as I can remember the Roper River mission always had a motor vehicle of some description: an old T-model Ford, an ancient Dodge car, and a buckboard lorry were among the earliest taken there for reasons which seemed obscure in view of the fact that we had only five or six miles of bush tracks on the lease.

Nevertheless, they were there, although as a youth I had no thought of how they were to affect profoundly my future life.

The Alawa tribesmen regarded engines which made a noise as inventions of the Devil, while being grudgingly respectful of the uses to which they were put by the white men.

A half-caste man, Edward Herbert, was first to begin my gradual conversion from walking to riding. He won my interest by demonstrating how petrol ignited and sparking-plugs worked. I remember the struggle which occurred between my primitive belief in the spiritual significance of unexplained fire and the desire to understand that these sparks, issuing from a plug which was neither on fire nor red hot, were under man's control.

Familiarity soon led me to accept, however, that this was not a supernatural phenomenon from which I should run as from a malevolent Mulunguwa, although I jumped as though one were after me the first time Edward short-circuited electric current through my body. Until he explained what had happened I was sure the engine had passed me a secret message that one dark night it would be out looking for me. Subsequently I had immense fun playing similar tricks on my tribesmen.

During the first year of the war I began work as a grease-monkey with Les Perriman, who came to the Northern Territory as a mission mechanic. He taught me the theory of internal combustion engines, and to him I owe my ability to take one apart and reassemble it even if the pieces are scattered far and wide.

I studied with Les for many months, learning the uses of pistons and rings and magnetos and generators and crankshafts and gudgeon pins and con-rods and a multitude of other things I had never previously heard of.

As my untrained mind came to rationalize the part played by each small piece in driving an engine and finally a vehicle, I was fascinated by the inventiveness and the genius which had made it possible.

In our tribal lives we had nothing mechanical, nothing more complicated than a woomera fitted to a spear shaft, and certainly nothing in which hundreds of parts complemented each other and were necessary for the efficient working of the whole.

Having mastered this intricate mechanism I was impatient for the day when I would first sit behind the steering wheel and control the mass of machinery as it rolled along one of the winding tracks around the mission.

I had, of course, often done this in make-believe, sitting proudly erect and turning the wheels while the vehicle was stationary in the mission garage.

On such occasions I thought, "This is easy. I could drive this thing without trouble."

I examined the three pedals of the T-model, one the forward gear, one the reverse gear, and one neutral, while I steered, confident that when the time came I would know exactly what to do.

Les Perriman, however, was in no hurry to give me a chance. The Ford did not have a self-starter and on his trips through the bush he took me along only as The Cranky Man, the man who wound the cranking handle, knocked the skin off his knuckles when it backfired, and thus became cranky. Driving seemed to be his eternal prerogative. I yearned to ask to be given a turn, but my natural aboriginal reticence prevented me.

Finally, one day when I least expected it, Les stopped the car on a track three miles from the mission and said to me simply, "You have a go!"

What an anticlimax!

If he had said to me the night before, "Tomorrow I will teach you to drive," I could have enjoyed at least a few hours of the prospect, planning it all in my mind, play-acting behind the steering wheel, practising with the pedals, happily impatient as a child on the eve of Christmas.

Instead, at one moment I sat beside him as The Cranky Man, and next moment I was chauffeur-in-training without an anticipatory thought, without my mouth watering once, sitting like a startled scout in the hot seat of un-preparedness.

Les sat quietly beside me as I fumbled with my fingers and wondered where to begin. He admired the scenery . . . "wonderful paperbarks" . . . "what a mighty river!" . . . deliberately leaving me to the mercy of this mechanical horse, politely unhelpful, the opposite of Sam Ulagang who had berated me with details when he taught me to break a colt.

Here was I upon the threshold of an experience never shared by any other Alawa tribesman, and Les had to talk about paperbarks and rivers!

Nevertheless, as I emerged from my first mesmeric trance, throwing off my muscular rigidity and gripping the wheel as though it were the neck of a Mulunguwa come to get my kidney fat, I was aware that Les watched me from the corner of his eye.

"Let's see what the scenery is like farther on," he said. Ah! That was a Ulagang sarcasm and it goaded me into action.

As I depressed the forward gear the T-model monster began to move, and when it did I advanced the hand-throttle on the steering column for more revolutions of the engine.

Alas! No doubt the mistake was a small one, but it had distressing consequences. I must have moved the lever too far, for the car gathered speed quickly like a horse breaking into a gallop, swerved alarmingly in a patch of sand which occurred most inopportunely at that spot, took the bit between its teeth and attempted to jump a small tea-tree at the side of the track.

Unfortunately it failed, though trying valiantly, and came to rest on the bush with the front wheels in mid-air like a fractious colt astride a bronco-panel it had failed to leap.

I was appalled, and yet thankful now that I did not have an audience of critical tribesmen who had never seen a car in any such predicament. Their laughter would still be ringing in my ears.

Les Perriman was first to speak.

"Trying to climb trees! Must be goanna oil in the sump," he said.

Ulagang could not have sneered more loftily.

I sat there speechless without knowing what to do next. Finally I said, "What will I do now?"

"You're the driver," Les snapped. "You put it here, you get it off. And don't waste too much time; there are no bowsers out here."

When we hit the bush I had instinctively pressed the neutral pedal and the engine continued to run. The waste of petrol seemed to be worrying Les more than the attitude of the car.

I thought for a moment, and then pressed the reverse pedal, advancing the throttle control as I did so.

Presto! The rear wheels bit into the ground and pulled the front-end off the tree. Within moments we had four wheels on the ground again.

I expected Les to shift me from the driver's seat at once and take us home on a course which would be less like a steeplechase. But perhaps he had been shocked more than was apparent, for he said nothing as I turned the car and began to drive carefully back to the mission, my tracker's eyes searching the road ahead for sandy patches and tea-tree scrub.

Once or twice I thought he was holding on to his seat rather more grimly than necessary, but after that first upset

I could have driven for the Queen. I have never had another accident in many thousands of miles along bush pads and hundreds of thousands behind the wheel of a speeding ambulance.

Yet I do not like driving. Les Perriman must have influenced me. I would much rather sit beside someone else and quietly enjoy the scenery, seeing the kangaroos as potential targets for my spear instead of a danger to my vehicle.

With Perriman's departure I became the mission mechanic. I had a full-time job maintaining engines in boats, pumps, mills, cars, trucks, and lighting plants.

My salary was exactly as it had been when I was a stockman—nothing! But I had food and clothes for my growing family, and enough tobacco to keep me satisfied. Life seemed good.

It was during this period in nineteen hundred and fifty-three that strange things happened which were to change the entire course of my life. Like a chicken anxious to see the world, I began to break out of the shell that confined me mentally and physically to the Roper River.

Nothing that occurred in the first thirty years of my life had inspired me with boundless faith in the goodness of white men. On the contrary, I had evidence of my own to convince me that the terrible stories told around the camp-fires by the Elders were not exaggerated. I expected nothing from any man other than a missionary whose skin was not black, unless it was censure and cruelty.

Yet two white men, spontaneously, led me out of the dark.

One was a policeman, and one was a doctor of medicine. They showed me kindness, encouraged me when I was despondent, matched their wills against mine, and dangled before me the vision of a splendid new life for me and my family in a world whose fringes I had barely touched.

Constable Dan Sprigg, of the Northern Territory Police Force, and Dr "Spike" Langsford, of the Northern Territory Medical Service, were first to set my feet on the bottom of a slippery slide which led to Citizenship, with my name transferred from the humiliating Register of Wards to the power-without-glory of the Electoral Roll, with gilt-edged invitations for Mr and Mrs Phillip Roberts to Government House . . . Waipuldanya of the Alawa tribe and Hannah Dulban of the Wandarang tribe . . . with a house which I could call home, unpretentious and yet a castle which sheltered a family of eight, with trips to far-away cities and foreign lands, and with white men seeking to talk to me, to discover voluntarily something of the culture I had left behind and they had always spurned.

A revolution came to my life.

One year I was a primitive blackfellow living by the tribal law, a tribesman incarnate, a Djungayi in the pagan Kunapipi ceremony in which we worshipped the Earth Mother and the Rainbow Serpent.

Next year I was an embryo citizen in another world, not wholly forsaking my Dreamings for Christ, but determined to embrace The New Way, determined that my children should have clothes and canned food and academic learning and the right to say "No" when ordered gruffly to act against their wishes.

Dan Sprigg helped me up. "Spike" Langsford helped me up. Stanley Port and Les Perriman helped me up. So did Miss Dove. So did my Uncle Stanley Marbunggu . . . more than any man who is not an aboriginal can understand. Sam Ulagang was a demonstration teacher, a Master of Method. Barnabas Gabarla, my father, showed me the Tribal Way. My totems provided, my Larbaryandji country provided, and the Elders watched over us all, keeping the laws, apportioning food and responsibility according to the Dreamtime Plan, making me understand that if my skin should ever turn white my heart would remain black.

Even now when Larbaryandji calls the urge to return is strong indeed, almost undeniable when I lie between man-made walls, beneath an unnatural blanket of iron which prevents my seeing the moon and the stars.

But I was shown the road ahead.

The Green Light is flashing and I want to cross the intersection before it changes, before I hit another clump of tea-tree.

Chapter Fourteen

I REACHED the Parting of the Ways on the day in nineteen hundred and fifty-three when I was sent upstream to Urapunga cattle station to fix the engine of a boat that had been under water for four months.

I recovered a motor, which was a mess of rust and slime, a dreary prospect for Maraliowi the grease-monkey I had working for me. Ah, yes, I had come up in the world in a short time and now rated a personal assistant who was in charge of the Department of Distasteful Duties.

The engine had to be stripped to the last washer, the corroded distributor and carburettor replaced, and new piston rings and valves fitted. After a long wait for spare parts, which were imported from Darwin, I had it together again three months after I began, and hopefully pressed the self-starter.

Nothing happened.

Then I found that the distributor wires were incorrectly linked to the plugs. When these were changed the hoped-for explosion occurred and the motor was soon running like a new one.

A few days later I sailed the boat up to Roper Bar police station and there met Dan Sprigg, "Spike" Langsford and his wife, Rita, who was a nursing sister.

One afternoon the doctor and the policeman came down to the boat and talked to me for more than an hour. When they left it occurred to me that I had been under some kind of cross-examination. On the following day Sprigg returned alone and I learnt what it was about.

"What are you going to do with your life, Phillip?" he asked.

"I don't know," I said. "I'll probably go back to the mission and stay there with my family." At that stage no other possibility had entered my mind.

"Are you happy?" he asked.

"Yes, I'm happy," I said, although I wasn't sure what a white man meant when he asked an aboriginal about happiness.

Then he said bluntly: "Look, you can't go on living like a blackfellow all your life."

"Like a blackfellow! I am a blackfellow," I said, perhaps with a little asperity.

"You know what I mean," Sprigg said. "The colour of your skin can't change. You'll always be a blackfellow in that respect. But there is something inside you that can change: you can begin to work and live and think as an intelligent man instead of a primitive."

I wanted to ask him, "Is that desirable?" but forbore to do so because I could see that he was genuinely interested in my welfare.

Instead, I asked: "How and where do I start?"

"Doctor Langsford wants a driver-mechanic," he said. "He is going on a long tour around the Northern Territory, visiting all the government settlements and mission stations and cattle stations to examine and treat the natives. If you go with him you could teach him something about engines and perhaps he will teach you something about medicine. In that way you would learn how to help your own people . . . better than that Doctor Blackfellow business."

I said I would think about it and let him know. The prospect pleased me. I had not been away from the Roper since the war. I had never been to Tennant Creek or Alice Springs nor to the Kimberleys out west.

I would visit all these tribes if I decided to go: the Mudbra at Victoria River Downs, the Gurindji at Wave

Hill, the Karama, the Djamindjun, the Gulawarang, the Wailbri, the Ngaringman, the Wandjira, the Muriwang, the Garanguru, and the Warramunga: dozens of aboriginal nations, all of them with kinship phratries to which I would belong as soon as I arrived. I would have new uncles, new fathers, new cousins, and even new mothers-in-law whom I must not speak to nor even gaze upon.

Next day I told Dan Sprigg that I was willing to go.

"That's good," he said. "Doctor Langsford is a man who started at the bottom and is now at the top in his profession. Be like him. Learn from him. Once you start on the road never look back. Never return to the tribal ways. Read and work. If you remember that and keep the laws, then one day you may be famous. You may even have your name in print."

That possibility seemed remote. I was still a tribal aboriginal, an obscure black man whose name had been written only in the footprints around our bush camps.

"Albert Namatjira, the Aranda artist, is famous," Sprigg said. "One day Phillip Roberts . . . Waipuldanya . . . may be equally well known."

"Might-be," I said, but believed it not.

My big adventure began from Katherine a fortnight later. Dr. Langsford and his wife arrived in a Land Rover and asked me to check over the spare parts for a long trip over lonely tracks which had neither garages nor tow trucks, delicatessens nor milk bars, hotels nor motels.

We were going into the vast north-west corner of the Northern Territory, a land of more than one hundred thousand square miles, but containing fewer than one hundred white people.

This was the land of cattle, of immense distances, often of two hundred miles between neighbours, and of Victoria River Downs, once the world's largest cattle station. Compulsory resumptions by the government had reduced its holding from thirteen thousand square miles to a mere six thousand. But with more than three and a half million acres remaining it could still be regarded as quite a property.

Its neighbour, Wave Hill, was equally big. This, in fact, was a country where "miles" related to property and not to distance, which was expressed in time elapsed: "Inverway is half a day from here."

It was necessary, therefore, that we should be self-supporting and able to extricate ourselves from any emergency. I checked over the spare parts, the tools, the shovels, picks, and axes until satisfied that not even the Great Sandy Desert could beat us. We had reserve tanks of water and fuel, three rifles, none of which ever fired a shot, cameras which were shooting constantly, and an Alawa tribesman who, if we had a breakdown, was supposed to be able to hunt food and walk for help.

During the first week my job was confined to driving and maintaining the vehicle. But that changed when we reached Victoria River Downs where a group of about one hundred natives had to be medically examined.

One day Dr Langsford showed me a strange apparatus and said, "This is a microscope. It magnifies germs and other small things we can't see with the naked eye. Tell me what you can see in the glass."

I looked through the eye-piece and was astonished by what I saw in this magic mirror.

"Ah! Billabongs, rivers, hills, mountains," I said. "This is a picture of the country."

"Not quite," he said. "In the mass you see there is something important. Can you pick it out?"

"A special landmark?" I could think only in terms of photographs.

"A landmark, yes—if you like," he said. "But a landmark in a different sense."

I looked again, but could still distinguish only the ravines and the trees and the creeks and the contours of what I imagined to be the Australian countryside. Like a white man in the bush who is unable to see camouflaged wallabies and birds, which stand out clearly to me, I was blind in this world of lenses and prisms and matter so enlarged that I could not identify it.

Finally Dr Langsford drew a diagram of hookworm ova. He explained that it could not be seen except in a microscope, but that it was visible on the slide now before me. After another search I distinguished what he had drawn: the unmistakable evidence of a hookworm germ taken from a native patient who had been examined that day.

This impressed me deeply. I knew how hookworm had ravaged my people. I had seen the ugly manifestations of it along the Roper, and now for the first time I saw what caused it.

When he had finished his examinations that day Dr Langsford noticed that I was still fascinated by the microscope. I had returned to it many times and peered long and intently into the glass. He brought some slides to me and said, "Here, have a few practice runs." He showed me how to adjust the mechanism and left me to play with it.

I experimented with other things: a hair from my head which looked like the mooring-rope of an ocean liner; the roots of hair which resembled the branches of a denuded tree; a grain of sand which looked like a mountain of quartz.

This was magic indeed, basic magic in the infinite enlargement of material I understood. My first lesson in the practice of medicine left me wide-eyed with wonder and anxious for more.

Other lessons followed. I learnt how to sterilize hypodermic syringes in boiling water and how to load them.

I watched hundreds of my aboriginal people file past Dr Langsford and his wife as they conducted Mantoux tests in a tuberculosis survey. After each use of the needle he passed it through a flame before injecting the next patient.

"That is a funny idea," I thought. "Why is it necessary to have a needle red-hot before piercing the skin?"

Later I was to understand that this, too, was one of the many precautions taken by all doctors to ensure that germs were not passed from one patient to another.

I wondered about our own lack of hygiene. I wondered how much disease had been transmitted in our camps by the use of common drinking vessels which were never washed. When I saw Dr Langsford treating a patient I wondered about the efficacy of our own medicines: of budiga, guyia, and tea-tree leaves. I wondered if a solution of boiled white-gum bark applied to a man's skin was really any help in treating leprosy.

Some of the aboriginal people were afraid of the white Medicine Man. They understood circumcision and witch-doctoring at its worst . . . but not this man who came with the steel and glass mosquito.

Dr Langsford would say to the frightened ones: "Come on my boy, come and get a little mosquito bite. No more go inside, just outside, just in skin."

After one man had been bitten he muttered, "Mandaidj."

I translated for the doctor: "All right."

The doctor then said "Mandaidj" after each injection. As this was the only word he spoke at all, the people began to assume that he knew their language, and most of them came forward without fear, apparently in the irrational belief that a man who could say "All right" in the Mudbra dialect must know what he was doing.

But one day at Moolooloo a group of bush people who had been brought in for treatment ran away immediately they saw Dr Langsford with his red beard and his tableful of paraphernalia.

With another native, Bobby Bulgar, I was sent out in the Land Rover to bring them in. We found them in the dry bed of a river, crouched low while they walked and ran, trying to avoid detection while putting as much distance as possible between themselves and the white devil they had seen at the station. They were terrified, and I had to talk for a long time before persuading them to return with us.

Nor were they reassured when I began: "This doctor wants to take some of your blood. . . . "

"A-a-a-a-h! O-o-o-o-o-w!"

"Don't be silly. It won't hurt you," I said. "He also wants to listen to your heart with the stethoscope—the wireless pipe."

"E-e-e-e-h! O-o-o-o-o-w!"

"Don't be silly. You won't feel anything."

"That needle cheeky-one," they said, "Got 'im sting like wasp."

Finally I pacified them with a little witchdoctoring of my own. All aborigines believe that the vital essence in a man's life is his wind. Until recent years we had never known that the heart circulated blood constantly through the veins and arteries to keep the body alive. We believed that blood was dormant everywhere inside the skin.

But the wind was another matter: the heart, acting like a bellows, pumped it in and out of a man's body so that the spirit inside him could breathe. This was a fundamental belief and one that I knew I could exploit.

"The doctor wants to find out if you're losing your wind," I said. "He wants to listen to the wireless pipe and make sure you've got plenty to keep you going."

Thereafter the issue was never in doubt. They climbed into the back of the truck at once and were soon jostling one another for the lead in the queue, their arms and chests staunchly bared for any test the doctor might like to make.

"Me got plenty wind?" the first man asked him.

"Big mob," the doctor said. "Like hurricane inside."

The old man inhaled deeply and patted his cicatrized chest fondly. His face was transformed with a delighted smile. "Good-one," he said. "I got big-mob wind." No present I could think of would have been more valuable to him at that moment.

As these people were passing before him, I watched the doctor closely as he worked quickly with syringe, stethoscope, and his expert hands, searching always for the swellings in the vital ulna nerve near the elbow which would indicate leprosy.

189

When such a man came before him he said simply, "Old man, you've got that sickness. By-'n-by we'll take you to Darwin in the big aeroplane. What do you say to that? None of these other fellows here have been in an aeroplane. Just you. You'll be able to tell them all about it when you come back. Ah, well . . . I'll see you in Darwin."

Another leper had been located. His name was recorded, and on the next routine flight by the aerial ambulance he would be picked up and taken to the leprosarium . . . if, meanwhile, he hadn't run away.

Next day as the doctor called out the result of his Mantoux tests and Mrs Langsford entered them against the patient's name in a card-index system, I was fascinated by his patois.

"Plus Five, Negative!"

"Positive!"

"Have we got electric current in our body just like a motor car?" I asked.

"Not quite," he said. But he laughed as he examined the next man and said to his wife, for my benefit: "Flat battery!"

On we went to Wave Hill and to Hooker Creek settle-ment on the fringe of a desert Never-Never as big as any in the world. While we drove, and at our dinner-camps and night-camps, I explained to him as much as I knew about the petrol-filled arteries, the electrical nervous system, and the mechanical complex of arms and joints which kept our vehicle alive and moving.

"It can't live without petrol and it can't live without water," I said. "And we wouldn't get far without air in the tyres."

Dr Langsford told me about the human mechanism. "We need fuel and water and air, too," he said. "Without them we would die. The big difference between mechanical things and human beings is that we have a brain which enables us to think. Cars haven't got one."

"I'm not so sure," I said. "I've driven cars which were wilful and temperamental and had to be fought every inch of the way. Others are tractable and prepared to be guided."

Some of the aborigines we found at Hooker Creek were woolly primitives, north-western Wailbris who had come out of the desert from Tanami and beyond, an inhospitable, perishing wasteland where they nevertheless found enough water to stay alive.

I had heard about these nomadic tribes who still lived out there in conditions similar to those of my forefathers on the Roper more than a century ago, without contact with any other race, using the wooden and stone-headed spears we had forsaken in my grandfather's day. But whereas the Alawa had ample food and water—rivers and a boundless ocean containing fish, turtles, crocodiles, and dugong—life for the Wailbri and the even more primitive Pintubi must have been extraordinarily hard. I am pleased that we did not have to earn our crusts as desert tribesmen.

The history of the Pintubi is lost in antiquity. The remarkable story of how they have survived will probably never be written. As late as nineteen hundred and fifty-eight, government patrols found groups of them who had never before seen white men, or such commonplace articles as mirrors, combs, clothes of any kind, or basic foods—tea, flour, and sugar.

In ten thousand square miles of spinifex and sand straddling the borders of the Northern Territory and Western Australia a patrol found sixteen alleged sources of water, only four of which were permanent. The Pintubi followed failing seepages by digging into the hard ground with sharp sticks. One hole excavated with these crude implements was fifteen feet deep but contained no water.

Mullah rats with white-tipped tails are one of their major sources of food. The country is so poor and water so precious that kangaroos and rabbits are scarce. The rats are supplemented by succulent grubs found in the roots of the witchetty bush, the gum from mulga bushes and eucalypts, Yellimbaya seeds from which they make meal, galahs, cockatoos, desert sunflowers, and big yallah yams which yield both food and water.

Water is life to these people. In their dialect they have no word to distinguish between "water," "life," and "camp." The three are synonymous. Some of the seepages yield the merest trickle, often as little as one gallon in twenty-four hours. Entire clans live on such meagre storages, so that to the desert men the location of water is a tribal secret never betrayed to visitors from other tribes.

I wondered what they thought of me, a sophisticated black man who sprang from the same virile race which conquered the continent perhaps fifteen thousand years ago. What did they think of an aboriginal who had his hair cut, whose face was smooth, who wore clothes and shoes, who drove a motor vehicle? But if these things perplexed them, what must those who still live out in the No-White-Man's Land think about the aeroplanes that fly over their tribal country? What possible explanation could they have for these monstrous mechanical birds? How could men who had never seen a wheel explain machines that had forsaken wheels for wings?

And yet among these truly Stone-Age men and women I found my own proofs that we had common ancestors. A naked, woolly, utterly filthy old man approached me soon after I arrived and through an interpreter he asked, "What skin are you?"

"Bungadi," I said.

"Ah! I am your uncle," he said. "These are your nephews."

And within a few minutes young men who had not long been out of the desert were calling me "Uncle."

It was in this country that I first saw the tracks of an Abominable Foe-Man, the huge imprints of feet which I thought could belong only to some prehistoric cave-man. After all, stranger tracks had been seen in the Himalayas, and credence given to reports that they might be of human origin.

But my bewilderment was short-lived. Perhaps it was just as well that Bobby Bulgar was with me and able to explain, or I may have been down in the creek, crouched low and making good time away from there.

"Camel tracks," he said.

In a few minutes we caught up with the animal which had made them, a humped giant of dusty fawn, ruminating placidly, neither abominable nor foe, but a fine-furred friend to the Afghan teamsters who had brought it to the arid heart of the continent to transport supplies across the gibbers, across the sand dunes, across the spinifex infinities to the women of the west.

At every opportunity I continued to practise with the microscope, and soon I was using it like an expert pathologist. Dr Langsford showed me how to read slides and to test faeces for hookworm, threadworm, and tapeworm. Finally I was honoured by being asked to do this job at each station we visited.

One day the doctor said, "Phillip, would you like to listen-in to a chest on my stethoscope?"

Would I! This simple wireless-pipe which permitted auscultation of the heart and lungs had intrigued me for weeks.

I adjusted the ear-phones while Dr Langsford placed the receiver against the chest of an old aboriginal man.

"What do you hear?" he asked.

"Loose nuts and bolts," I said. "The tappets are noisy. Sounds like a worn gudgeon bearing. And a lot of piston slap."

He laughed, but I was serious. To me, the human body was an engine which misfired or sparked on all cylinders according to its age and maintenance. I could decide by listening to it whether an engine was in good running order. This one seemed to me at least to need a valve-grind.

"Forget about motors and then tell me what you hear," the doctor said.

"I can hear waves surging on to a beach, roaring on to the sand, some breaking more heavily than others. Here comes another now. . . ."

The old Wailbri tribesman who had suffered the indignity of having another aboriginal listen to his chest with a white man's device looked at the doctor and then put a forefinger to his temple.

"Might-be that feller need little bit oil along head, ain't it?" he said.

During my three months' stay with Dr Langsford he paid me from his own pocket. He was working long hours for the government health service as a medical officer in a remote part of the world where the help of another man was often necessary. The government, however, had decided that he did not rate a personal factotum. He therefore paid me himself.

I have always been grateful because that trip marked the turning point in my life. Although I was to return to my tribe at Roper River I would never forget the experience of being with a doctor on patrol. It gave me an understanding of the great need my people had for medical care. Later, when the chance came again for me to contribute to this, I did not hesitate, and in the year nineteen hundred and sixty-two I am still working as a hospital orderly and ambulance driver.

But not only did Dr Langsford pay me a salary. On our return to Darwin he paid air and train fares for my wife and family to join me there on a holiday.

This was the first time Hannah Dulban the Wandarang, wife of Waipuldanya the Alawa, had visited any settlement bigger than Roper River mission.

The shops, the endless rows of houses, the neon lights, the hundreds of cars and trucks: all these fascinated and frightened her. Fear finally overcame fascination, and she asked to go back home, back to the open country where the wallabies came from the Fat and Juicy Place, back to Larbaryandji, the tribal land of her husband, back to the barramundi and the turtle eggs and the lily roots. She wanted to be away from the City of Big Things and Bad Things: Opperlong Casserty on the wide screen, clandestine liquor in the bushes and mosquito-ridden swamps behind Bagot Settlement, salacity and immorality among heterogeneous groups whose lack of tribal entity had demolished their Dreamtime laws.

"Fares please, Doctor Langsford." And he paid for Hannah and the children to return to the Roper. He wanted to pay for me, too, but I thought it was time I cast off my civilized clothes and became an aboriginal again . . . before I lost my ability to track and to hunt and to walk endlessly on.

I told Hannah: "I will join you at the Roper. I will walk from Mataranka. I am in need of a hunting holiday."

Soon after Christmas, in the heat and electric fury of a tropical summer, I met an old native trader on the banks of the Waterhouse River near the point where it is adjacent to the Stuart Highway.

"I am wanting spears for a journey," I said. "Two shovel-spears and two fish spears. I have money and tobacco to exchange."

"You will travel far?" he asked.

"To Larbaryandji," I said. "To the Alawa beyond the Roper Bar. To my family who are there. To my father Barnabas Gabarla. To my Uncle Stanley Marbunggu. To Sam Ulagang the Hunter and Horse-breaker. . . ."

"It is a far place," he said. "You will be many moons on the track."

"By the white man's way it is one hundred and fifty miles," I said. "By my reckoning it will take only two moons. I have many friends to see on the way: the Mangarai at Elsey station where The Old Maluka lies buried; the Nalakan in the Roper Valley; the Yangman at Moroak; the Ritarrngu at Urapunga."

"You will have gifts to carry?"

"Yes," I said, and thought: "I'll bet I'll be laden like a pack-camel once this old gossip tells the world where I am going."

"I will get you the spears," he said.

For two months thereafter I lived as my ancestors had lived, hunting wallabies and goannas as Sam Ulagang had taught me, spearing barramundi as I had learnt to do as a child, digging lily roots from the billabongs, cooking my food with fire I made with a Budular firestick.

I waded creeks and swam rivers, floating my clothes and gifts ahead of me on a Wanbiribiri raft of sticks, paperbark and vines, a shovel-spear facing backwards from me as I swam to meet the probing snout of any crocodile that might decide to follow. I had to be ready to jab it quickly, to fight for my life in muddy rivers with foul-breathed monsters.

They left me in peace, to hunt as I wished, to fish when the fish were ready to be bitten, to walk naked through the rain and the intermittent sun, to shiver and sweat and at night to crawl under the crude humpy I built of sheet-bark I pulled from the trees.

I was an independent man again, living off the un-contaminated land, a tenant of my Roper River heritage, freed from the harness of civilization, freed from slavery to Flour, Sugar and Tea, my wits sharpened to the pitch of a human animal, my old fears returning as I walked, watching behind me always for the Burgingin pygmies, my eyes piercing deep into the heart of every bush to examine its secrets before I passed.

The rains came and I was saturated. Forked lightning split the trees around me and was thunderously applauded by the raucous hounds in heaven.

At Elsey station, the Never-Never home of Aeneas Gunn, a man said to me: "You are travelling to Roper Mission. My poor old mother is there. I would like you to take this gift to her."

He handed me a piece of calico and a notched Message Stick. He pointed to one of the cuts and said, "Tell her I am thinking about her." He touched another cut and said, "Say that I am well." And another: "Say that her grand-children are well." There were several other cuts on the small stick and I was given a message relating to each of them.

At Moroak a man said to me: "You are travelling to Roper Mission. My poor uncle is there. I would like you to take this gift to him." He handed me a Message Stick and said: "Tell him . . ."

At Roper Bar a man said to me: "You are travelling to Roper Mission. My poor old wife is there in the hospital. I would like you to take this gift to her." He handed me a Message Stick and said: "Tell her . . ."

As I predicted before beginning my holiday I was an unpaid postman laden with Christmas parcels long before I reached the Mission. Each of them was accompanied by a Message Stick, which meant that I had to remember dozens of personal details about them all.

The last forty miles of my walk was through constant bog. I was often ankle deep and sometimes knee deep in mud and running water, and I was encumbered like a Santa Claus. The Wanbiribiri rafts had to be bigger to carry the presents across creeks and rivers. When I stalked a kangaroo I always had to return to the parcels I had left under a tree, sometimes miles from the point of the kill.

But if word from the old trader on the Waterhouse had gone forward to my intermediate staging places, it had also reached my destination at Roper Mission.

Roger Gunbukbuk, the man who had broken his hips as a boy when he fell from a horse, came out to meet me with Dennis Murulbur.

"The poor old man is sure to be carrying presents," they said. "We had better help him in."

One day as I waded through the mud, alert as ever for the evil spirits which might dwell there, I became aware of a black figure moving in the distance.

"Mulunguwa on the prowl," I thought. "I'll have to be careful."

Then I saw two men wave to me and I recognized my friends.

No suburban postman on his final Christmas Eve delivery was ever more relieved than I to be helped with his burden.

Five months earlier I had left the Roper as the sophisticated assistant of a white doctor, skilled in machinery, having since acquired a cursory knowledge of what made the human engine purr.

Now I returned as my forefathers had always returned from the hunt: on foot, near-naked, carrying the spears which had sustained me while I walked and swam one hundred and fifty miles, the spears which had protected me from the Burgingin pygmies and the crocodiles, and gave me illogical comfort when the Yamindji thunder-giants fought and old Gubidjidji the Rain Man was making the heavenly women cry.

Chapter Fifteen

MY welcome home was like none I had known before, overwhelming and embarrassing in the profound respect my tribesmen showed me.

They knew I had travelled to distant aboriginal nations with a white doctor. Word had sped ahead of me that I was his medical assistant, a man who could dress wounds and use a microscope and a hypodermic syringe, but I scarcely expected they would naively credit me with abilities I did not possess.

The extent to which I had been raised in their estimation was impressed upon me one morning while I was helping Sister James in the mission hospital.

I was treating suppurating sores on the arms of a small girl when I heard an old man at the door inquiring for the doctor.

Sister James said: "The doctor isn't here. He is coming next month on the medical plane."

"I want Doctor Waipuldanya," he said gravely.

"Doctor Waip——"

"Wadjiri-Wadjiri," he said, using my other name. And then, when he saw the Sister was still puzzled, he added: "Phillip."

"Oh, Phillip!" Sister James said. She began to laugh. "He's not a doctor . . . not yet, anyway."

"You-ai!" the old man corrected her indignantly. "Him properly Alawa doctor now, all-a-same white-feller way." He would never understand that a doctor must train for six years in a University and pass many examinations.

"Well, anyway, what's the matter with you?" Sister said impatiently. "Perhaps I'll do?"

"No-more, no-more, must have Doctor Waipuldanya!"

Sister James was a qualified nursing sister with years of experience. Her knowledge was immensely superior to mine. She had certificates to prove it, and I had none. That didn't impress the old tribesman: she was a woman and I was a man, and therein lay an absolute distinction to any aboriginal.

I finished dressing the piccaninny and walked out as he was repeating his demand: "Must have Waipuldanya. . . ."

"What's the matter, old man?" I asked, assuming my best bedside manner. Sister James seemed a little miffed.

"Ah, Waipuldanya . . . Doctor . . . I am crook . . . properly crook. . . ."

"Where?"

"Here . . . on my leg . . . I need rubbing-medicine."

Having rejected the Sister and insisted on my treating him, the old man had now prescribed for himself.

Sister James laughed again, her professional huff dissolved. She handed me a bottle of liniment, and I applied some gently to his eager thigh.

Next morning he was back with a dozen of his friends, all with sore legs, all wanting me to treat them with rubbing-medicine. Now it was impossible to stop the spread of my fame as a doctor.

"My leg properly-better, no-more-little-bit," the old man said. "Doctor Waipuldanya fix 'im. He good man all right, that doctor. I savvy that time he fix 'im motor car engine, make 'im go like new one. He doctor of car, now he doctor of man, too."

My life at the mission, thereafter, was like that of a famous specialist at a cocktail party. Men and women plagued me night and day with their pains in the chest, pains in the tummy, pains in the head, sore legs, sore arms, and sore eyes.

"Doctor Waipuldanya fix 'im?" they asked.

What could I do but hand out rubbing-medicine, binjy-medicine, and aspirin? I cured more potentially fatal illnesses with aspirin, if the patients were to be believed, than even the druggists claimed possible for their pills.

That was the situation a month later when I heard that Dr Jim Tarleton Rayment was to visit the mission with a portable X-ray plant to conduct a tuberculosis survey. My esteem was soon to be put to the test in pacifying men, women, and children who regarded the machine as an infernal invention of the devil which miraculously looked inside their skins and magically drew a picture of their bones.

During my visit to Darwin with Dr Langsford I saw an X-ray plant being operated, but I had not seen a developed negative. I was a little disappointed when I first did: from such a complicated camera I had expected extraordinary photographs, at least in colour and three-dimensional. What I saw instead was a rather fuzzy black and white outline of a skeleton. But I was suitably impressed when I realized that the camera had taken a picture of bones inside a man's skin which could not be seen by the human eye.

"Ah, yes," I admitted to myself, "that's clever all right."

When Dr. Tarleton Rayment arrived I was introduced to him by the mission superintendent, Percy Leske. He was a pleasant man, fond of trying to play the didgeredoo and failing in such a comical way that we all laughed uproariously. I think it was a great blow to his pride when his ten-year-old son, Jimmy, began to play it. It was a blow to my pride, too, because I had never been able to get a sound from one.

"I know all about you from Dr Langsford," he said. "I would like you to be my assistant. We will work here at the mission, and then go to Rose River, Groote Eylandt, and Umbakumba." I was happy with the arrangement, and so we began shooting.

Dr Rayment showed me how to load the casettes and how to develop the film in a portable canvas dark-room.

These duties kept me busy, but I still had to find time, after the first few photographs had been taken and exhibited, to pacify people who were afraid.

"Get ready . . . now hold your wind," I would say. And grown men struggled manfully not to betray their terror.

They were familiar with portraits which showed the skin, face, eyes, nose, mouth, and body, and joked about them. But they did not joke about a bone picture. That was different, something they did not comprehend.

I held up the first negative I developed and said to an old man, Jackie Ilianyinyi, whose chest it showed: "There you are, old man; that's what you are like inside your skin."

He looked at it perplexedly for a moment and then began to wail. "Ah! Poor feller me!" he shouted. "I'm a devil, a spirit."

To the aboriginal mind, bones mean death, and death means devils or spirits. Many of the people believed that by looking at their bones they were seeing their spirits.

"I'll be like that when I die . . . only bone!" a woman cried.

"Ah-h-h-h-h! We'll all go like that some day. Poor feller we!"

"Like buffalo," another said, remembering a skeleton.

"No-more, no-more. Him like kangaroo, standing up."

"Debbil-debbil! A-h-h-h! Only debbil-debbil inside our skin."

The X-ray photographs showed them, too starkly, what they must expect in the future: death, decay of the flesh, and exposure of their bones on the Gulla-Gulla burial platforms.

I explained patiently and repeatedly, reassuring every person who saw his own photograph: "This is a magic machine. It sees inside you, but it is not looking for spirits. It finds disease. It helps to keep you alive. If The Sickness is there the doctor will be able to see it and treat you with medicine before it is too late."

Few of them were convinced. And the Nungubuyu at Rose River were even more terrified than the Alawa. They had had less contact with white doctors. Several ran into the bush when the first photographs were shown.

But I was enjoying it all. Dr Rayment had trained me to operate the machine. I knew how to reduce the exposure to three seconds for a child or increase it to five seconds for a man. I mixed the developing and fixing chemicals and later he showed me how to read the negatives. Within a few weeks I regarded myself as a trained X-ray technician.

Whether I was or not, Dr Rayment allowed me to do much of the photographing unaided. At Groote Eylandt I was joined in this work by an Andilyaugwan tribesman, Billy Nabilya, who subsequently went to Darwin to become a trained laboratory assistant and then went back to his country to work among his people.

It was inevitable during a survey such as this that we should find many cases of tuberculosis. Infected people were flown into Darwin hospital for treatment. Most of them survived and were returned happily to their tribes. Men and women I photographed years ago are still brought in for regular routine checks. In this way the spread of tuberculosis, which had been decimating my people, is kept in check.

During this period my knowledge of elementary medicine expanded rapidly and my reputation grew alarmingly. Every day we treated dozens of people for sore ears, blepharitis, trachoma, yaws, and other diseases common among aborigines. Sadly, we continued to find a large number suffering from leprosy.

As Dr Langsford had done, Dr Rayment explained to me how to detect its presence by examining the ulna nerve near the elbow, by physical changes which may have taken place on the face, nose and limbs, especially if lesions were apparent.

Because it had killed my mother and been responsible for banishing my brother from society for twelve years, I began to regard it as my personal enemy. But our weapons to combat it were inadequate. Although we did what we could, I felt a sense of frustration every time we found a new patient. I thought it was unreasonable that medical scientists who had developed cures for other malignant diseases, and had such clever apparatus as the X-ray machine for spying behind the human skin, should remain baffled by a malady which pre-dated Christianity.

Later that year, after a few months' work in the Darwin laboratory, I flew with Dr Rayment and the X-ray equipment to Yirrkalla, on the extreme north-eastern tip of Arnhem Land, to conduct a chest survey among the Jabu, the Gomaid, the Dalwangu, the Mangalilli, the Gobaboingu, and the Jambaboingo.

These northern Arnhem Landers, according to the historians, are direct descendants of the Dravidians from India and Ceylon, who are believed to have crossed to Australia either on rafts or a land bridge which was said to exist many thousands of years ago.

Their blood then became mixed with that of the Malay and Macassar traders who came down in ocean-going prahus long before the first white navigators visited the South Seas. It has since been diluted with blood from a hundred other tribes, but the traces of Asia are still visible in some of their features.

I had made earlier visits to Yirrkalla and knew enough of the mother tongue, Jambaboingo, and the father tongue, Gobaboingu, to be able to interpret for the doctor. As with my own Alawa people on the Roper, three hundred miles away, I explained to these wild men and women why we had brought the X-ray machine and what we proposed to do with it.

When Dr Rayment was recalled to Darwin I stayed to help the mission sister in breaking down the old tribal prejudices to medical skill. A month later I took my precious equipment aboard the mission lugger, Larrapan, and sailed west to Elcho Island and then to Goulburn Island, where Dr Rayment rejoined me.

At Goulburn Island I had my first contact with the Maung tribe, which must have been something like the first meeting between Negroes and Indians. Although I had lived all my life only four hundred miles from Goulburn Island, I had never heard of the Maung. Nor could I speak their language. Goulburn Island is separated from the Roper by the rugged Arnhem Land escarpment, and until I arrived there had never been any contact between our tribes.

We were similar only in that they had black skin and so did I. The Yirrkalla tribes observed the Kunapipi, so I at least had that in common with them, but it was unknown on Goulburn. I might just as well have been in the West Indies. I was a foreigner in a foreign land—and yet, when our language barrier was eventually removed, I found that here also I had brothers and sisters, a father and a mother and, inevitably, a taboo mother-in-law.

We conversed in English, so that as an interpreter I was at first quite useless. But soon I could "hear" their talk and within a month I knew enough for us to be able to discard English. In this way, during several years' work with the Arnhem Landers, I learnt fourteen separate languages.

Nor was that as easy as it may appear. There were times when, except for the useful contribution I felt I was making to their acceptance of medicine, I was tempted to abandon it all. Our languages have become complicated with many impurities imported from other cultures. I was often confused by different meanings for the same word. In the Jabu tribe at Yirrkalla, "boiyuga" means "fire," but at Maningrida it means "wild apple." The Andilyaugwan word for "fire" is "ungura." The Ngulkpun at Mainoru call it "ngura."

Relate this kind of confusion to only one hundred words in fifty tribes and the number of permutations becomes incalculable. But, of course, I had to worry about more than one hundred words, and in the Northern Territory alone there are at least two hundred remaining tribal groups.

Not one of them has a dictionary!

Although I was separated from my family for long periods, I was now happier than I had been since reaching adulthood. I had a sense of achievement and personal satisfaction. My life was beginning to mean more than I had ever dreamed possible.

While I lived as a tribal aboriginal along the Roper in the Larbaryandji land I still call My Country, a future of semi-nomadism was my only prospect. Sufficient unto the day were the kangaroos and wallabies thereof. Like the tribesmen in the Time of Dream, I was concerned only with daily food and water and my place as a Djungayi in the celebration of our rituals.

Yet now, having broken away from the tribal bonds, having come to appreciate that there could be more to life than hunting and tracking, I was conscious of a frustration. I identified it on a day at Croker Island half-caste colony when Dr Rayment said: "Phillip, I must return to Darwin. But I have a job for you—a job that you, alone, can do."

I wondered if this was a polite way of saying that he had no further use for me, or that he had lost faith in me.

We had worked together for many months, and I had always tried to be attentive. I had missed no appointments. I had never, in the unfortunate tradition of my people, forsaken the job for a hunting walkabout when I was most urgently needed. On the contrary, I had put all my tribal ways behind me and attempted to live and behave in the Whitefeller Way.

What he now proposed was that I should resume my life as a blackfellow!

"I want you to go on a big walkabout . . . " he said. This was the customary form of dismissal on cattle stations for an aboriginal whose usefulness had ended, and I was well aware of it.

I was stunned. Was my hand to be prised from the rung I was grasping and had reached after abnormal application? Was I to be cast adrift from the society I was trying to enter while on the very threshold? Was my grip on the New World to be loosened at the moment when I thought it was tightening? Could I be lifted up and thrown down like a yo-yo at the whim of a white man? Was I his to dispose of as he thought fit?

"A walkabout!" I was furious and shouted at him. "A walkabout!" My heart was leaden.

"Yes, a walkabout," he repeated. "A big walkabout. . . . " And then, aware at last of my disappointment, he said: "Phillip, this is a walkabout with a difference . . . a Medical Walkabout. I want you to go out and treat your people who are wandering in the bush . . . the nomads . . . the Maung, the Walang, the Iwaija families who live in Arnhem Land between here and Oenpeli . . . along Cooper's Creek . . . along the Murgenella and the Birraduk. You are the only man who could do it."

His voice was soft. His eyes sparkled as he watched the transformation of my face, the smile that replaced the grief he had seen. My spirit soared and in that moment I loved this white man who had been my friend as we worked together for the people we both loved, a white man who laboured for black men until, a year later, a heart attack killed him.

I had the answer to my frustration.

"I'll go," I said eagerly. "When?"

"As soon as you're ready," he said. "Take two men with you as porters and interpreters. I notice you've been speaking English to the Iwaija people here. You don't know their language?" He missed nothing.

"Just a little," I said. "Not enough. I'm learning."

"We have had reports of leprosy in the area," he said, "and I wouldn't be surprised if the victims are being hidden by the tribes. They're still not too keen about going to the leprosarium. If you find lepers you'll have to do some fast talking and persuade them to come in. Take a medical kit with you and treat all the sores and sickness you think you can correctly diagnose. I can't tell you any more than that. You've got a lot of walking ahead of you."

"How far?" I asked. "Not that it matters."

"Who knows?" he said. "If you find the tribes on the direct route between here and Oenpeli it wouldn't be more than about one hundred and fifty miles. But if you have to go looking for them . . . well, your guess is as good as mine. There are no roads, and the only way the job can be done is on foot."

Next day, with Dick Yamara and Jimmy Bunbiaga of the Iwaija tribe, I crossed the Bowen Strait from Croker Island to the mainland in a dugout canoe. Dick and Jimmy were to be my interpreters and guides in a country in which I was a foreigner. Within a few days I was thinking of myself as a black Dr Livingstone boldly crossing unknown land to bring succour to strange people. And I would be surprised if the difficulties I had to overcome were not often comparable with those faced by that great man who first penetrated the African wilderness.

Our troubles began after we had ported the canoe across the narrow isthmus that leads into the Coburg Peninsula and separates the Arafura Sea from Van Diemen's Gulf. Having reached the gulf, we decided to paddle along the coast for a few miles to native wells which Jimmy and Dick said contained fresh water. But each time we landed the well was dry. Before long the meagre supply we carried was exhausted. We paddled along silently under a blazing dry-season sun reflecting viciously from the water, silently because we wanted to keep our mouths closed and the salt-air out.

Late in the afternoon we found brackish water. I boiled some and after adding sugar drank it. It tasted like rather unpleasant cough mixture, but who was I to worry about taste when my thirst was raging?

At dusk, after I had been led to other brackish and salty wells, I began to have doubts about my guides' knowledge of the country. I ordered that we should paddle all night to the mouth of Murgenella Creek. When we reached it at daylight Jimmy said, "Water over here," and led the way to a well in the sand. That was brackish, too, but our luck changed a few hours later with a deep hole of clear fresh water.

I decided at once that this should be the starting point for our walk eastward to link up with the Iwaija, Maung and Walang nomads I had come to find.

The canoe was pulled into the shade above high-water mark and the undergrowth cleared away so that it should not be destroyed by bushfires while we were absent.

At dawn we began a walk into the Arnhem Land interior. For the first time in my life I was equipped with a rifle we had brought from Croker Island. Nevertheless, we each had a wire spear as well . . . you can't spear fish with a rifle.

Apart from these weapons we carried only tomahawks and my precious bag of medicines. We had neither food nor water, but Dick and Jimmy solemnly assured me there was plenty of both on our track. We each had one article of clothing—a loincloth—and we were barefooted.

Our journey that day took us through billabong country that changed dramatically from the arid coastal strip. Here was water in abundance, here were ducks and yams, wild buffalo, and wild cattle, Timor ponies, and deer, a land in which even a blind man would neither starve nor perish.

Towards dusk on the second day Dick, who was leading, stopped suddenly and said, "Ah! Tracks. Iwaijas."

"Travelling east," Jimmy said.

"Might-be south," Dick said, after he had circled the area.

"Could be north," I said.

As we had come from the west this diversity of opinion meant only that none of us were sure which way the tracks led. They were old, and superimposed upon them were the footprints of animals and birds. I was convinced that these were the people I sought. But which way had they walked? There were no signposts, no forwarding addresses, no defined paths, nothing except the enigma of north, south, or east.

"We'll sleep on it," I said. "One of us might have a dream to show us the way."

"They went east," Jimmy said adamantly.

"Might-be south," Dick said.

"Could-be north," I said.

We shot a young Zebu bull and grilled delicious steaks on the coals of our camp-fire, eating with our fingers as we sat cross-legged on the ground. And then, like the guests at a Roman bacchanalia, we toppled forward and slept, without blankets, without pillows, wild black men whose dusty bodies matched the colour of their earthen mattresses, sophisticated men who were returning to the animal habits of their bush ancestors, one of them a trained medical assistant who was going out to treat his fellows.

"Dr Rayment should see me now!" I thought, and fell asleep, my face in the dirt.

As the piccaninny daylight pulled back the first sheet of night I threw a piece of wood on the camp-fire and grilled myself another piece of last night's meat. The spluttering fat and the spiralling aroma soon tickled Dick and Jimmy awake.

"I bin dream . . . I bin dream . . . I bin dream . . . " Dick said sleepily as he stood up and stretched. "I bin dream about tracks going east, tracks going north, tracks going south, tracks going round in circles, tracks climbing trees, tracks going down holes, tracks in the sky, tracks on the salt-water. But none of them Iwaija tracks."

Jimmy said: "I bin dream about a track, too. I see this track going along . . . might-be east, I think . . . and I follow 'im. But then he stop. No man there, nuttin' . . . his track just stop in middle of stride and 'im disappear. I was just going to work out what happened when somebody woke me up."

I said, "I was dreamless. Nuttin' dream." But as the leader of the party, and having suggested that the tracks might have led north, I had to assert my authority.

"We'll go north," I said.

The dust on our bodies was allowed to remain there as sunburn cream. I have heard that black skins are supposed to be immune from the sun, but that is not so. I have often suffered, especially when I come out into the sun after wearing a shirt or working in a building for several months.

In the late afternoon we came to a billabong that was strangely barren of wild life. Nor, when we searched, were fish visible.

"Gumba!" Dick said.

"Gumba! Gumba!" The dialect word for underwater hunting!

We threw off our loin-cloths and dived down to the slimy bottom, prospecting the turtle-rich reed beds, mining the opaque veins of mud and waterlogged rubbish with bare hands until we felt the smooth surface of the ore we sought: turtle-shell, with slow indignant flesh attached to it, too tired to get out of its own way, too astonished to avoid the black fingers clutching a flipper, and rudely transplanting it from water to camp-fire coals.

On our first dive Jimmy, Dick, and I each got one, which we ate for supper. Then we went back into the billabong for tomorrow's lunch—another three—which we would carry alive in our swags until cooking time.

The crocodiles will get you if you don't watch out! The warnings of my youth were with me always as I floundered in the brown opacity. Tributary billabongs in Arnhem Land must be approached with crocodiles in mind and, indeed, on this occasion I felt the serrated tail and the horny back of a fresh-water fish-eater, a five-footer which stayed in its bed of ooze while I fondled its back. Experience had taught me that a submerged fresh-water crocodile will not move when touched. But in these circumstances it is difficult to be sure that the one you are caressing is not a salt-water man-eater. Gumba, therefore, is not without thrills.

Three days later, still walking barefoot, still without finding another trace of my nomadic patients, we turned south-east towards Cooper's Creek. At dusk we had been without food for twenty-four hours. I was hot and tired, distressingly dirty, with a raging thirst, and as hungry as the primitive hunter I had become.

As we approached our night-camp waterhole, fetid with drying mud and dying fish, Dick said, "Sh-h! Buffalo!"

He indicated the direction by pointing with the corner of his mouth, and there, in a wallow, were twelve wild descendants of domestic animals imported more than a century earlier by the first British settlers at Port Essington on the Cobourg Peninsula. When the settlers departed the buffaloes came south-east through the narrow isthmus and spread to the coastal plains around the East Alligator, the South Alligator, the West Alligator, the Mary and the Adelaide Rivers flowing down into Van Diemen's Gulf. Here they found the lush green pastures, the billabongs, the mudholes for wallowing . . . and an almost complete absence of human beings. Within one hundred years a few of these beasts had become half a million.

And there, fifty yards away, were twelve of them now, prime beef hanging in folds from their briskets and rumps, steaks for the camps of blackfellows. But be careful! Coolies might have driven and ridden their ancestors, but these were wild animals, majestically equipped with horned armament, eight feet from tip to tip, poised to penetrate the paper-hides of human intruders.

Quietly sneak-up . . . quiet-feller now. Dick discarded his narga in case it should become a peg on which he would be hoisted high by the mighty horns. There was little cover except for a near-by clump of pandanus. Jimmy and I hid behind it while Dick crawled, naked, on his belly, inching his way forward with the rifle, careful not to raise dust. Thirty yards from the wallow he sprang up and whooped, waited long enough to see that the startled beasts were running from him and not at him, and dropped a small bull with his first shot.

Camp-fire-grilled buffalo steak and yams, with lily roots and murky swamp water have probably never been written on any menu by a French chef. I doubt that they serve them at Maxims or the Savoy. But out in Arnhem Land where there are no tables, no plates, no cutlery, and no napkins except the hair and the beard on which to wipe greasy fingers . . . well, the absence of an *à la* or so does not seem to matter. After a few days of living like this, with grime adhering to my matted whiskers, I looked like a nomad who might never have seen civilization. I was a renegade from the basic precepts of the hygiene I had been preaching.

Next day we climbed Tor Rock, one of the few natural features in the area, and surveyed the limitless plain for Travellers' Smoke. We could distinguish this from bush-fire smoke only if walkabout natives were lighting fires as they moved against the wind.

Nothing we saw indicated that another human being shared with us the vast immensity of Arnhem Land, but our luck was soon to change.

Near the headwaters of Cooper's Creek Jimmy stopped and said: "H'm. I smell something."

We sniffed the air like wild animals trying to detect the scent of an enemy. I identified it at once.

"Fish cooking," I said.

"Who would be cooking fish out here?" Dick asked.

"They can only be the people we are searching for," I said.

Jimmy said: "But we haven't cut tracks. We haven't seen smoke except from bushfires. We haven't heard any people or dogs."

"Nevertheless," I said, "there are people camped somewhere within half a mile of this spot. Fish don't jump out of the water and cook themselves."

Five minutes later, as we walked on quietly, we heard dogs barking and children laughing. Then I saw that we were approaching a creek.

"There they are!" Dick said.

A piccaninny looked up and pointed at us. "Someone come," he shouted.

Men who had been sitting around a dying camp-fire jumped to their feet and reached for shovel-spears, the automatic reaction of any aboriginal who is surprised in the bush, but they relaxed at once when they identified Dick and Jimmy.

We were given the sign to approach the camp, without which another step forward may have been regarded as an intrusion.

The group of about twenty Iwaija people had been in the bush for a year, happily separated from the great civilization represented by the city of Darwin only two hundred miles away, aloof even from their own tribal people at Croker Island mission. The men wore brief nargas, and the women calico lap-laps, some of them made from old flour-bags. The children were naked. They were living entirely off the land, supporting themselves as the tribes had done long before Captain Cook crossed the equator.

I was still unable to "hear" the Iwaija tongue, but I did understand Dick's references to "doctor" and "medicine" as he explained to these simple people why we had walked almost two hundred miles searching for them. We were invited to stay, and that night I shared their camp-fire and their meal of fish, turtles, yams, and lily roots.

At sunset I began a medical examination. I had eaten their food with my fingers, without washing, but before the medical kit was opened I remembered my training. I "scrubbed up" in the creek, combed my hair and beard, and disinfected my hands with a most professional air. I laid out kidney dishes, medicines, antiseptics, soap, and towels.

"The surgery is now open," I told Dick.

"The doctor is ready," he said.

I treated and bandaged a ten-year-old girl whose entire body was covered with sores, and a seven-year-old suffering from yaws. I could smell the infection long before she was brought to me. Then they all discovered sores or pains and insisted on treatment. Fortunately I had plenty of aspirin, and they were content with that.

None of them were allowed to approach the doctor before washing thoroughly with soap.

"Doctor's orders," Dick told them. "You can't go near him while you're dirty."

This was inexplicable to them. An hour earlier we had been sitting in the dust together, taking turns to scoop flesh from a barramundi carcass with our grubby fingers. When the clinic closed, segregation ceased and I rejoined them around the fire.

Next morning I removed the bandages, now filthy, from the two girls, and treated them again. The condition of the one with yaws, seen in daylight, called for drastic action. I boiled a billyful of muddy water to sterilize needles, and from the capacious pockets of my bag produced a hypodermic syringe. And there beside a creek, around a nomads' camp-fire in a Never-Never corner of Arnhem Land, Dr Waipuldanya gave an expert injection of penicillin. Dick and Jimmy, my unpaid orderlies, and the girl's father were needed to hold her still while the black monster with the huge mosquito bite descended upon her.

My examination of the others disclosed no traces of leprosy, but I decided to wait at the creek until I had given the girl a full course of penicillin. After the second injection I explained to the old men that I would need to stay another two or three days.

But they had a better plan. "We'll walk with you," they said, "and you can treat her as we go along."

And so it happened that this odd retinue set out for the coast and our canoe—an Alawa medical assistant whom they insisted on calling "doctor," accompanied by two orderlies and twenty naked patients, all of us walking barefoot, hunting as we travelled, sharing the burdens of spears, rifles and medical kit, stopping twice a day to sterilize my needles and treat a girl who had become a complaisant patient.

Three days later, as we neared the coast, I saw that she was better. I had walked two hundred and fifty miles to cure her. My fee was a shy smile, but my reward beyond price. As I stepped into the canoe and Dick and Jimmy began paddling towards the mouth of the East Alligator River on our way to Oenpelli, the girl flashed her brilliant teeth, came to me slowly and whispered something which Dick interpreted:

"That mosquito doesn't hurt now."

"Jara, you mob!" Dick said.

"Wee-aa!" I said. "Goodbye." And I added: "Dju-Dju nama yallala. I'll see you later."

But I never did.

Chapter Sixteen

FOR having bitten a few people with steel mosquitoes my sins were visited upon me with cruel interest.

In nineteen hundred and fifty-seven the Northern Territory Director of Health, Dr Alfred H. Humphry, told me that scientists at Sydney University wanted a large number of anopheles mosquitoes for malarial research.

"I thought you should go to the Roper River and catch a few thousands for us," he said.

I agreed, and was flown back to my Larbaryandji tribal country.

How does one catch mosquitoes in thousands? I experimented with traps and nets, but had to abandon these methods as impracticable. I was finally convinced that the only way to do it was to catch them singly—after each one had embedded its sting in my skin!

With two pieces of rubber hose, some gauze and a bottle, I made a suction gun, exposed myself along the river bank and around billabongs where anopheles bred, and began sucking them through the hose and into the bottle as they bit me. Then I killed them with chloroform.

I was a human pin-cushion and soon had thousands, which I sent off to Darwin. One night I went out with a billygoat on a lead, and another night with a horse, because the scientists also wanted to establish which mosquitoes bit animals. While they were doing so, of course, furious clouds of their mates were dive-bombing me!

My Alawa tribesmen shook their heads sadly.

"Might-be Doctor Waipuldanya sick-along-head," they said. "Might-be more-better if we get that medical plane for him."

The spectacle of a man exposing himself to mosquitoes, sucking them into a bottle, and then leading harmless goats and horses out to be bitten was beyond their comprehension. But I was rewarded for my pain. One day a telegram came from Dr Humphry: "A conference is to be held at Noumea, New Caledonia, on hygiene among native peoples. Would you like to go? Expenses paid."

I accepted at once. A fortnight later, at Darwin airport, I climbed up the steps of an Air France plane for a direct flight to Noumea. I was the first aboriginal from the Roper River known to leave Australia since my people settled there in the Dreamtime, and I might have been the first from any tribe in the Northern Territory.

At the top of the steps a uniformed hostess said: "Bon soir, monsieur!"

"Uh?" My mouth dropped open.

"Bon soir, monsieur. Voici votre place, s'il vous plaît."

"Uh? Sounds like Iwaija," I muttered, and then took refuge in the barbaric pidgin phrase: "Me no savvy."

"Oh, I'm sorry," she said, in perfect English. "Good night, sir. This is your seat."

In Noumea I also had language trouble, but no difficulty in understanding the English text of a cable from Dr Humphry delivered to me while I was there: "Tarleton Rayment died suddenly in Sydney."

For the remainder of that day I could not concentrate on the lectures. My mind was back at the Roper with Dr Rayment, listening to old Jimmy Ilianyinyi wailing about the X-ray photograph of his chest: "Poor feller me! Me proper debbil-debbil inside my skin."

I was now more determined than ever to continue working in the field of medicine. To make it easier, an American lecturer, Lyn Keyes, told us in great detail how native medical assistants could help in promoting health and hygiene among their own people. He also gave us some sound advice on getting the co-operation of tribal witchdoctors.

Less than a year later I was putting this unique training into practice in my first head-on clash with a Dr Blackfellow since I had been "sung" on that walkabout at Mount Saint Vidgeon . . . in my boyhood . . . oh, so long ago.

Maningrida is a new aboriginal settlement that has risen in primeval bushland at the mouth of the Liverpool River in north-central Arnhem Land, as remote from The Whitefeller Way when I went there as Lambarene was for Dr Albert Schweitzer when he first sailed up the Ogowe River in the Belgian Congo.

Like the Ogowe, the upper reaches of the Liverpool, in the area around Havelock Falls, are a secret locked away by terrain so inhospitable that not more than two white men are known to have been there.

The river winds down through rugged escarpments and towering ranges which are seldom penetrated even by the Berara and Gunavidji tribesmen whose country it is: they stay on the plains adjacent to the estuaries of the mighty Liverpool and its myriad tributaries, forsaking the heart of darkness because, as one of them paradoxically told me: "It's proper blackfeller country."

The Arafura coast, with an estuarine harbour where it is fed by the Liverpool, was a convenient shelter for the Macassar traders. And now the river has something else in common with the Ogowe: blood containing the insidious heritage of leprosy.

Maningrida was my home for nine months while I cared for a group of twenty lepers, some of them in an advanced stage of physical rottenness, and treated hundreds of other people suffering from sores, yaws, blood poisoning, spear wounds, and terrible abrasions inflicted in tribal fights. The Berara and the Gunavidji are warlike people. I was not there long before the daily parade through my medical post in a tent looked like a casualty clearing station on a battlefield. I quickly had to learn the art of suturing.

In its early days the settlement did not have an aero-drome. I went in by boat with Dr John Hargrave and, when he returned to Darwin, stayed on to administer sulphone drugs and dress the sores of the large group of lepers he diagnosed: men, women, and children with deformed bodies, elongated ears, ugly lesions, and withering fingers and toes.

One of my first operations, performed with a pair of scissors, was to amputate a finger hanging by the skin at a right-angle to the rest of the hand.

None of it was pretty. Some of the manifestations of the disease were horrible in the extreme. But it had killed my mother and I regarded it as a personal enemy.

The aerial ambulance could not land there to evacuate the patients. Boat crews could not be expected to treat and dress them on a long sea voyage to Darwin. The only answer to the urgency of their plight was for Doctor Waipuldanya to hang his imaginary shingle on the flap of a tent and, later, at the entrance to a bough shed where I established a daily clinic for the bare-breasted women, naked children, and woolly men coming out of the forest. I shared this duty with the wife of the settlement superintendent, Mrs Ingrid Drysdale.

If there was cause to worry about a patient's condition I had immediate access to my mentor, Dr Hargrave, three hundred miles away in Darwin. The settlement was equipped with a magic box, a wonderful radio transceiver through which we could report symptoms and receive treatment instructions. From my tent in the wilderness I often spoke personally to Dr Hargrave in his Darwin office:

"Good morning, Doctor. This is Phillip. Jabirr is not too well. Temperature is high and pulse is weak."

By flicking through a card-index Dr Hargrave had Jabirr's case history in front of him before I finished speaking. He would know exactly what drugs had been given.

"Good morning, Phillip. I think you had better stop Jabirr's drugs for two weeks, then resume in divided doses until he is back to normal routine."

In this way we were relieved of the responsibility to worry about patients whose condition fluctuated.

Hannah and our four eldest children—Phyllis, Rhoda, Connie, and Margaret—came out to join me. We lived in a tent provided by David Drysdale, the superintendent, and later in a house of bush timber which I built in my spare time.

One weekend I took the family on a hunting walkabout. I threw off my clothes, changed into a narga, picked up spears and woomera and walked towards the edge of the clearing which defined the boundary of the settlement.

Beyond was the virgin tribal country which only the Berara and the Gunavidji knew, the lower reaches of the Liverpool where they built bark and log canoes, the corroboree grounds where pagan ceremonies identical with others danced thousands of years ago were still observed. Beyond lay the kangaroos and the wallabies, the goannas and snakes, and the multitude of fishes in the tidal estuaries.

Each morning when I stepped from the front porch of my house and walked towards the clinic I wore a clean shirt, a clean pair of shorts, socks and shoes. This was adornment befitting my professional status as a Medicine Man. But now my dress was indistinguishable from that of any of my wild patients. To complete the similarity I carried spears.

I had not hunted for a year or more. My food had been served on plates, and I was accustomed to eating with a knife and fork. It was sophisticated food sold by butchers and grocers and bakers, tinned and packed in foil, aseptic and often deep-frozen. Although I ate and enjoyed it, I was always conscious that something was missing: the tang of game freshly killed and cooked in a camp-fire, the deep satisfaction of living by my wits as my forefathers had, and I had, along the Roper.

221

At the end of my hunting training years ago Sam Ulagang said: "Now he is fit to look after a wife and kids. He is a Hunter First-Class."

I did not want to lose that ability, or Sam's approbation.

But as I moved across the clearing with Hannah and the children behind me I was conscious of spontaneous laughter. Bush people who had been coming to me for treatment were hysterical with delight and astonishment.

"Look at the doctor . . . look at the doctor!" they yelled. "H-a-a-a-ah! H-a-a-a-ah!"

"He no-more bin got 'im boot, no-more trouser, no-more shirt!"

"He got 'im spear! H-a-a-a-ah! We bin follow quick-time, see if he spear 'imself."

"Might-be good tucker, eh?"

Their ridicule was incessant and insufferable. They were saying, in effect: "What does this silver-tail know about hunting? He wouldn't know up-wind from down-wind, a wallaby track from a goanna's, the sharp end of a spear from the blunt end!"

They laughed until I was out of sight.

That evening I walked back through the clearing in silence so complete that it was complimentary. Across my shoulders and around my neck I wore the badge of rank of a Master Hunter: a dead wallaby. My wife and daughters carried barramundi transfixed on the three points of a wire spear.

No aboriginal likes to feel that he has been made to appear a fool. I had been angry that morning and determined that I would show these primitives that not only the Berara and the Gunavidji could hunt. The stalk after wallabies had been long and tiring. I missed one—they would never know that!—but got the next. Now it was their turn to be annoyed at their own stupid judgment.

At the clinic next morning I reappeared in clean clothes, and began treating the daily parade of sick and injured as though nothing had happened. They continued to address me as "doctor," but in their voices I detected the inflections of a deeper respect than they had previously shown me.

A group of young men sat in the dirt a few yards from the tent. I overheard part of their conversation.

"Hey, boy, this feller proper doctor and proper hunter, properly-way."

"Might-be him blackfeller with whitefeller way, but he know blackfeller way all right."

"Hey, boy, you bin see that barramundi he got? Fat one . . . fat one . . . juicy one."

"And, boy, you bin see spear mark on that wallaby, eh? Right in heart he bin hitt'im, middle-one."

My mild revenge was sweet indeed, but not sweeter than the lightly grilled meat I ate with my fingers, black-feller way, nor half as sweet as the tribute they paid me a few days later.

Tommy Galbaranga the Left-Hand Man came to me and said: "Soon big-mob bin go walkabout. We bin go to the bush people at Margulidban and to Gubungu on the Blyth River. L-o-o-n-g way, no-more-little-bit. You come, too, eh?

To be asked to join another tribal group on a hunting walkabout was flattery of the sincerest kind. My shirt buttons threatened to explode as my chest swelled with pride.

"I'm sorry," I said. "There are many sick people here and I must look after them."

The Left-Hand Man had thought of that, too.

"Missus Drysdale," he said. "She properly good doctor. And big-mob sick people in the bush at Margulidban and Gubungu. Leprosy allabout."

This was a challenge I could not resist, especially when Mrs Drysdale agreed that she could look after the clinic alone. Within a week forty bare-breasted, bare-chested, bare-footed men, women and children, with the inevitable retinue of dogs, carrying only our spears and my medicine kit, left on the first stage to Narmongara billabong, the first leg of a walkabout that will live with me always as one of the best holidays of my life.

Narmongara billabong, thirty miles from the settlement, was almost perfectly circular, a deep clear pool where fish abounded and no aboriginal would ever starve.

Around the fire that night Galbaranga told me how it was made:

"Way back in the Time of Dream two young boys who had just been circumcised were camped here," he said. "Before the ceremony they were told by their uncles that they must not eat fatty food . . . no-more fat goanna, no-more fat wallaby, no-more anything tucker that got fat along binjy."

I was astonished. Here among the Berara and the Gunavidji, separated from us by hundreds of miles of escarpments . . . the Blackfeller Country . . . here among people with whom we had had no tribal contact I found a belief identical with our own and equally as old.

I remembered the time when I was Made a Man, twenty years before, and been put under the same taboo by Stanley Marbunggu, my tribal uncle. No! There had not been direct contact, but Kunapipi the Earth Mother and Wedarragama the Rainbow Serpent had penetrated north and west to the Liverpool, spreading the same ancient laws that we keep today.

The Left-Hand Man went on: "All right. Those two boys disobeyed the law. They killed fat goannas and began cooking them. But the Rainbow Serpent, the Whirlwind Man, smelt the fat and came along to investigate. 'What that noise?' one of the boys said. 'Him nuttin', only whirlwind,' the other said. 'Huh! Whirlwind nuttin'.' Wedarragama got properly-cranky-feller. He make that whirlwind go quick-time. The Elders had told these boys: 'Run away if you see a whirlwind, otherwise you'll be swallowed.' They took no notice. 'Whirlwind just crazy wind," they said. Then Wedarragama struck. The two boys were lifted up and taken away to the Dreaming Place, never to be seen again. The ground disappeared as the whirlwind spiralled into it and Narmongara billabong was formed."

Several boys travelling with us had listened wide-eyed to this recital. Galbaranga turned to them. "Whirlwind properly-cheeky-one," he said. "Suppose you see one, you hide. And keep the laws of your people."

Yet in a land where fat was taboo to some we lived on the fat of the land: wallabies, ducks, fish, goannas, turtles, and turtle eggs were brought in by the hunters and contributed to the common pool. My belly became distended from over-eating and I was glad of the opportunity to walk it off next day on the way to Annamaiyera.

It was there, near the mouth of the Cadell River, that we saw a truly remarkable phenomenon. As we approached Annamaiyera an aeroplane flew over. Parachutes billowed and fell slowly towards a point less than a mile from us.

A young man who was old enough to remember the war shouted and began to run. "A-h-h-h! They're bombing us!" he yelled.

A small boy said, "All the bits are coming off that plane. It's breaking up."

I had seen parachute drops of medical supplies to missions and settlements whose aerodromes were water-logged by the tropical monsoon. "They're not bombs, and the plane is not breaking up," I said. "There must be white men near here and they are being supplied with food."

"Flour, tea, and sugar?" a small boy asked.

"Yes."

"Ah," he said, enlightenment dawning in his primitive mind. "It's a big canteen?"

"Yes," I said. "The Air Force canteen."

The Left-Hand Man was incredulous. "No-more! Can't be that!" he said.

"Why?"

"What would they want to drop food here for?"

"For the white men to eat," I said.

"But . . . here! Tucker everywhere! Can't walk about without standing on tucker. Can't swim because too many fish. Turtle eggs allabout in the sand, with big tracks leading to them. Wallabies . . . they must have rifles?

Yams, lily roots, goannas, grubs . . . what's wrong with them? Why fly a plane out here to drop food?"

He just couldn't believe it. And yet it was true.

An hour later we found a camp near the beach inhabited by ten Navy men who were surveying the estuary of the Cadell. They welcomed us generously, although perhaps regarding us somewhat as men from Mars who had walked off the unknown planet in the bush behind the nearest tree, beyond which they had not penetrated. We knew that to be so because we examined their tracks.

The evidence of a huge meal was spread around them: empty sausage tins, empty spaghetti tins, empty pork and beans tins, opened tins of coffee, and the unmistakable smell of meat freshly grilled.

"You've had properly big feed," Galbaranga said.

"Including T-bone steak," one of the sailors said. "Landed to us here on the beach only two hours after it left a refrigerator in Darwin."

"And just in time," another said. "We were nearly starving. The first square meal for a week."

One of the sailors handed an orange to each of the children with us. "Fresh from heaven," he said, and then added for the benefit of his mates: "Poor little perishing devils. Probably haven't had a decent feed for months."

I was nettled by this patronage and said: "We've got plenty of food."

"Where? You're not carrying anything unless it's in that small bag?"

"In the bush," I said. "In the rivers and creeks. On the beach. Food everywhere."

"Blackfeller food?"

"Yes, blackfeller food. Fish and eggs and fresh meat."

"Fish and eggs and . . . Hey, Bluey, did you hear what he said? How do you catch the fish . . . on lines?"

"No. With wire spears," I said.

"What kind of eggs do you get? Crows' eggs?"

"Turtle eggs."

"What are they like?"

"Like eggs."

226

"What about catching some fish for us?"

Galbaranga said: "All right. How many?"

"One each," he said.

Young men ran off to the river with their pronged spears, and an hour later returned with a dozen big fish. The sailors' eyes were eloquent.

Meanwhile one of them said to me: "What's in the bag?"

"Medicine," I said.

"Medicine! Jumping cats! Hey, Bluey, did you hear that? This guy's got medicine. Say, pal, it's not black-feller medicine, is it?"

"Whitefeller medicine."

"He's a doctor," Galbaranga said proudly. "He's travelling with us."

"A doctor! Hey, Bluey, did you hear that? This guy's a doctor! I'll go hopping to hell and back. . . . A doctor! Out here!"

"You're not a witch-doctor, are you?"

I may have been offended, but the man was friendly and smiling . . . and frankly incredulous.

"I'm a trained medical assistant," I said. "My name is Phillip Roberts. I was taught by Doctor Langsford and Doctor Rayment and Doctor Hargrave." I thought the sailors deserved this explanation.

"What kind of medicine have you got?"

I opened my precious bag at his feet. "Penicillin. Sulfa drugs. . . ."

"Binjy medicine," Galbaranga said.

"Binjy medicine! Hey, Bluey, did you hear that? This guy's got binjy medicine. What kind?"

"Sulphadiazine. I've also got bandages, and ointment for sores, and antiseptics."

"Could you treat Bluey?" he asked.

Bluey, although addressed several times, had said nothing.

"He's awful crook . . . he's got dysentery," the talkative sailor explained.

"Yes, certainly," I said. I gave him a dose of sulpha-diazine and enough for treatment on the following day.

The first sailor said, "I think it's the brackish water. We've all had mild dysentery."

When I repeated this to The Left-Hand Man he said: "Why are you drinking brackish water?"

"Because there's no other."

Galbaranga laughed. Some of the young men giggled. "There's fresh water right where you're standing," he said. "This is an old sand-well of ours."

With two others helping him he scooped away a few feet of sand. Fresh water surged into the hole. Galbaranga lowered his head and drank thirstily. "Number one," he said.

"Well I'll go hopping to . . . Hey, Bluey! Fresh water; look at it running, clear as crystal!"

When first we walked into their camp these men had treated us kindly, but were inclined to pity, perhaps because of our dirty bodies and our nakedness. Now we were being shown deep respect, and especially Doctor Waipuldanya. This was evident when the garrulous one said: "Hey, pal, would you mind treating our sores? We've been out here so long we're going rotten."

I agreed. And there in the bush, hundreds of miles from the nearest hospital, ten white men lined up before one who, to them, was a naked black nomad. I treated them for dysentery, sores, wounds, headaches, and stomachaches.

My fee was a cup of coffee.

While I was busy Galbaranga organized another hunt for the sailors. The party returned with two kangaroos, several dozen turtle eggs, more fish, four ducks, goannas, and a snake.

"What are the goannas and the snake for?" a sailor asked.

"Tucker. Number one tucker," Galbaranga said.

They did not want to offend him, but I knew by their quickly masked horror that these were items that would never reach the naval menu.

We resumed our walk and camped that night a few miles away at Juddala billabong. Here we found so many ducks that small boys were able to kill them with sticks.

After a big meal Galbaranga and I sat together to watch an impromptu concert. A pair of beating sticks and a didgeredoo appeared magically. Songmen chanted corroboree lays, young men performed interpretative dances, and one of them hilariously mimed a perishing white man hunting for food and water, and vainly watching for an aeroplane and parachutes.

Galbaranga rolled on the ground in an agony of delight.

"Look at that!" he roared. "He's sitting on water and dying of thirst! A-h-h-h! H-a-a-a-a!"

"Look now! He's got a tin opener but no tin to open!"

When the miming ended Galbaranga said: "Can you beat it . . . can you beat these whitefellers! They're proper clever . . . they can make aeroplanes . . . and motor cars . . . and tinned food . . . and big bombs . . . and refrigerators . . . and ships that sail under the water . . . but they can't find food in the bush!"

"It's all a matter of environment," I said. "They don't have to find food—they buy it in shops. We have never had shops. We must therefore hunt to live."

Then I told him something of what I had read about atomic bombs and hydrogen bombs which the white man had also invented. I told him of their terrible destructive power, of their ability to devastate entire cities and nations.

Galbaranga said sagely: "If they start dropping them it mightn't be a bad thing to be an old bush blackfeller. We'll still be living off the land, but they'll have to learn."

"You might end your days as a great teacher," I said.

"Teacher? Me?"

"Yes. Teaching white men how to survive."

I was back at Maningrida ten days later, having walked one hundred and fifty miles. I returned alone, hunting as I travelled, because I was concerned about the patients at the settlement. The "big-mob of sick people" and the "leprosy allabout" which Galbaranga had used as bait to take me with him did not materialize. One day at the Blyth River we saw travellers' fires in the distance. I delayed my departure to wait for them, but they turned away. The forty Berara and Gunavidji people stayed there to conduct a burial ceremony for a man who had died a year earlier.

One day soon after I resumed work in the clinic a Berara tribesman, Toby Barl-Badla, told me about a boy who was sick in the camp but had not been brought up for treatment.

"Why?" I asked. It was a rule that all sick people must report to me.

"He's the son of a Doctor Blackfellow," Toby said, and I was conscious of the fear in his voice. "He is the most powerful Doctor Blackfellow on this part of the coast, a Number One man among all the Berara and Gunavidji people, a man of Very High Degree."

My mind flashed back twenty years to that fearful day at Mount Saint Vidgeon when I had been "sung" to death by a malevolent Doctor Blackfellow and saved at the last minute by our own Medicine Man—old Gudjiwa.

I remembered my terror and the herbal mixture of wattle bark, yams, and wild honey he forced down my throat. I remembered that my stomach had rebelled while he danced around me, beating the ground with green bushes, yelling imprecations at the evil spirits which sought my destruction, chanting to me, chanting to my ancestors, placating our pagan totems with extravagant promises of tribute and calling malediction on the alien spirits that had brought me to the verge of Djarp—the predestined path leading from life to death.

I remembered that Gudjiwa sucked blood from my arm . . . blood which came from nowhere but did not cease flowing. I remembered the nausea, the involuntary contraction of muscles, and my imbecilic raving.

I remembered, finally, that Gudjiwa had produced a red star-shaped shell from his mouth, indicating that he had taken it from my body. And I remembered the immediate relief from convulsions, my convalescence, and my subsequent fear of ever again being "sung."

230

"I'm about to do some singing," I said. Toby was startled until I added: "I have a score to settle. We will see whether my medicine is more powerful than that old man's. Tell him to come up here and bring the piccaninny."

"He is a very skilled man . . . properly-clever-one," Toby said.

"Nevertheless . . . we shall see."

"He doesn't obey orders. He gives them."

"We shall see about that, too."

Throughout the years I worked with scientific medicine I had often thought of the possibility that one day I might meet a Dr Blackfellow on equal terms. I yearned to demonstrate my superior skill, not only for the sake of healing but also because I was determined to demand tribute as a reprisal for the indignity inflicted upon me in my youth. Now that the opportunity had occurred I did not intend to let it slip from my grasp.

The old man's name was Malagwia. Toby gave him my message but returned alone.

"He acted like a managing director who has been told what to do by the office boy," he said. "Just waved me away."

"Maybe he will learn humility tomorrow . . . if the boy is sick enough," I said.

Next morning, as usual, I visited the camps to treat people who were too old or too feeble to attend the clinic. I was squatting on my knees, bathing the eyes of a woman almost blind with trachoma. Her name was Mary Djabaibai, and she spoke passable English. Presently I was aware that another shadow had been added to those on the ground around me. A child whispered to Mary and I saw that she stiffened.

"Who is it?" I asked.

"Malagwia! The Doctor Blackfellow."

I ignored him. He began to mumble in a dialect I did not understand. He watched intently as I treated Mary. When I finished I stood up and faced him. He looked at me belligerently, unwavering eyes locked on mine.

"Do you want something?" I asked.

Mary translated.

"My little boy over there . . . he's sick."

"You're a Doctor Blackfellow," I said. "Why don't you cure him?"

Mary was diffident about translating such defiance from a stranger to the most powerful man on the coast. She waited for a signal from him before answering.

Finally the old man made an admission that must have been wrung from his heart. The boy was his only child.

"I have tried," he said despairingly.

"Then you will bring him to the clinic," I said.

"I can't."

"Why not?"

"Because too many people would laugh at me . . . a Doctor Blackfellow seeking treatment for his child from a blackfellow who is a Doctor Whitefellow."

"If I go to your camp they will still know."

"That is different," he said irrationally. "I can't stop you visiting my camp on your medical rounds."

I was out of patience with him, but I knew the boy's welfare must take precedence over my pride.

"I'll come now," I said. He smiled for the first time, a smile of relief but also of victory.

We assisted Mary to her feet and I supported her along to the old man's tent so that she might continue to act as interpreter.

There I saw a ten-year-old boy lying on a dirty blanket. The sole of his leathery right foot was badly gashed. Flies adhered to the wound. He was holding his leg and whimpering softly.

I bathed the cut, and put a thermometer in his mouth. One hundred and two degrees! I touched his groin and was conscious of immediate protective withdrawal.

"Blood poisoning," I thought.

Malagwia watched every move I made. He was fascinated by the thermometer while trying to assume indifference, and furious that his own standing in the community prevented him asking about its uses. That would have betrayed ignorance, which was unthinkable.

I said to Mary: "Ask him again if he wants me to cure his son."

"Yes. He does."

"Ask him if he thinks my medicine is more powerful than his."

"I dunno," the old man replied. "I want to see you try."

He was defiant to the last and testing my confidence. If my treatment failed and the boy died he would be able to blame me for his death. That would severely prejudice the medical programme for all the tribal groups in the Maningrida area.

I had no doubt that Malagwia would prevent the spread of the story of my treating his son by threatening to "sing" Mary if she gossiped, but I was determined that he should be humbled at least in her presence.

I examined the foot again and said to him: "Now you show me how to draw out the pus."

"I can't do that," he admitted grudgingly.

"Show me how to make the swelling subside."

"I can't do that, either."

"Then if I do those things and cure this boy you must accept that my medicine is stronger than yours."

He made no such admission. How could an experienced specialist, a man skilled in the use of bark-juice and mumbo-jumbo, admit subservience to an apprentice? How could the most influential man on the coast admit that he was beaten by a foreigner?

I washed the foot thoroughly and then produced a hypodermic syringe from my bag. I sterilized the needle in flame from the camp-fire.

Malagwia's eyes were goggling. "What is that for?" he demanded brusquely.

I realized at once that my answer called for diplomacy.

"There is powerful magic in this syringe," I said. "Proper Doctor Blackfellow magic. If I inject this fluid into your son it will force out the devil that is inside his leg and killing him."

He was satisfied and nodded happily for me to go ahead, convinced that his own profession and not mine was at work. I might have lost his co-operation by telling him that the syringe contained penicillin which would fight infection in the leg. He watched intently, consumed by an overwhelming curiosity but keeping it indifferently in check.

At that moment his wife appeared from the shadows and began to cry.

"Shut up!" he told her roughly. "Can't you see that a Doctor Blackfellow . . . one of my colleagues . . . is trying to cure our son."

"I'm not a Doctor Blackfellow," I said.

"You-ai! Proper Doctor Blackfellow." He had cleverly switched the situation to his own advantage and I realized the uselessness of argument.

I gave the injection and bandaged the gashed foot. When I had finished and stood up the old man held me by both shoulders in fraternal greeting . . . the intimate acknowledgment of equals.

"I am busy in the clinic. You will have to bring your son to me each day for more injections," I said. "It is better there . . . in the clinic I am a more powerful singer. . . ."

Malagwia relented. "All right," he said. "I will bring him."

Not only did he bring the boy, but four days later when the pain and the swelling in the groin had gone he presented himself and his wife for treatment, pointing to eruptions on their legs and arms which I had noticed earlier but which, because of his own standing, I had ignored.

So I examined and diagnosed, treated and cured a Doctor Blackfellow, his wife and his son. Each time I dressed Malagwia's sores I thought: "One of your fraternity tried to murder me, years ago." But that thought was always replaced by another: "And a Doctor Blackfellow in the Alawa . . . old Gudjiwa . . . saved me."

234

I was told later that Malagwia had never "sung" a tribes-man to death. He had been touched by some primitive Hippocratic ideal that it was better to cure than to kill. In this way he had built up an enormous practice and by aboriginal standards was an immensely rich man. Calico, tobacco, weapons, and food came to him in a flood of fees which appeared to be bottomless. I had seen him on his bill-collecting rounds in the camp. Anything he de-manded of a patient, even if it be his wife, was given to him at once.

His drugs were herbal mixtures which he extracted from plants and bushes, sap boiled fom bark, stones and bones, wax and ochre and feathers and fur: anything he thought could be imbued with the magical power, when combined with blood-sucking and mesmerism, to cast out malevolent spirits from the bodies of his ailing compatriots. In spite of this beneficence he was feared by the tribes as only a Doctor Blackfellow can be feared.

When his son had completely recovered and his sores and his wife's sores had vanished he came to me and magnanimously bestowed the ultimate accolade.

"Doctor . . . " he said fervently. "Doctor . . . "

I was overcome.

He was a Medicine Man who had treated hundreds of his people. Some may have been cured, for faith is a great healer. I could not doubt that his people regarded him almost as a Dreaming in whom they believed blindly.

But he could not cure his son. He could not cure his wife. He could not cure himself. For that, while still trying to dissemble, he had to submit to a dispenser of other drugs . . . taken from herbs and bushes and bark and Mould! . . . in whom three white doctors had reposed a certain faith.

The wheel had turned.

EPILOGUE

•

Northern Territory of Australia

•

Government Gazette No. 19B of May 13, 1957

•

I, James Clarence Archer, the Administrator of the Northern Territory of Australia, in pursuance of the powers conferred upon me by the Welfare Ordinance 1953-1955, do by this notice declare to be wards the persons named in the Schedule to this declaration, being persons who by their manner of living, their inability without assistance adequately to manage their own affairs, their standard of social habit and behaviour and their personal associations, stand in need of such special care and assistance as is provided for by the said Ordinance.

•

The Schedule contains the names of 15,211 aborigines —but not one white man—who thus became wards of the government.

The name "Phillip Waipuldanya" appears on page 236 of the Schedule. The names of my wife and children are there too.

In the year nineteen hundred and fifty-seven the government's advisers considered me to be a person who was in need of special assistance.

I was unfit to manage my own affairs.

With fifteen thousand others I became a ward.

I was not free to do as I liked.

I was thirty-five years old, but I had a legal guardian— the Director of Welfare—who was empowered to say that I may or may not do this or that.

In reality, however, I was left to do as I pleased.

236

I was at Maningrida when the Chief Welfare Officer, Ted Evans, came out from Darwin. I showed him around the settlement and he saw the work I was doing.

Later he said: "Phillip, I would like to recommend you for citizenship. It seems to me that you are well able to look after yourself. Will that be all right with you?"

"No," I said bluntly.

I was afraid that the law which prevents white people entering aboriginal reserves without permission would apply to me if I accepted citizenship. I knew that such a restriction existed.

If I was to be deprived of any freedom, the right of access to the missions and settlements and reserves where my own people lived was the last I wanted to lose. I was afraid that I would need a pass, perhaps in triplicate, to see my tribesmen.

During the next few days I discussed the proposal with Trevor Millikens, another Welfare Officer who was at Maningrida. He told me that it would not affect my right of entry to the reserves. That was confirmed by others.

One day in Darwin I came face to face with the Director, Mr. Harry Giese. He introduced me to some friends he had with him and said: "We are trying to get Phillip to accept citizenship."

Later when one of his officers approached me again my resistance crumbled. "Yes," I said. "I'll be glad to."

Northern Territory of Australia

•

Government Gazette No. 25 of June 15, 1960

•

I, James Clarence Archer, Administrator of the Northern Territory of Australia, having received the advice of the Administrator's Council, in pursuance of the powers conferred on me by the Welfare Ordinance 1953-1959, do by this notice amend the notice appearing in the Northern Territory Government Gazette No. 19B of May 13, 1957, declaring certain persons to be wards by omitting from the list of names the following:

Phillip Waipuldanya, Bungadi group, Alawa tribe.

Hannah Dulban, Ngamayang group, Wandarang tribe.

Phyllis Mutukutpina, Burlangban group, Alawa tribe.

Rhoda Bululka, Burlangban group, Alawa tribe.

Connie Ngamirimba, Burlangban group, Alawa tribe.

Mavis Wanjimari, Burlangban group, Alawa tribe.

This typical piece of public service dialect meant that my entire family were citizens. The two youngest girls, Margaret Gabadabadana and Miriam Jardagara, were Born Free.

What difference has citizenship made to my life?

I am entitled to enter hotels and ask for a drink of beer without danger of being arrested by the police on an "abo. drink liquor" charge. But that is a privilege which does not mean much to a teetotaller.

My name and Hannah's name are on the Electoral Roll. We will be fined if we do not vote at Federal elections. That is something new.

There was a touching gilt-edged invitation from the new occupants of Government House: "The Administrator and Mrs Roger Nott request the pleasure of the company of Mr and Mrs Phillip Roberts. . . . "

Otherwise, little has changed.

I am still a medical assistant with the Department of Health. We have a new house at Nightcliff, a Darwin suburb. My children attend an aboriginal school, and are learning to read and write.

Tribally, of course, there has been no change at all.

My responsibilities to the Alawa people remain as they were. To them, I am Waipuldanya or Wadjiri-Wadjiri of the Bungadi skin. I am a Djungayi and will remain so. . . .

. . . If I return to the Roper River while a Kunapipi is in progress I will be expected to examine the body decorations of the men in my group and to act as Master of Ceremonies.

. . . My daughters' uncle, Johnny Nunguru, will say whom they shall marry. Citizenship has not given me that right.

. . . Nor has it helped to resolve the conflict between my inherited pagan beliefs and the Christian religion I was taught by the missionaries.

. . . Yes, I believe in God. But I also believe in the Earth Mother, the Rainbow Serpent, and my Kangaroo Totem. They gave us all we have: my tribal country, our food, my wife, our children, our culture. Nothing . . . nothing . . . will change that. It is inherent in me, the heritage that has come down with each generation since the Time of Dream and was burnt into my mind and body with sharp steel during my initiation.

How can a tribesman who has two religious ceremonies each of which lasts six months forsake his beliefs for one that lasts an hour?

How can I forsake spontaneous ritual, the beating sticks, the Songmen, the decorated dancers, for drab intonation?

The missionaries have been trying for half a century to destroy our faith and convert the Alawa to Christianity. There are a few who profess it. I am one. My father, Barnabas Gabarla, is one . . . a lay preacher.

But the truth is that we have accepted the alien faith so as not to offend white men who have been good to us.

We are grateful for the help they have given us in material things. We are grateful because they took us under their protection and gave us refuge from the cruelties inflicted by the first squatters.

Yet if they try for another five hundred years they will never take the deeply religious Kunapipi and Yabudurawa from us. They have been passed on to the new Generation of Men.

And Always Shall Be.

Citizenship would not save me from my tribal responsibility if the Elders arrived one day with a Diwuruwuru stick decorated with feathers and sacred markings and said: "Waipuldanya, you are to be a Mulunguwa, an executioner."

I would have no choice but to obey the tribal law either by committing the murder, by forfeiting all my worldly goods as a fine if they were prepared to impose one, or by being killed myself.

It would be pleasant in such a situation to be able to say: "I'm sorry. I'm now a citizen in the Big White Way. I cannot do what you ask. I must obey the white man's law."

The fact is that such a thought would not even occur to me.

I Am a Blackfellow!

I hope the situation never eventuates.

I do not expect that it will.

But if it does I will be an aboriginal first and a citizen later.

The immutable laws of the Alawa were brought into the mouth of the Roper by Kunapipi long before the God of Israel spoke: "Behold, I am the Lord. I do not change."

Nor do we.

DJU DJU NAMA YALLALA!